P9-CEY-264

The DRAWING BOOK FOR KIDS

365 Daily Things to Draw: Step by Step

Woo! Jr Kids Activities

No part of this publication may be reproduced in whole or in part, shared with others, stored in a retrieval system, digitized, or transmitted in any form without written permission from the publisher.

Copyright © 2017, Woo! Jr. Kids Activities / Wendy Piersall. All rights reserved.

Woo! Jr. Kids Activities Founder: Wendy Piersall
Production Coordinator: Cassidy Piersall
Cover Illustration: Michael Koch | Sleeping Troll Studios www.sleepingtroll.com
Interior Illustration: Avinash Saini

Published by:
Wendybird Press
2050 S. Eastwood Dr.
Woodstock IL, 60098
www.wendybirdpress.com

ISBN-13: 978-0997799378
ISBN-10: 0997799374

How to Use This Book!

All you need is a pencil, eraser,
and a piece of paper!

Follow each drawing diagram step by step:

Tips:

Draw lightly at first, because you might need to erase some lines as you work.

Add details according to the diagrams, but don't worry about being perfect! Artists frequently make mistakes - they just find ways to make their mistakes look interesting.

Don't worry if your drawings don't turn out the way you want them to. Just keep practicing! Sometimes drawing the same thing just a few times will help.

Once you've finished your drawing in pencil you can trace it with a black fineliner pen and color or paint it to your liking.

You can draw a new item or character every day for 365 days - or use your creativity to combine multiple drawings into an entire scene.

Turn the page for some cool composition ideas!

Put Drawings together to Create full Scenes!

– Underwater Scene –

#14
Crab

#16
Starfish

#18
Stingray

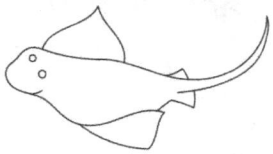

#282
Mermaid

#21
Hammerhead Shark

#23
White Shark

#24
Whale

– Fishing Scene –

#29
Fishing Pole

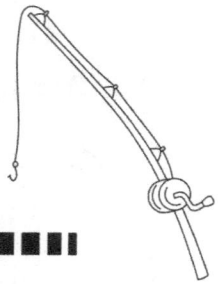

#30
Fish

#79
Waterfall

#292
Boy

Put Drawings together to Create full scenes!

– Outer Space Scene –

#196 Round Alien

#197 Happy Alien

#198 Squid Alien

#203 Rocket

#201 U.F.O.

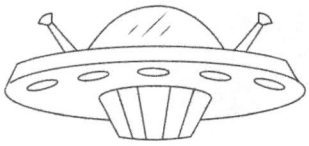

#206 Planet

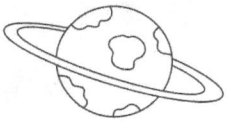

#279 Astronaut

– Flying Fairies Scene –

#97 & #100 Butterflies

#110 Flower

#205 Rainbow

#284 & #286 Fairies

#287 Bird

#288 Toadstool

ADD Perspective to your Drawings By using the vanishing Point and a Perspective grid!

The "vanishing point" is a point on the horizon in which a set of parallel lines appear to converge into a single point.
For example, railroad tracks appear to converge in the distance in this photograph:

To use a perspective grid, lightly draw guide lines with a pencil as shown below with a ruler. Then use the grid as a guide for how to angle your lines accurately to convey perspective as shown in the bottom demonstration.

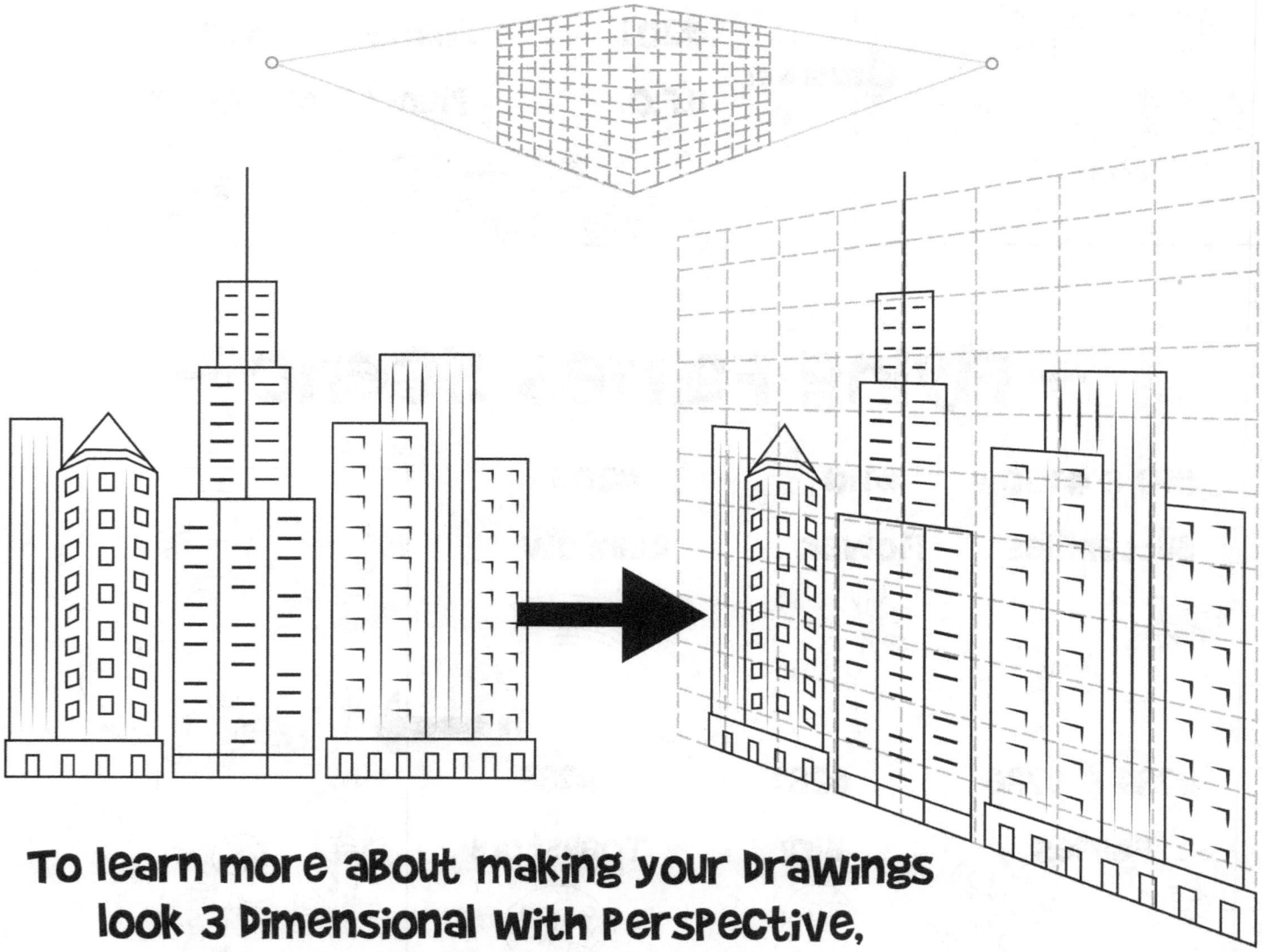

To learn more aBout making your Drawings look 3 Dimensional with Perspective, read our free tutorial at:

WWW.Woojr.Com/Perspective

Free Download!

Like this book?

Join our VIP mailing list and get a *FREE* 70 page printable PDF *Holiday Activity Book for Kids*! It includes crosswords, word searches, picture matching, and coloring activities for ages 4-10!

Holidays include:

- Martin Luther King Jr. Day
- Valentine's Day
- St. Patrick's Day
- Easter
- Earth Day
- 4th of July
- Halloween
- Thanksgiving
- Hanukkah
- Christmas

Get started here:

www.woojr.com/VIP

1

2

3
4

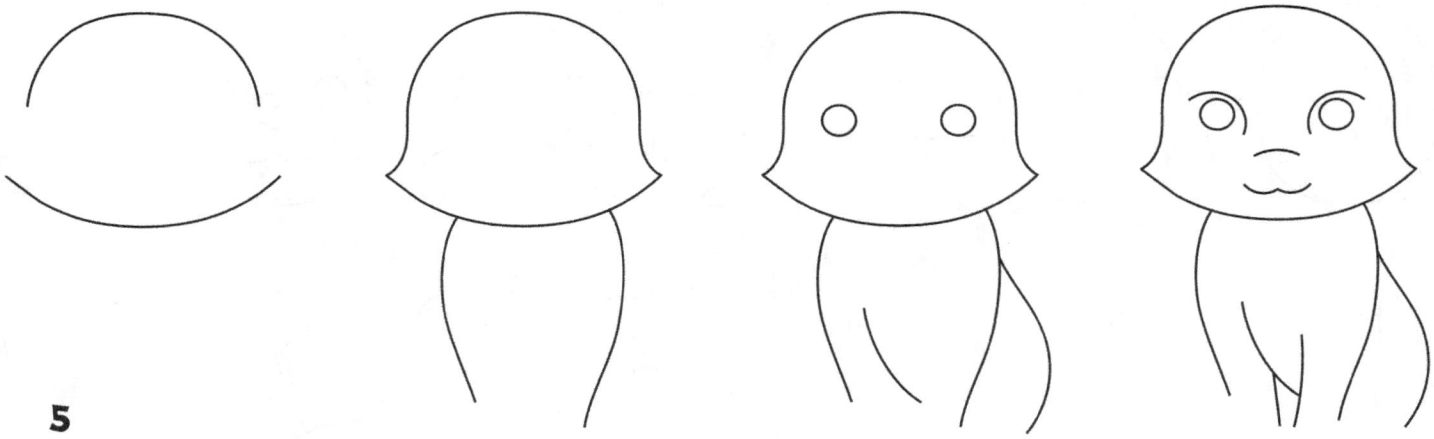

5

6

7

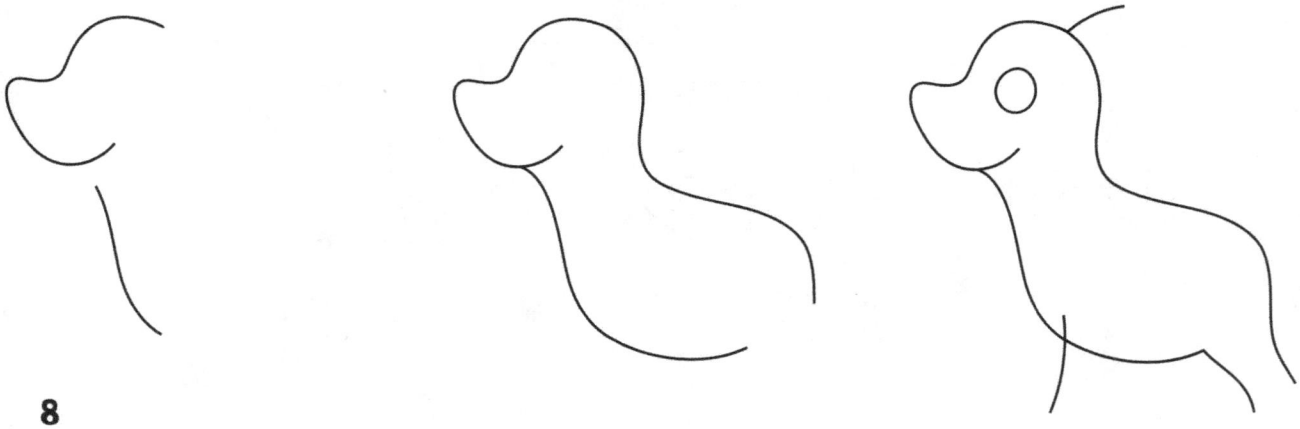

8

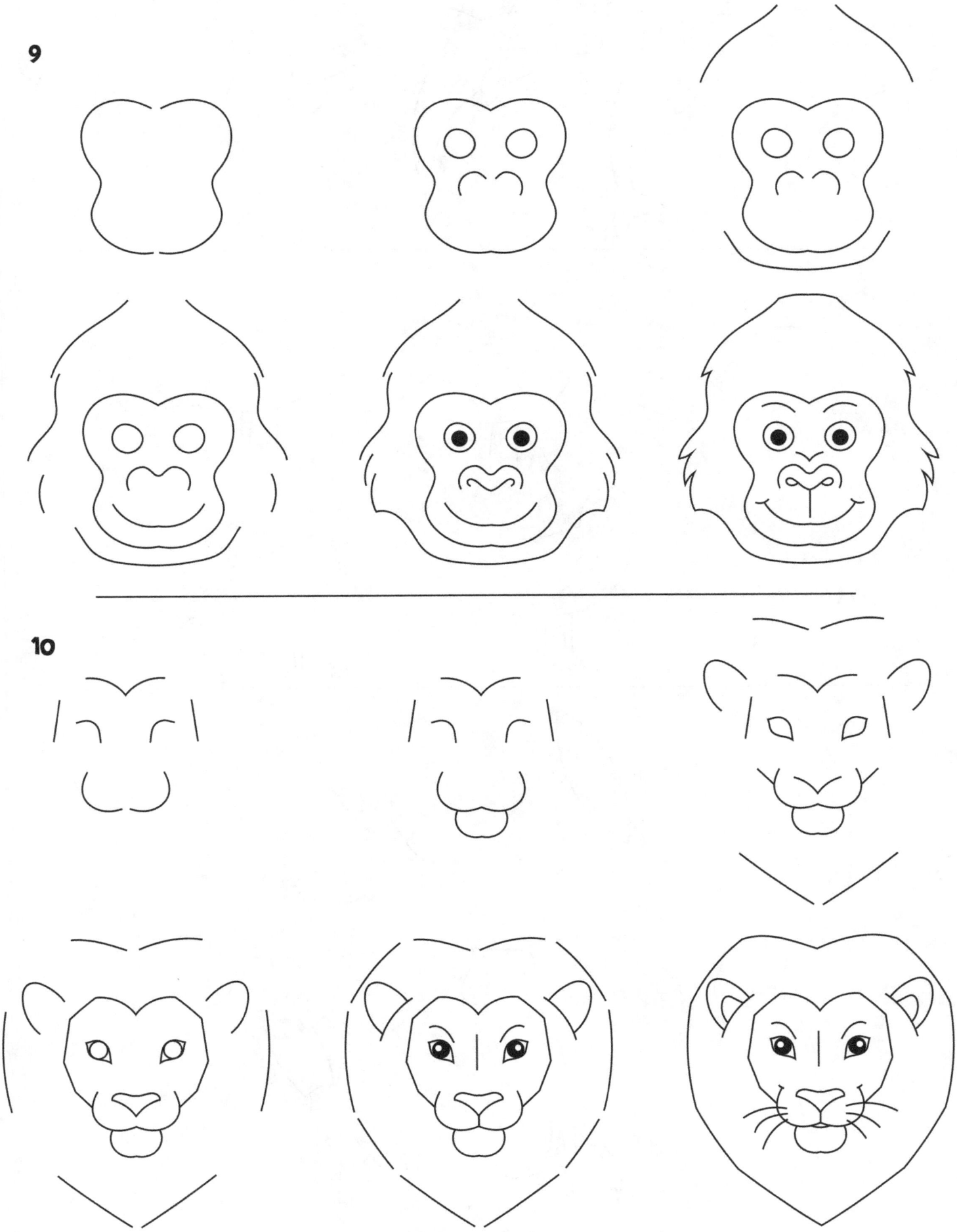
9
10

11

12

13

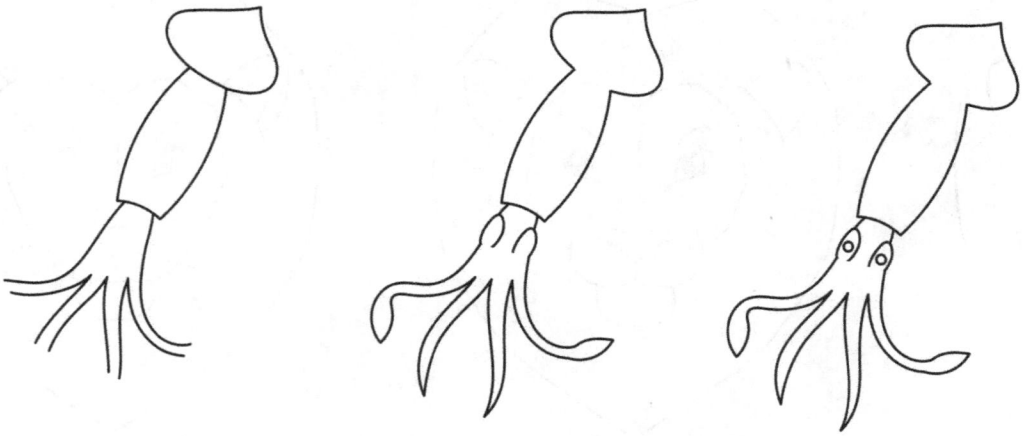

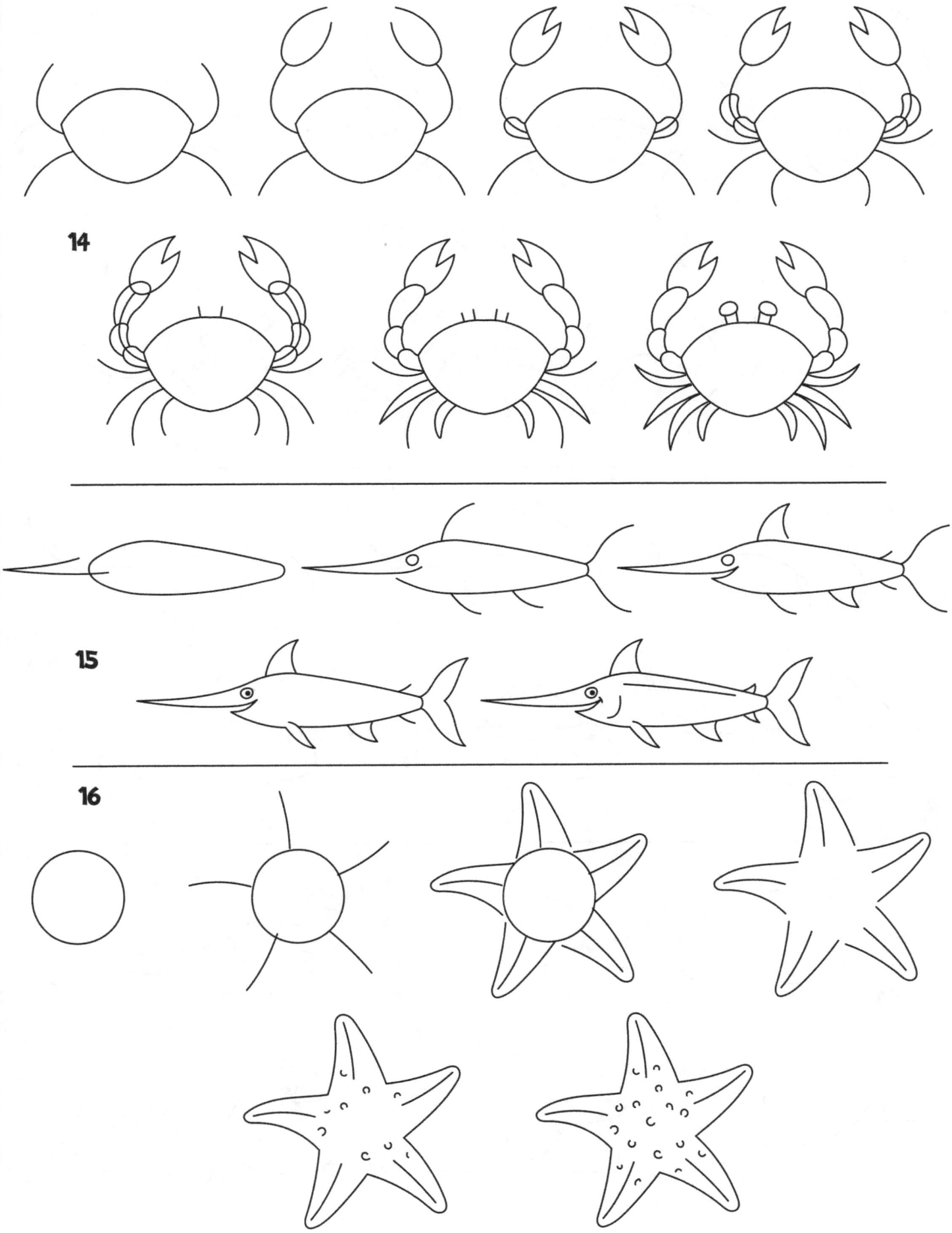
14
15
16

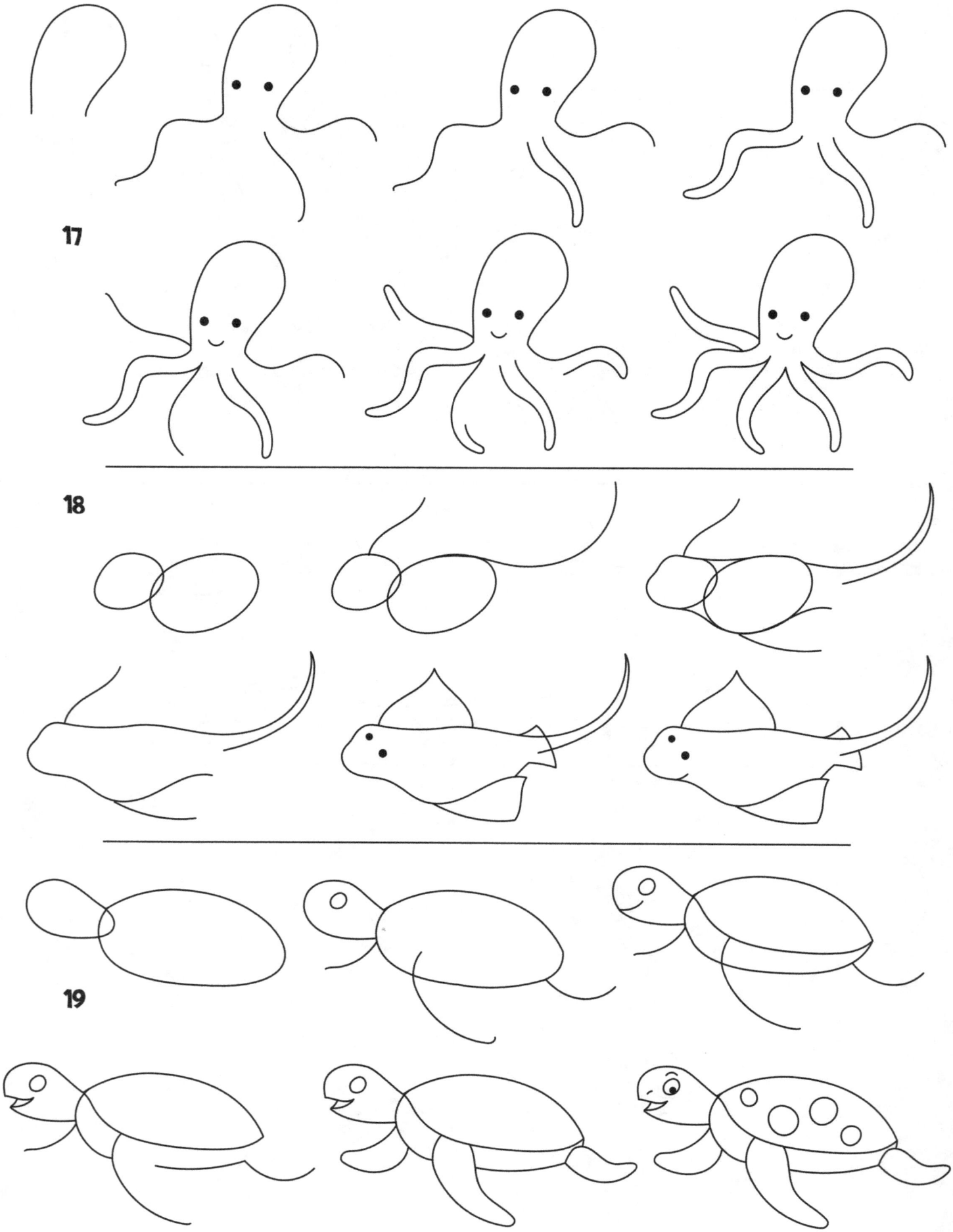
17
18
19

20

21

22

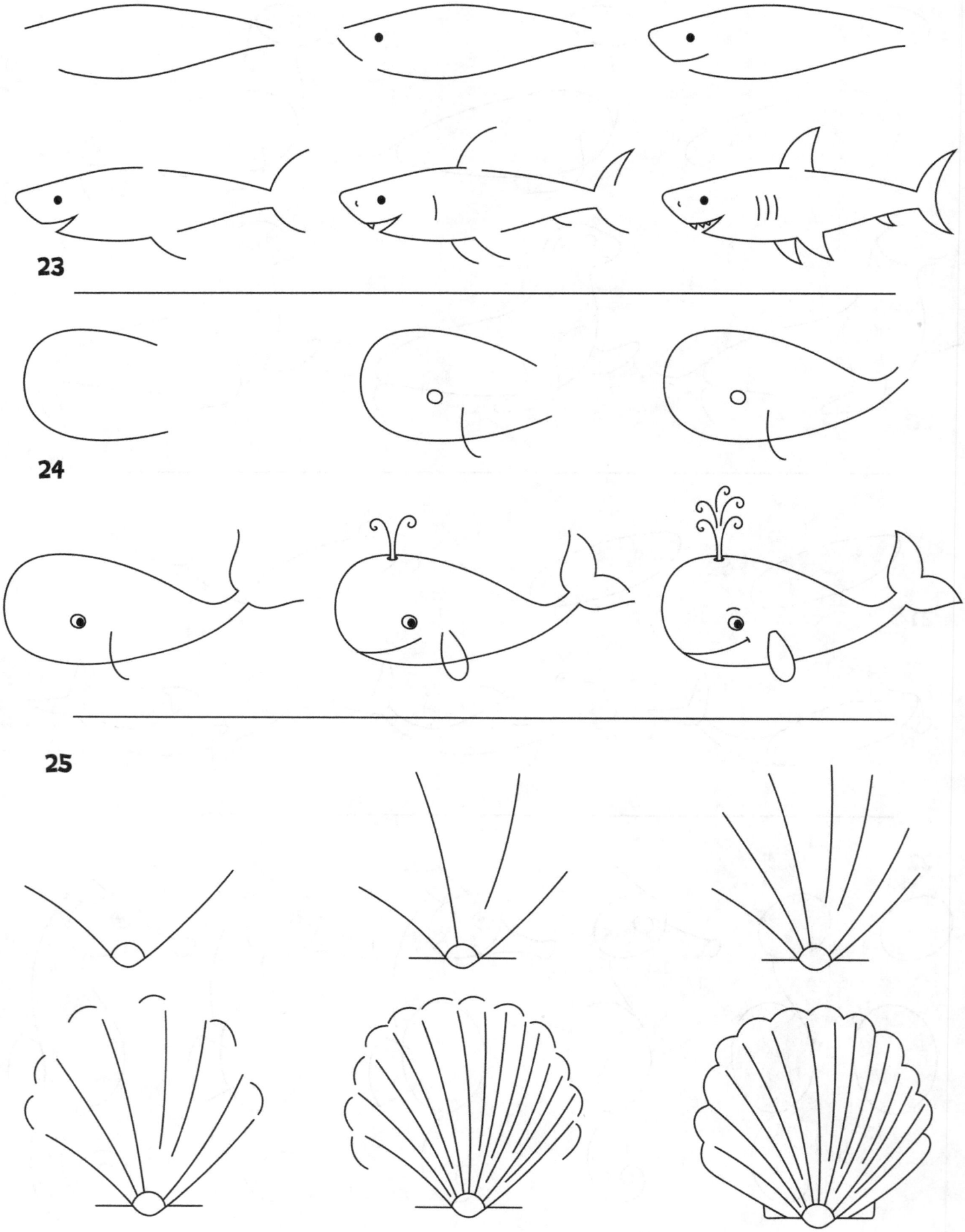
23
24
25

26

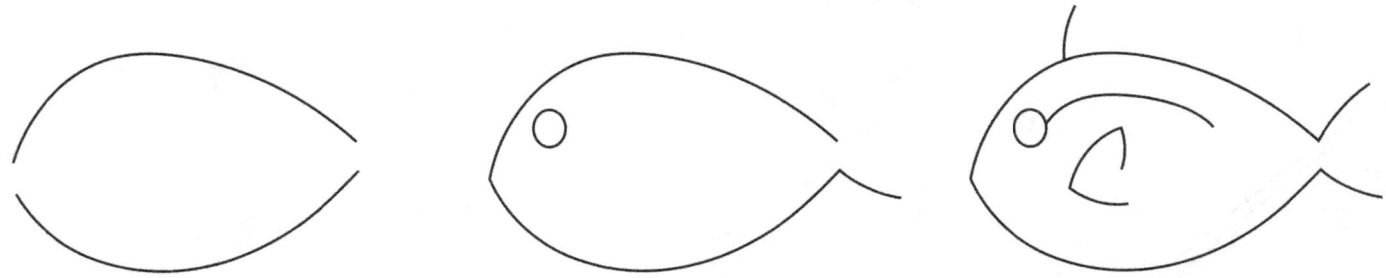

27

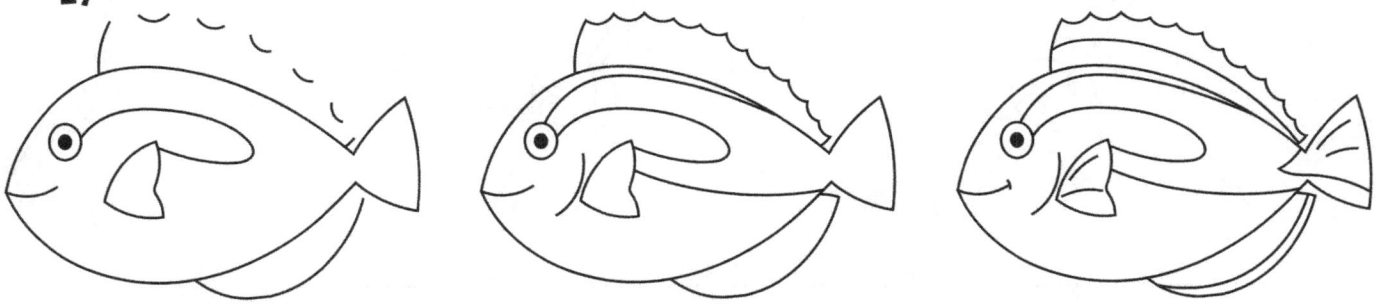

28

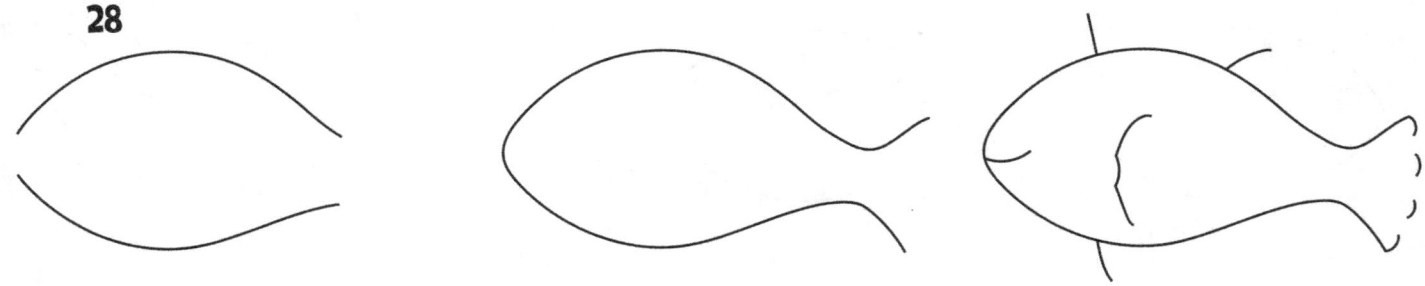

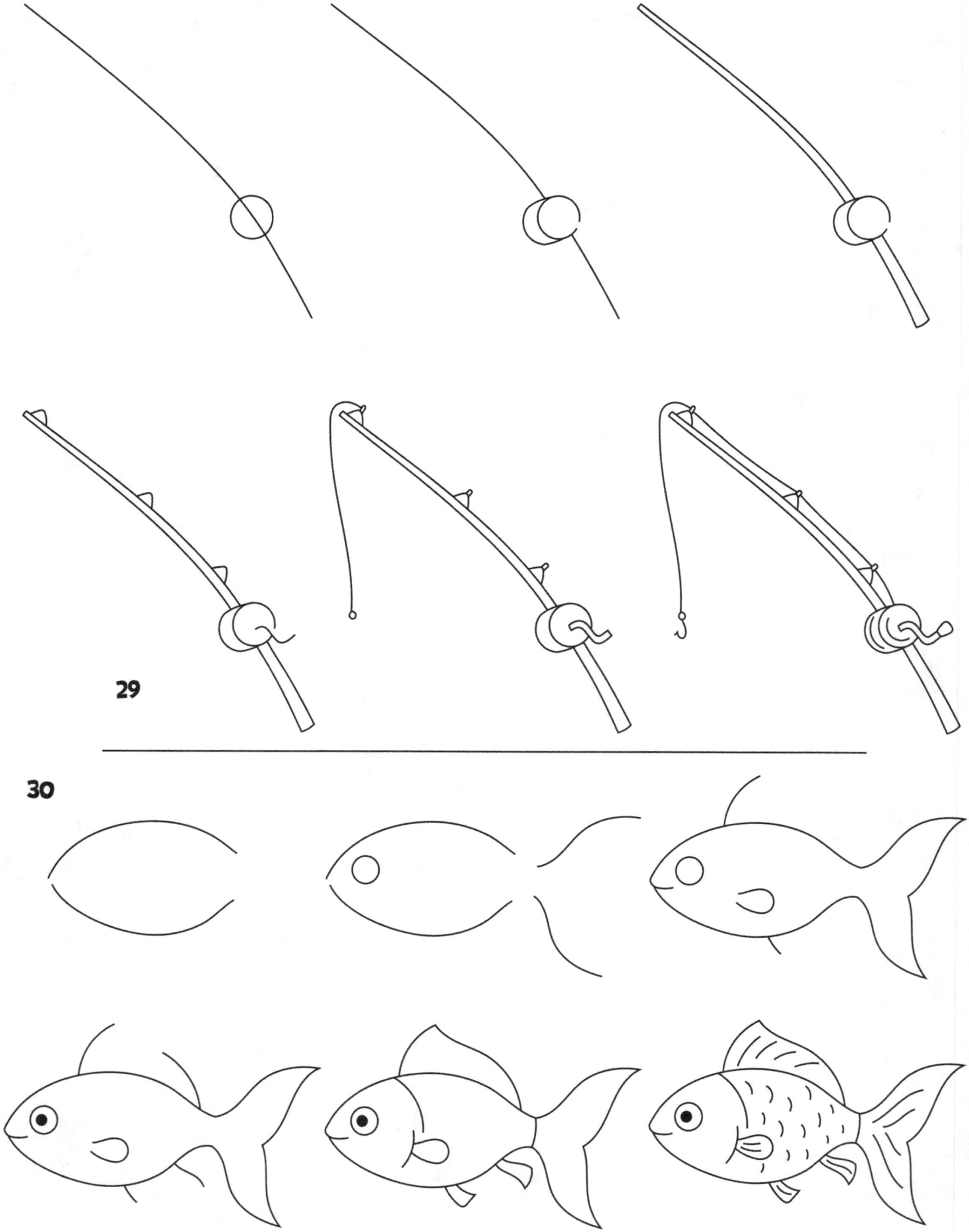
29
30

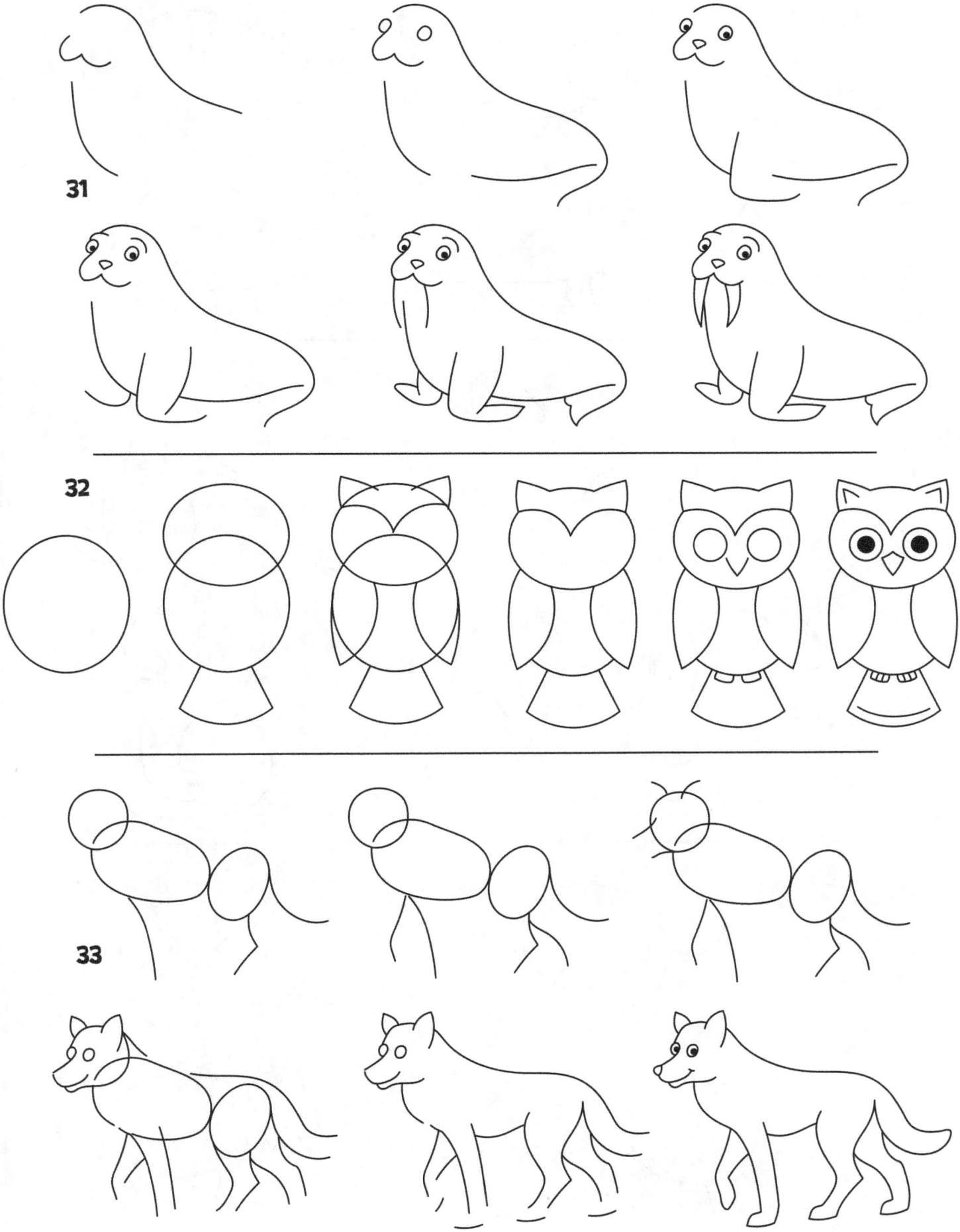
31
32
33

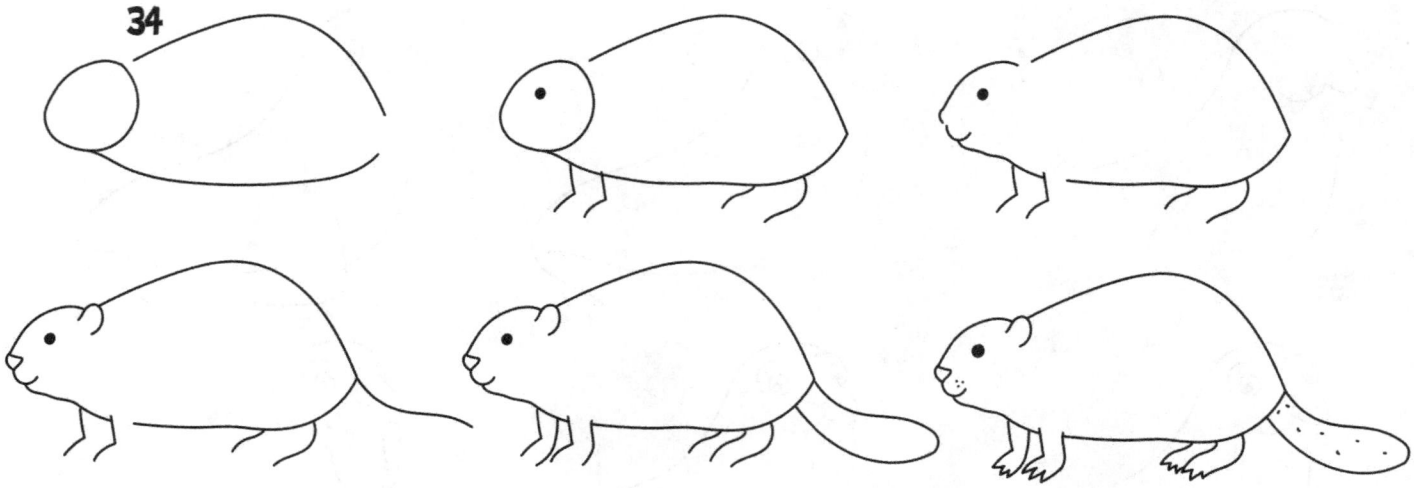
34

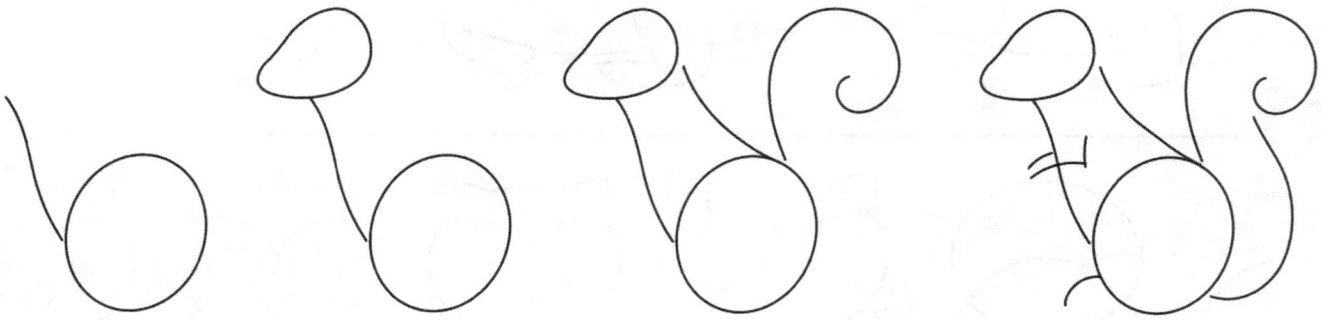

35

36

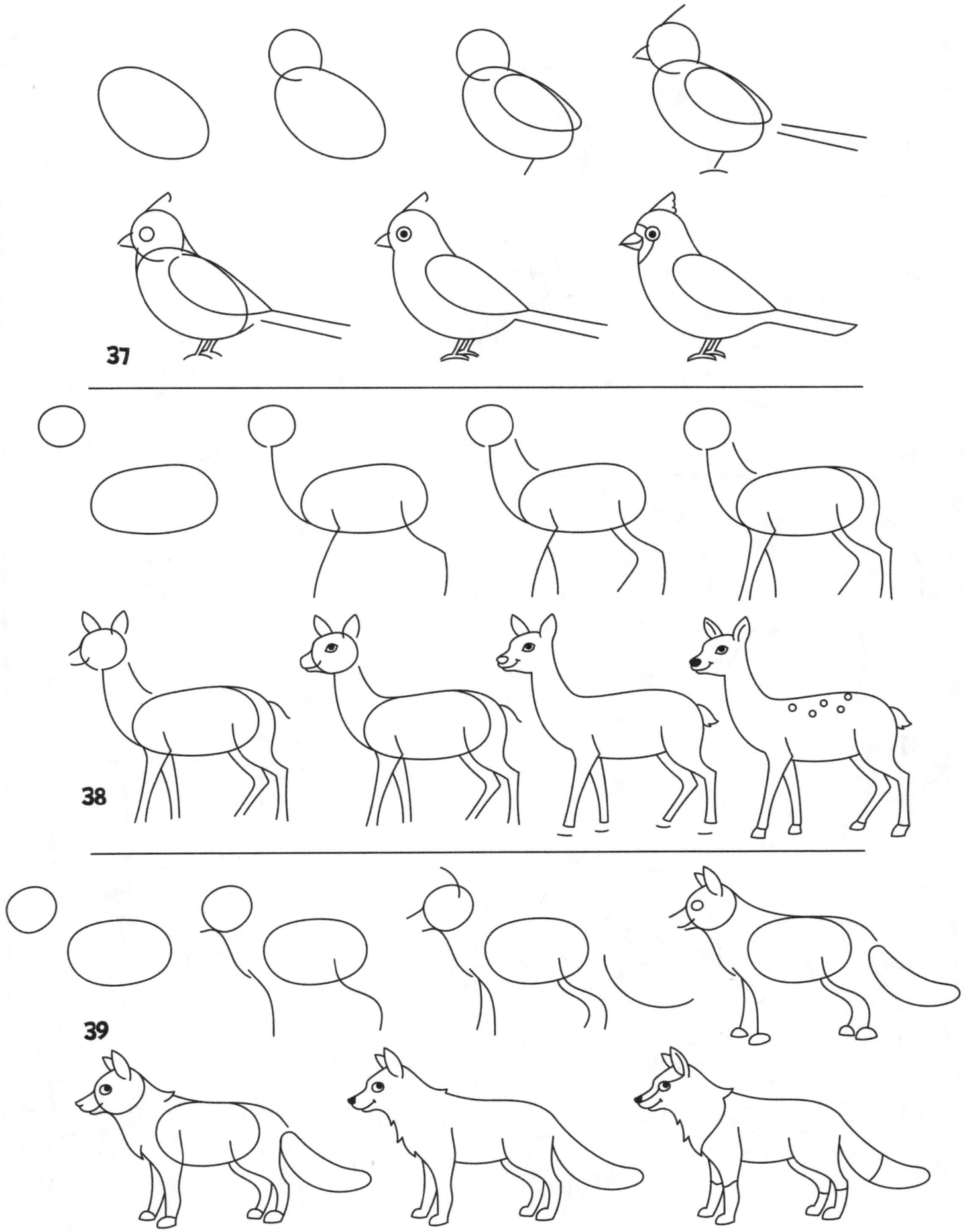
37
38
39

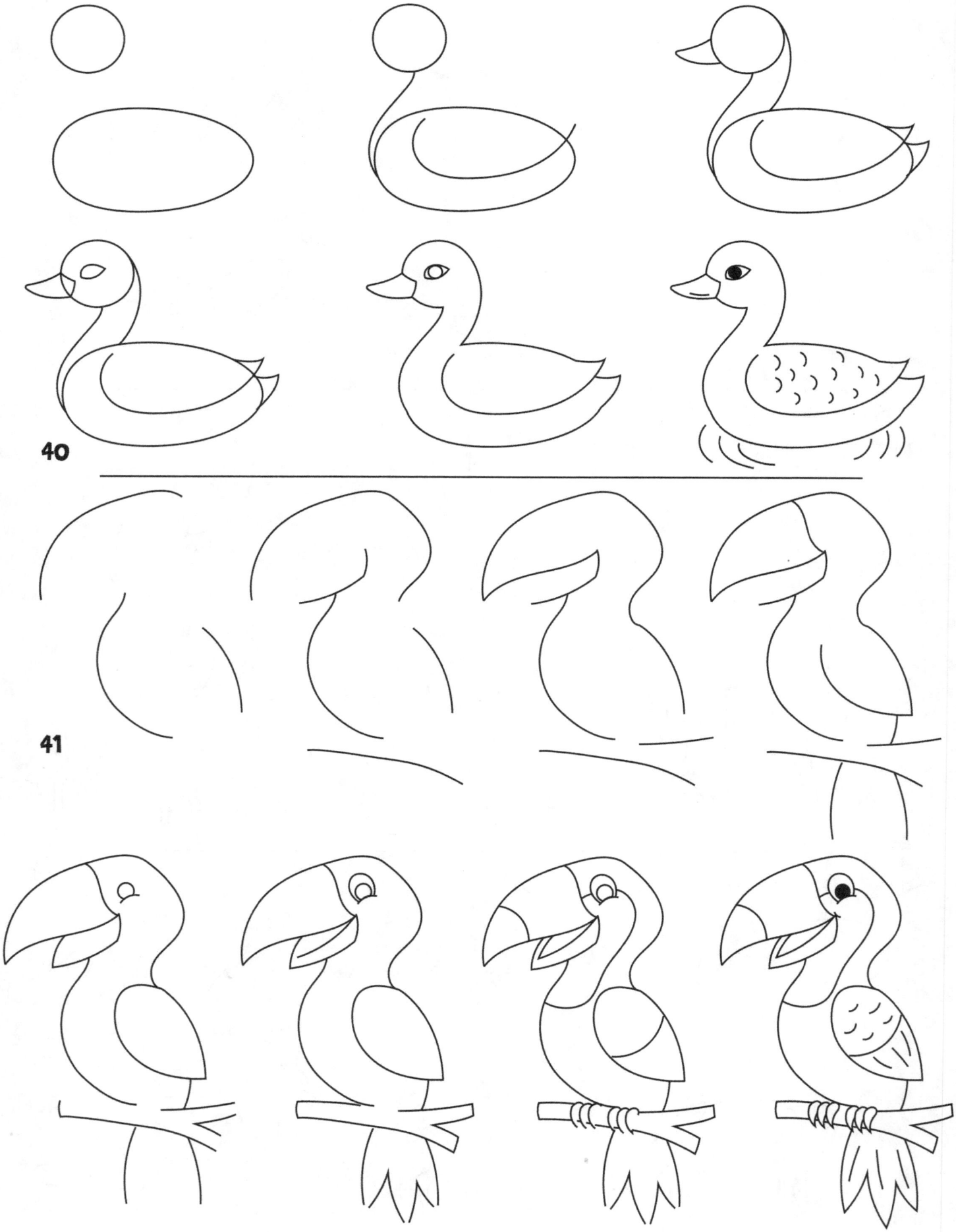
40
41

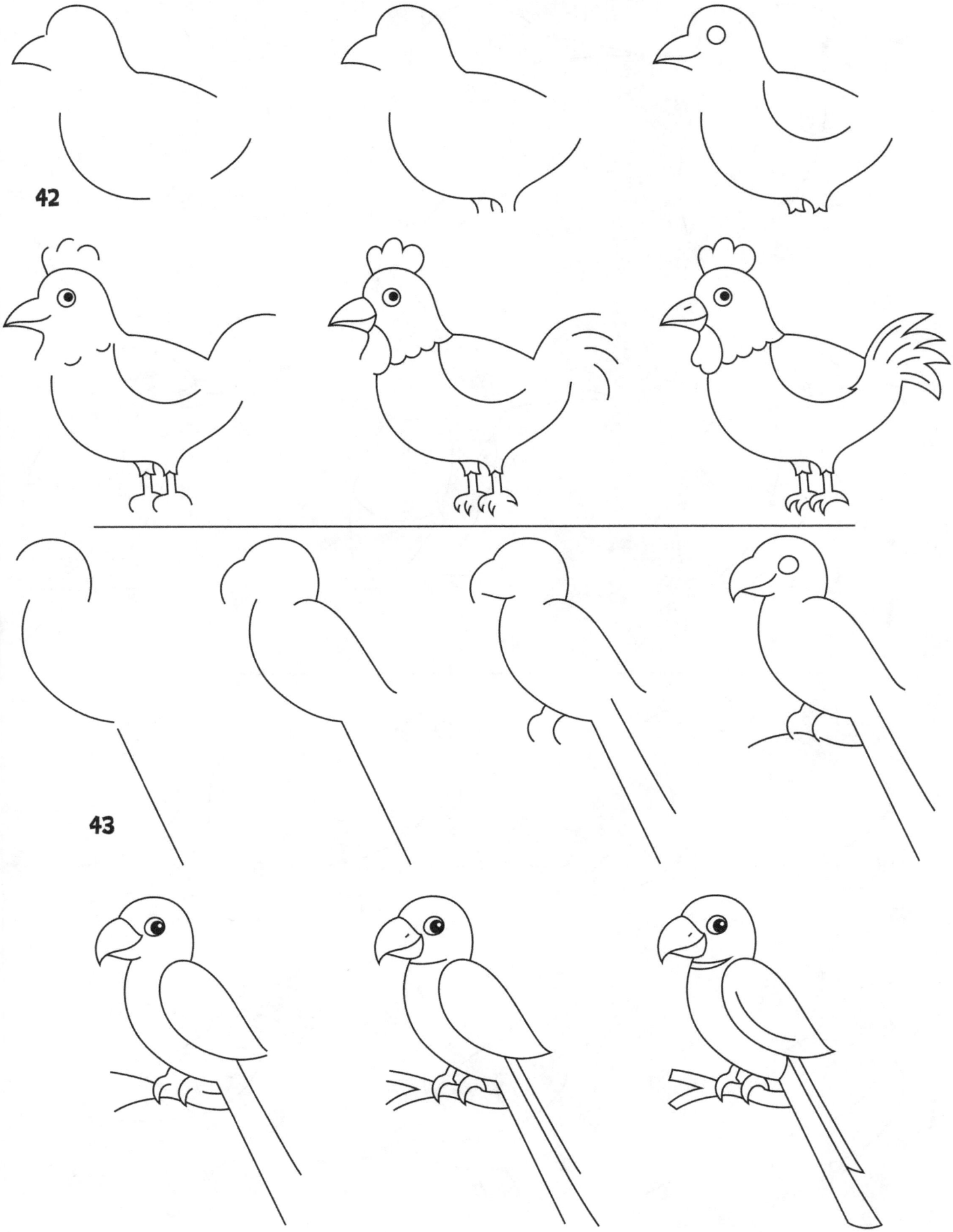
42
43

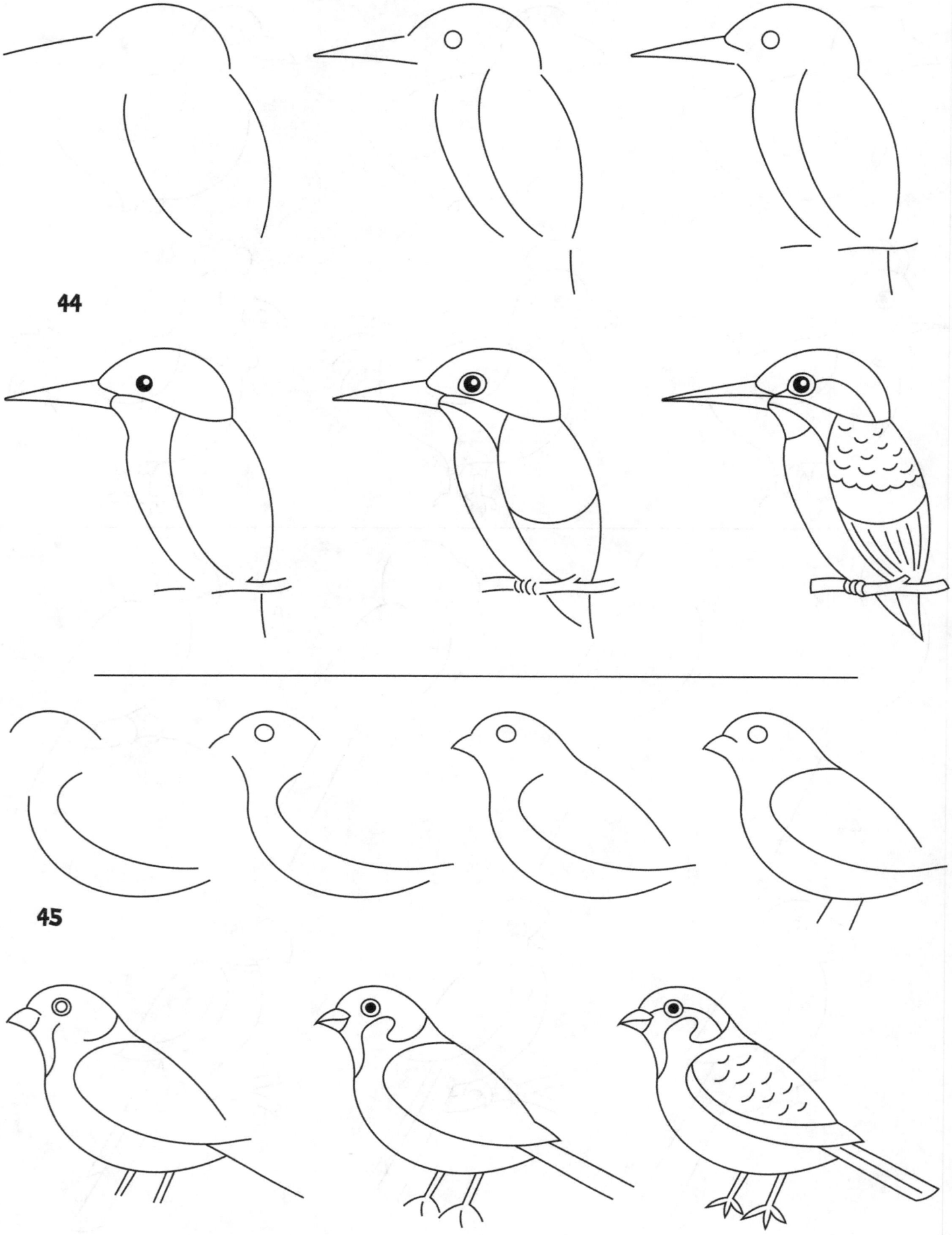
44
45

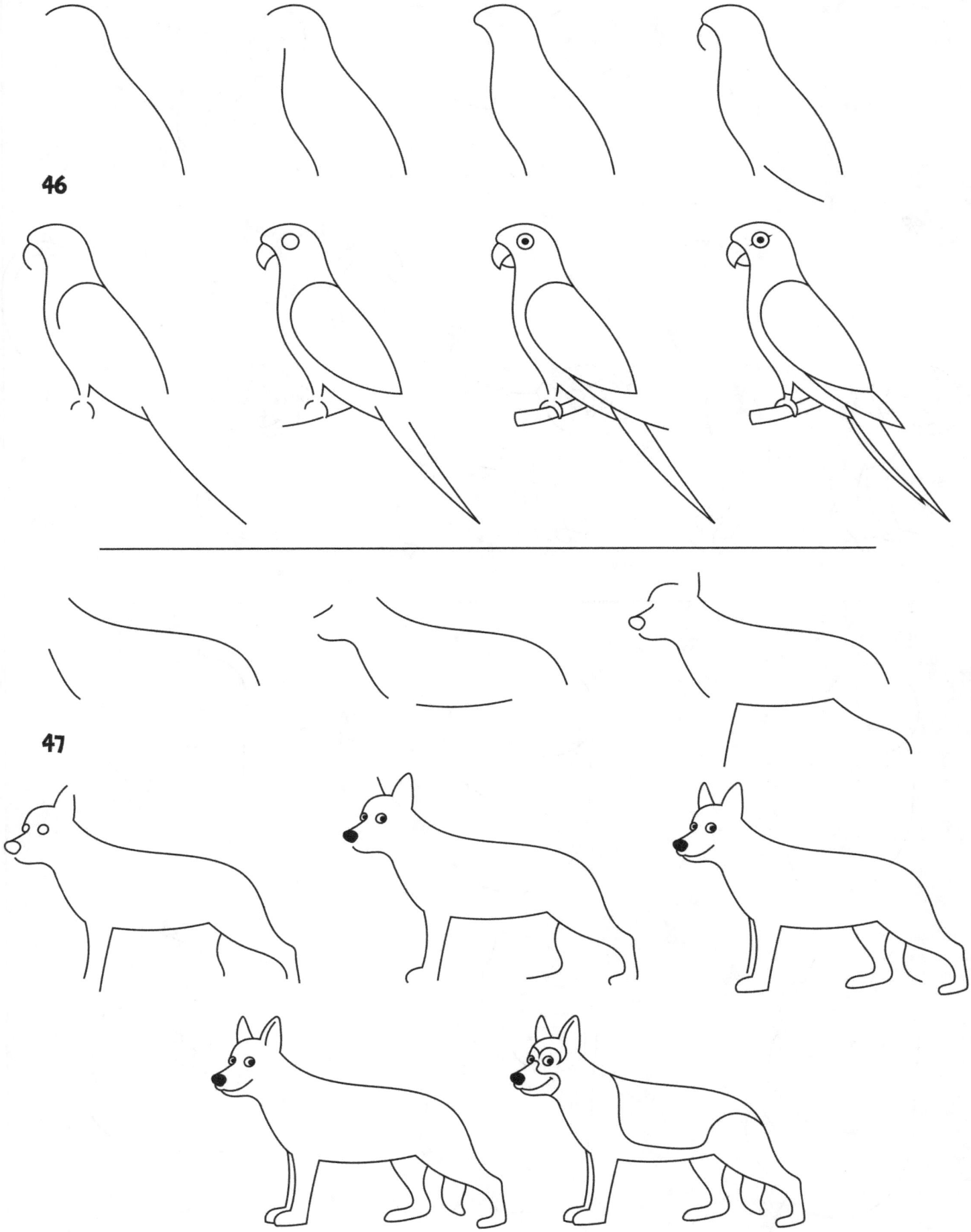
46
47

48

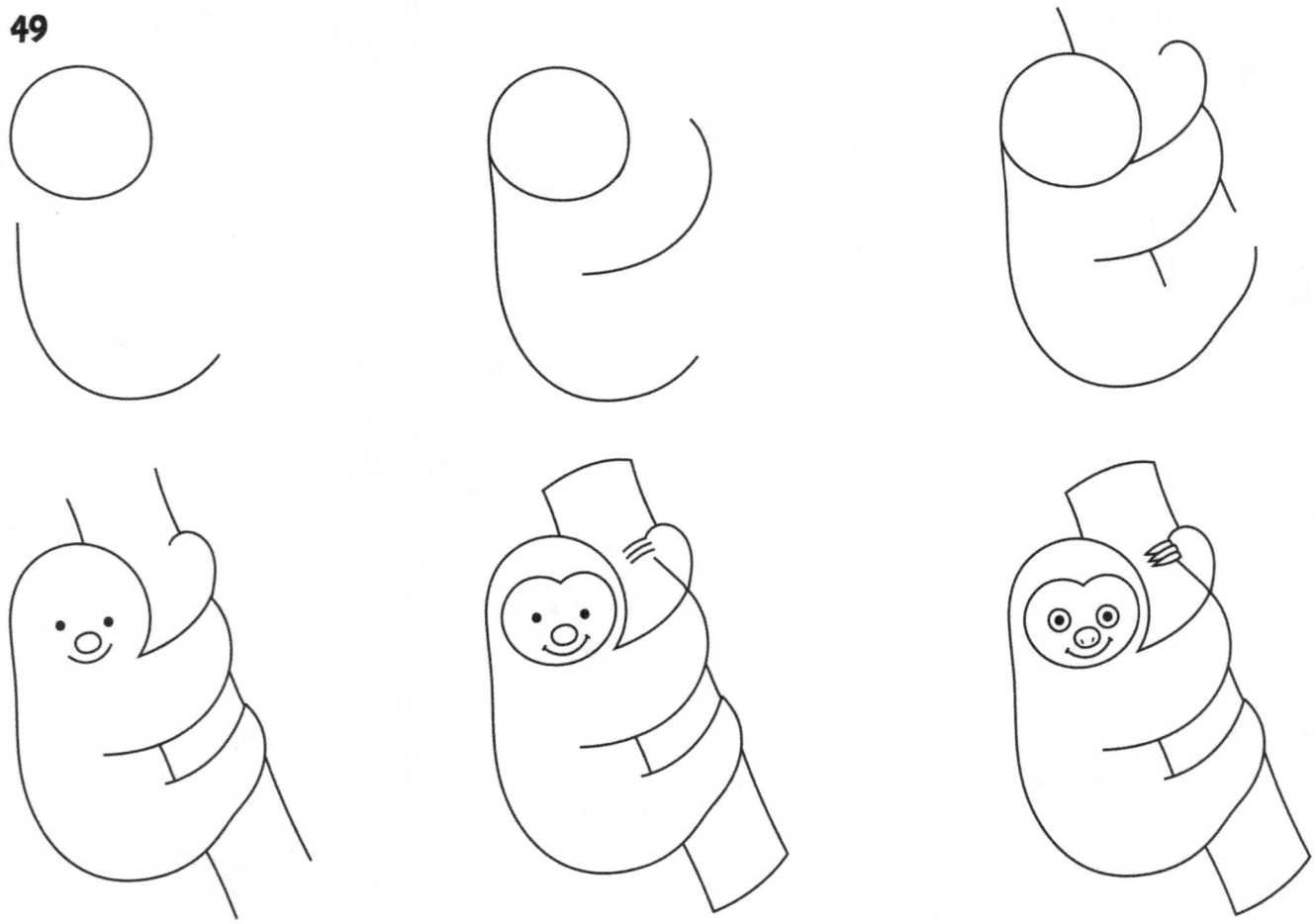
49

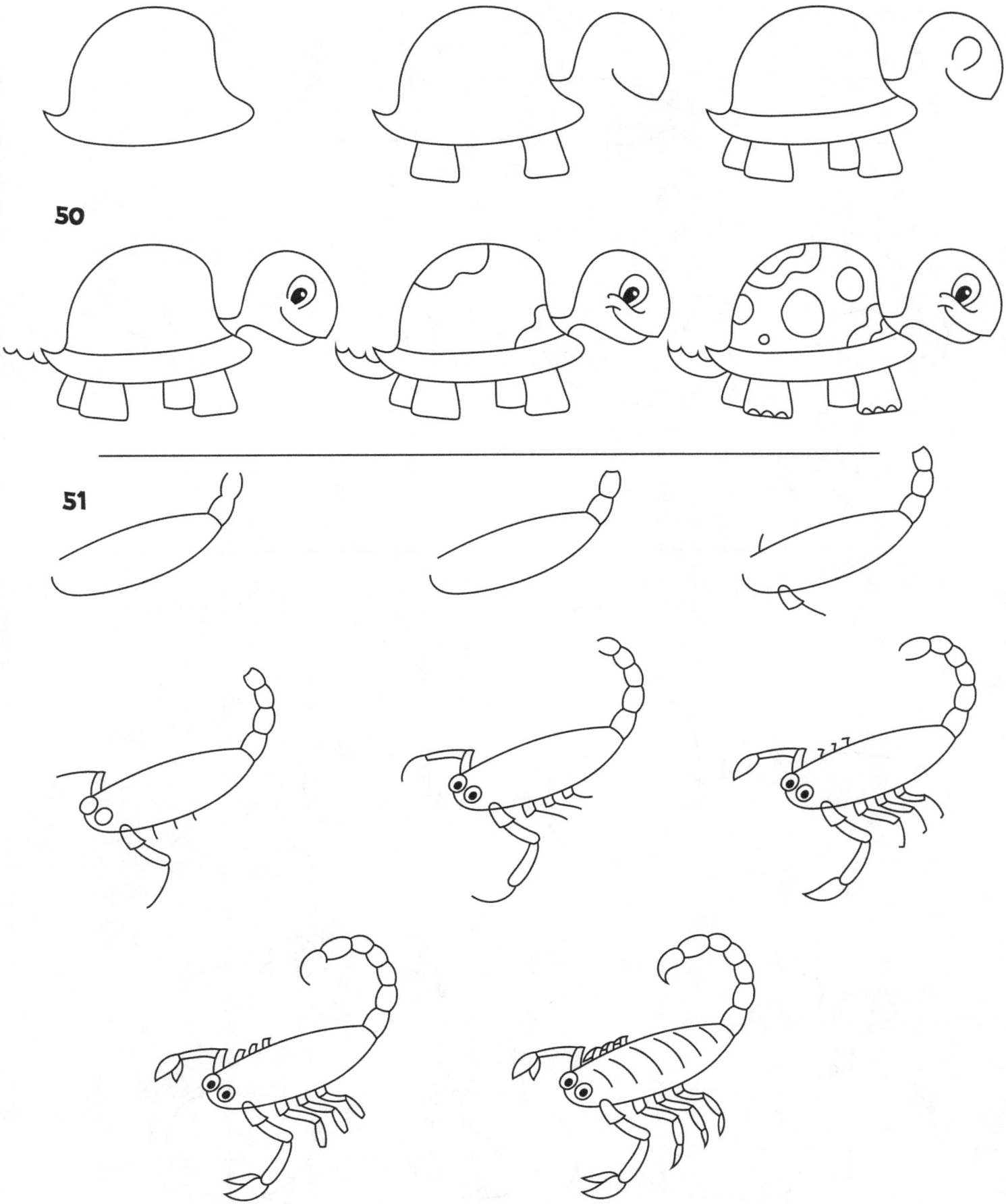
50
51

52

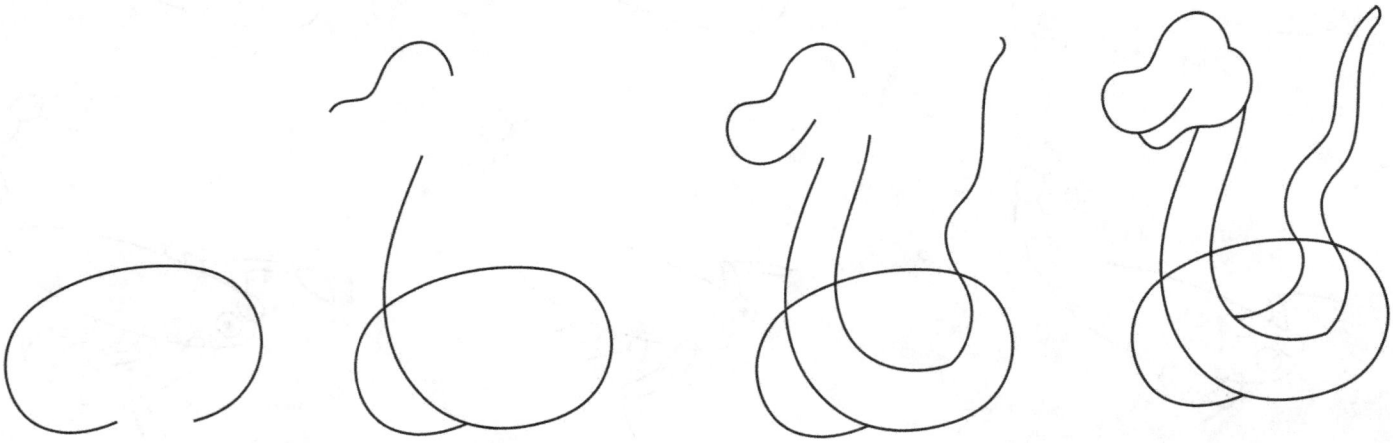

53

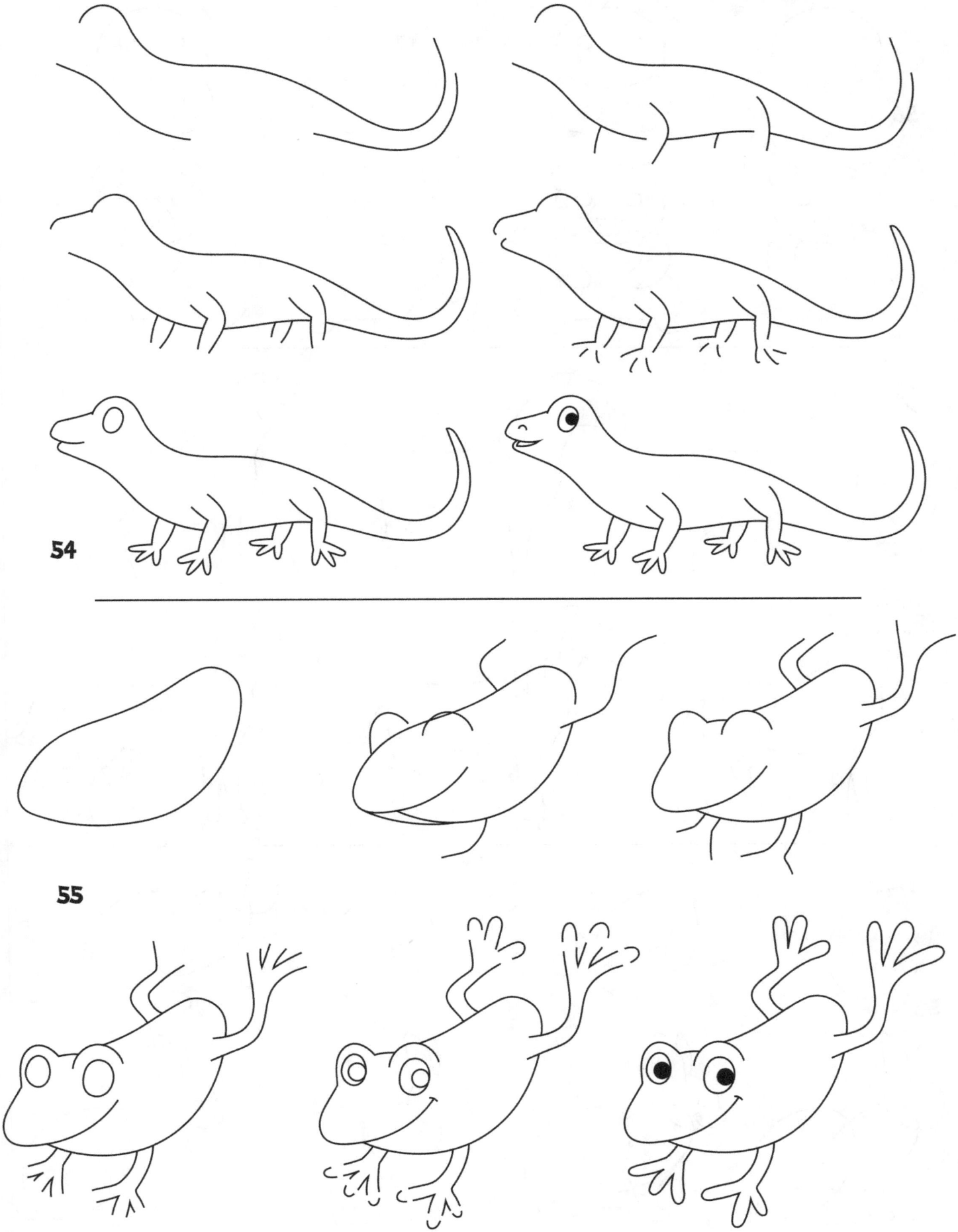
54
55

56
57
58

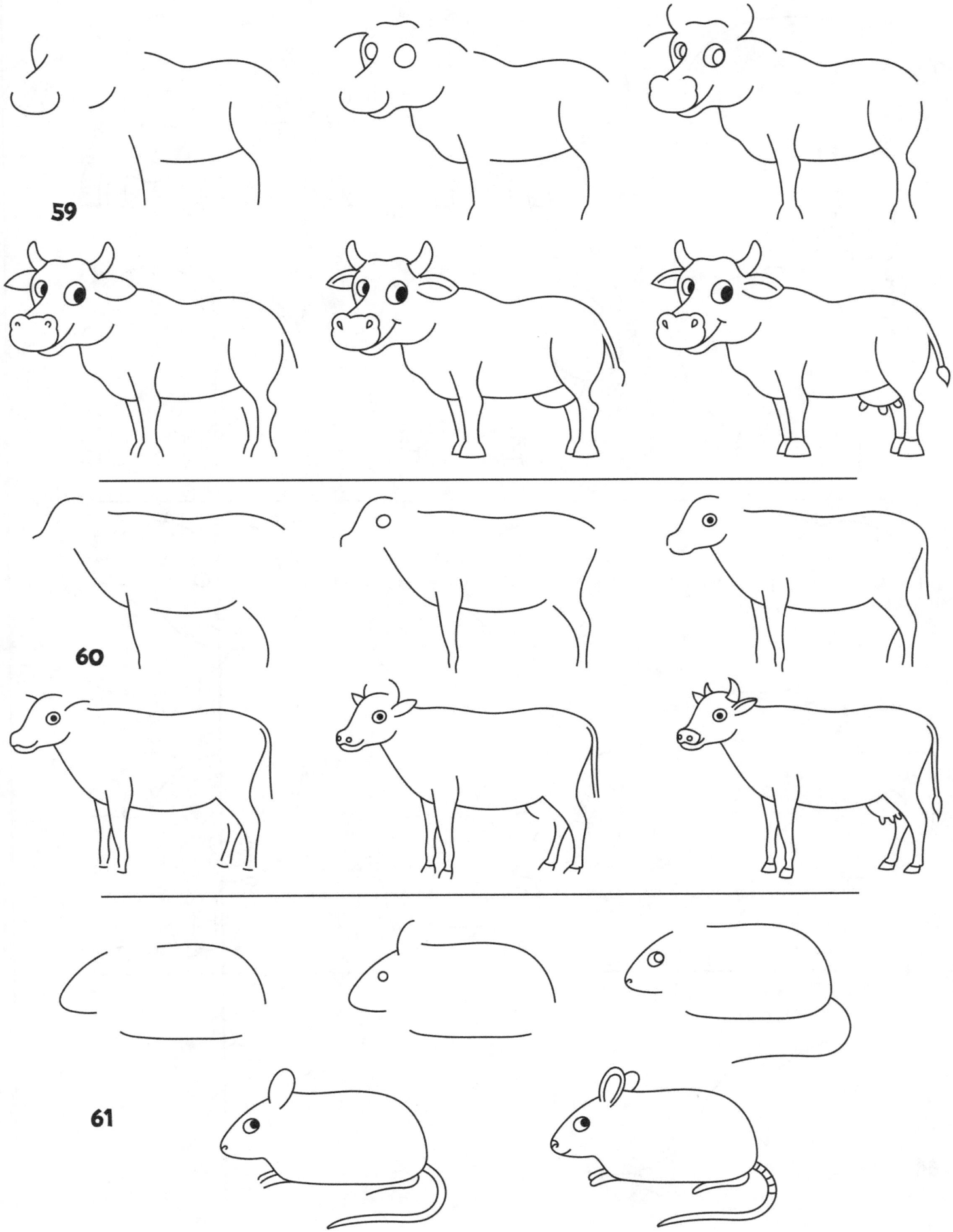
59
60
61

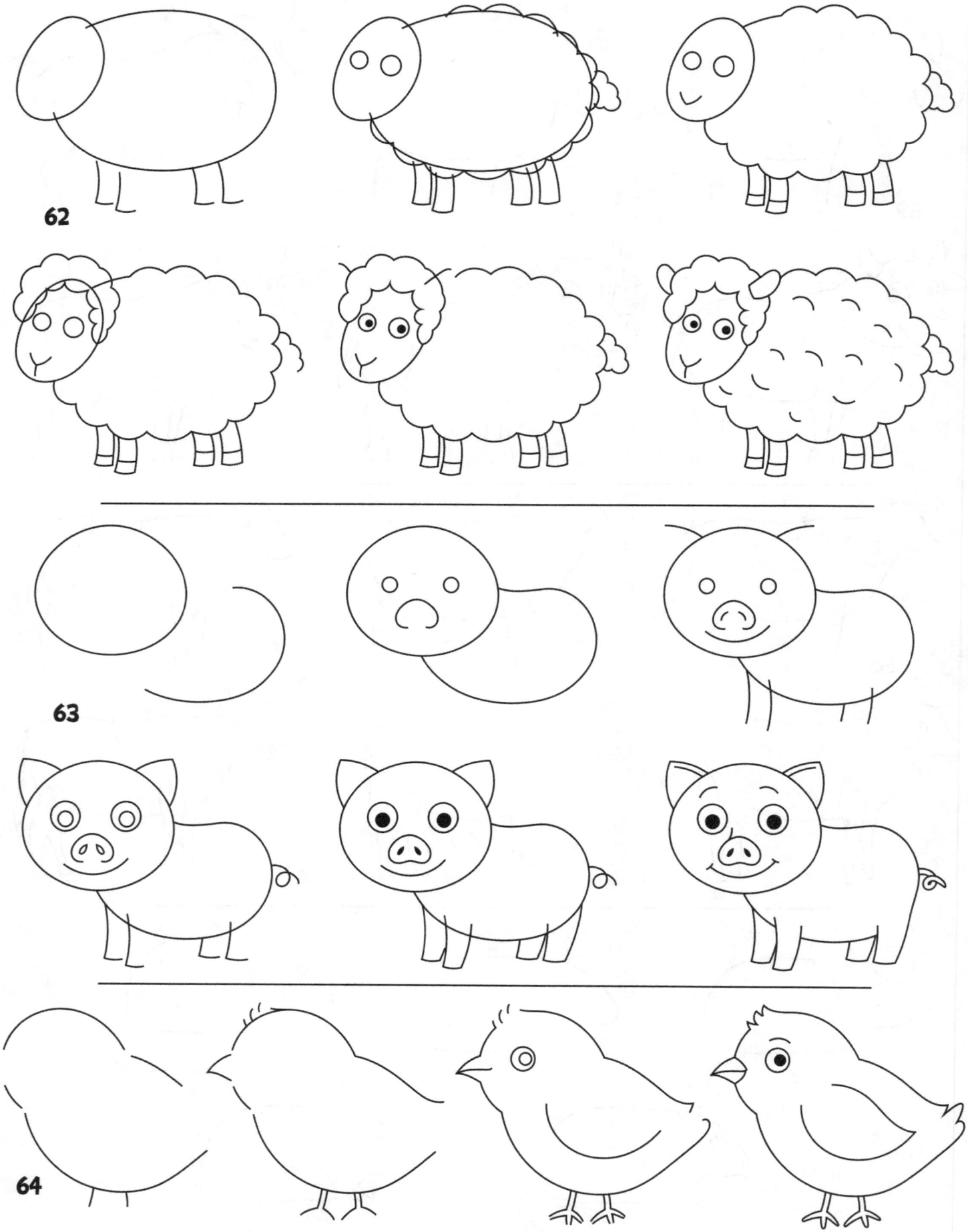
62
63
64

65
66

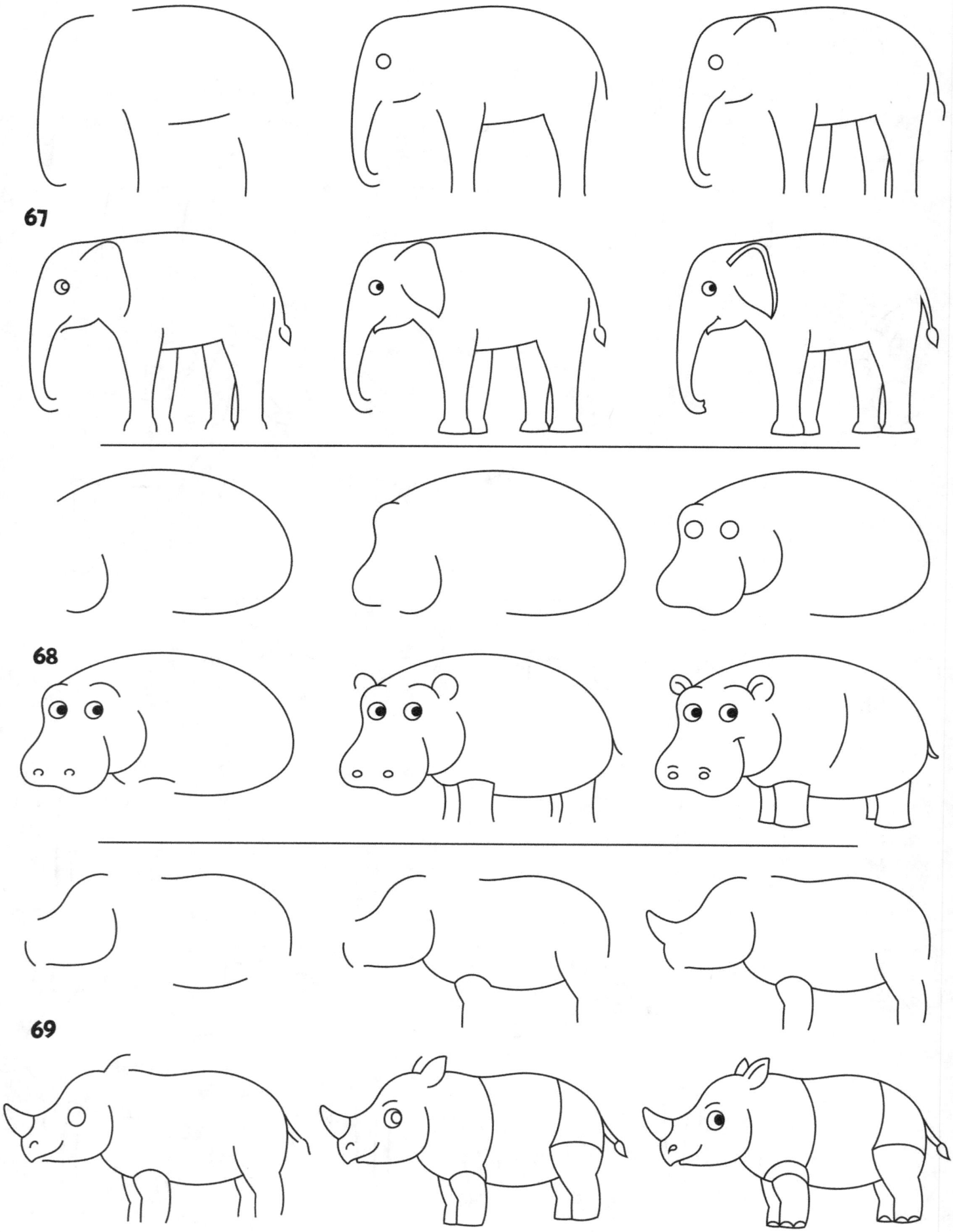
67
68
69

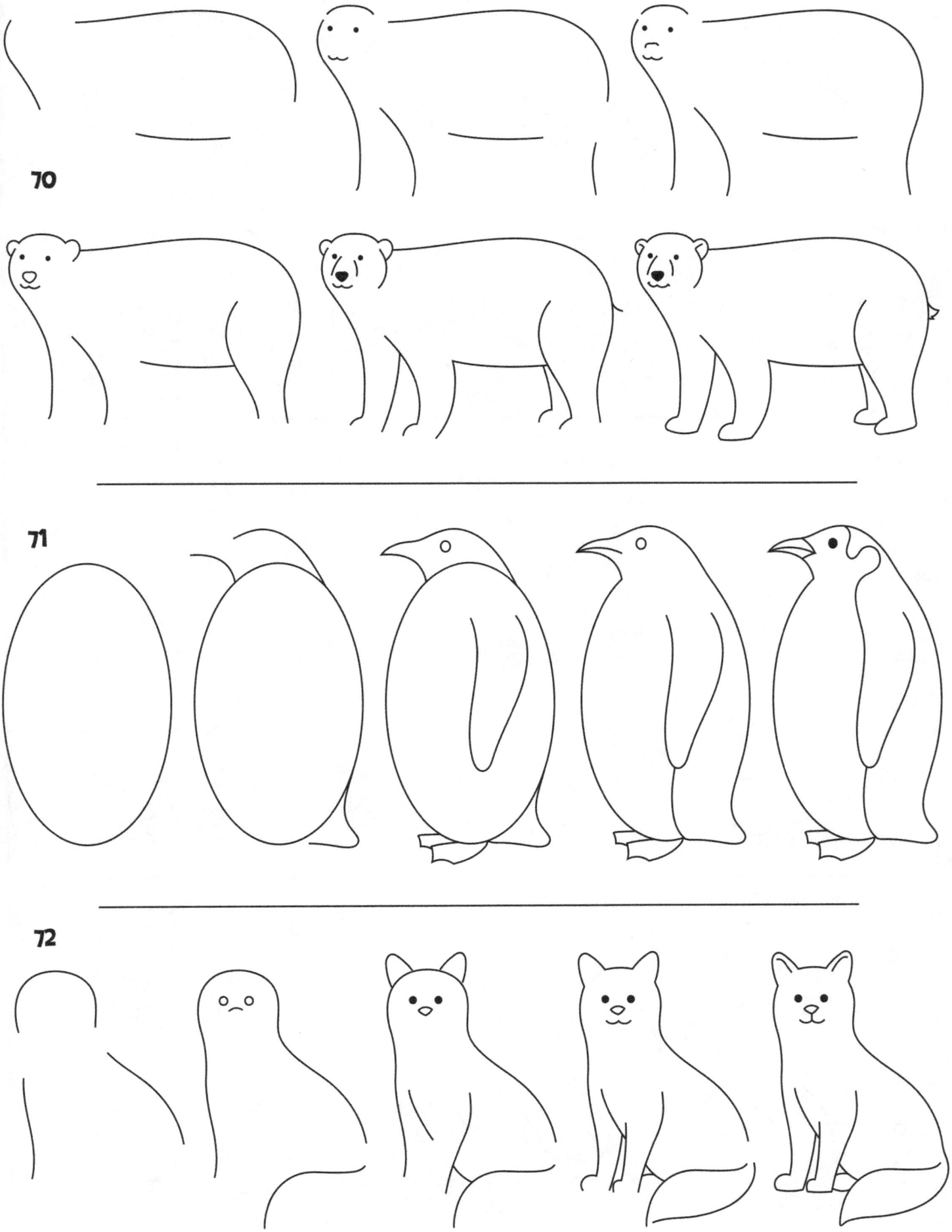
70
71
72

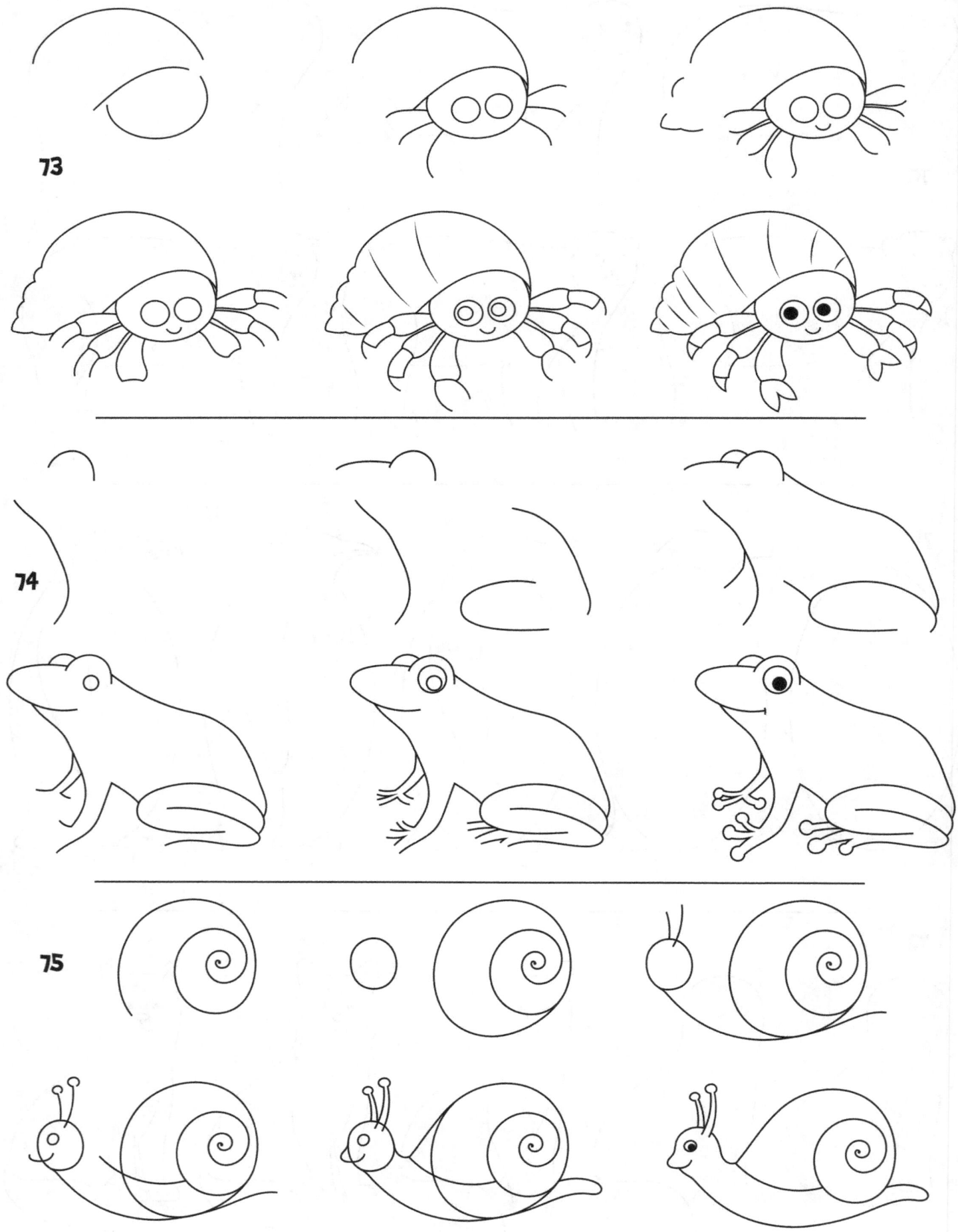
73
74
75

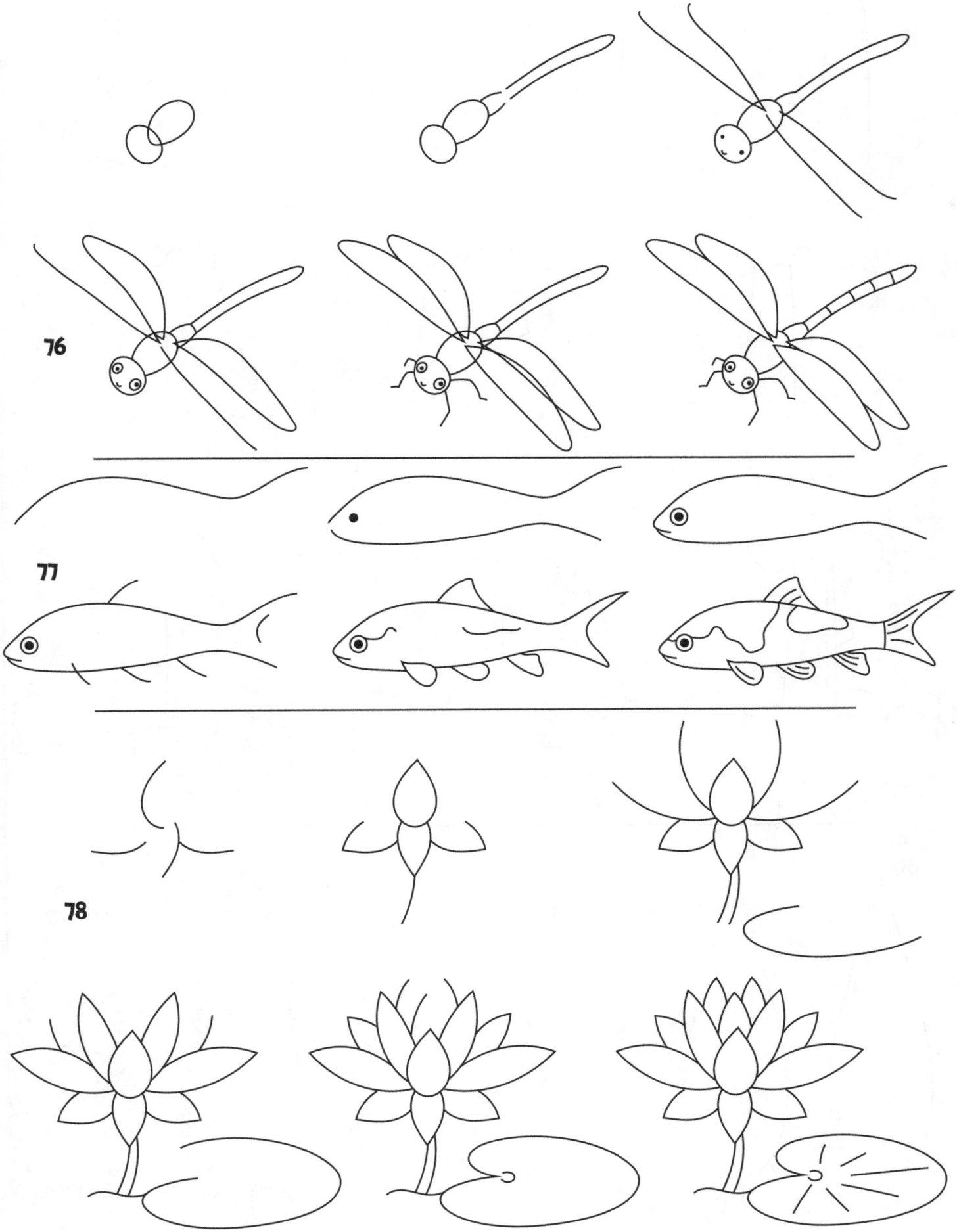
76
77
78

79

80

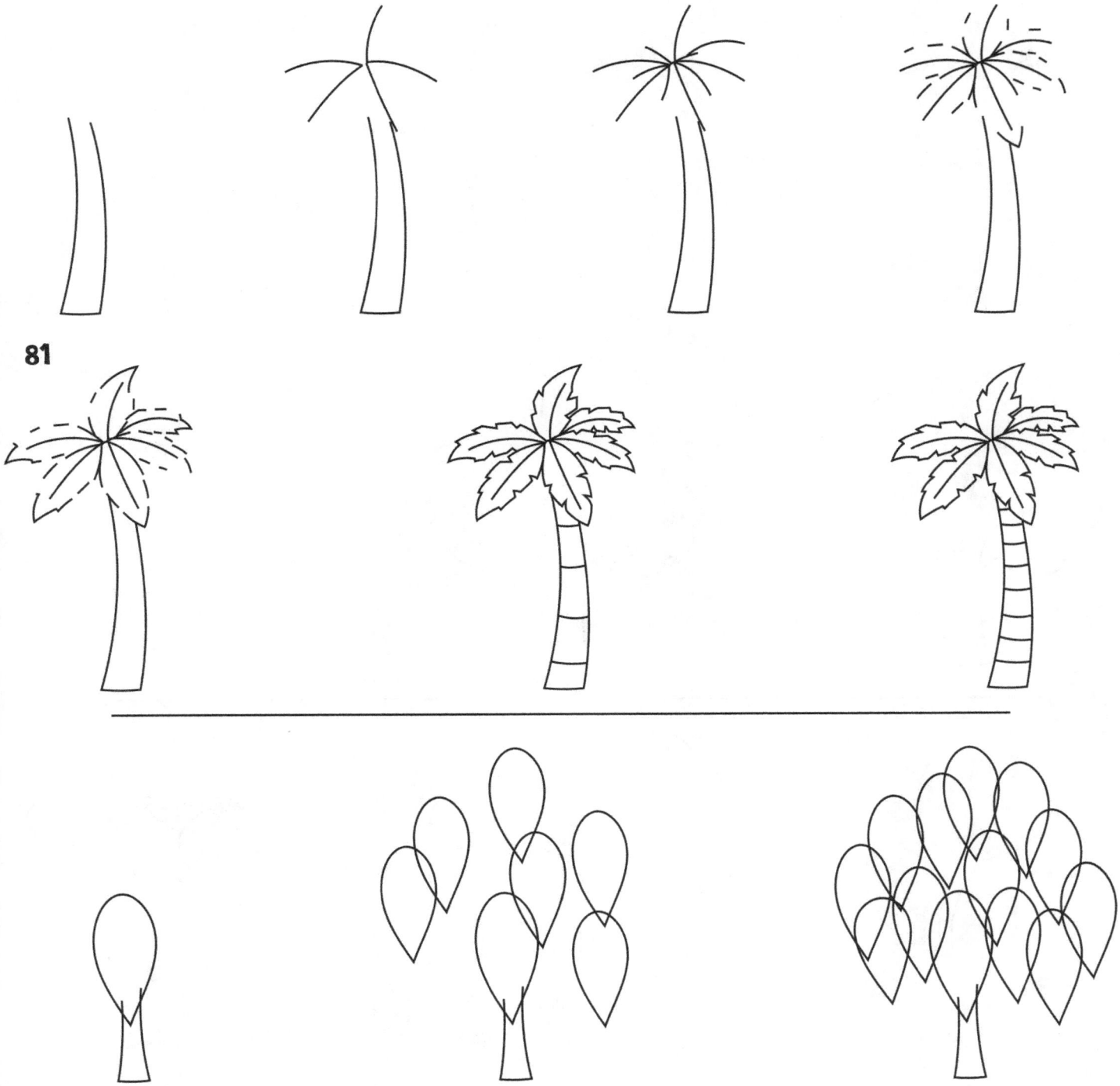
81
82

83

84

85

86

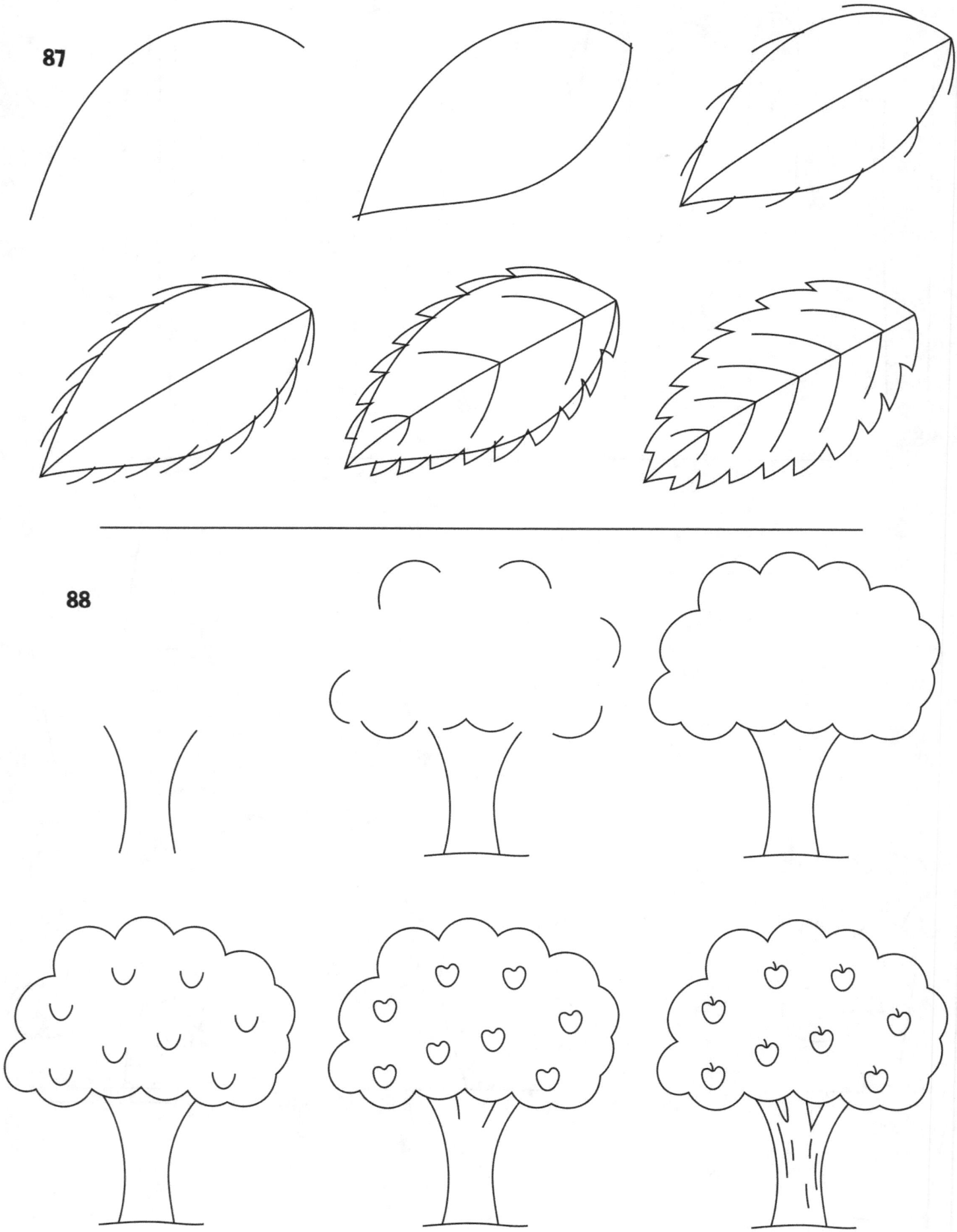
87
88

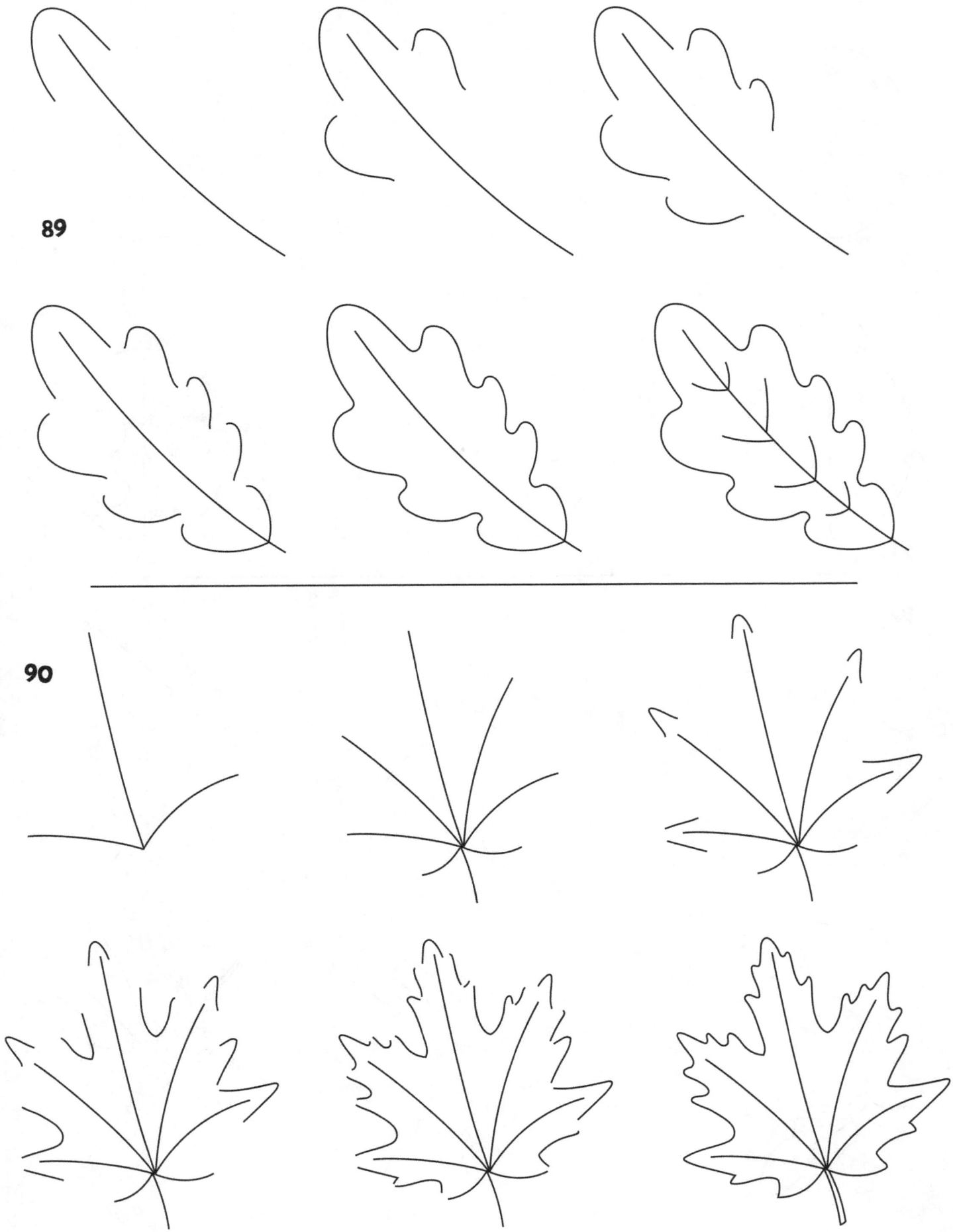
89
90

91

92

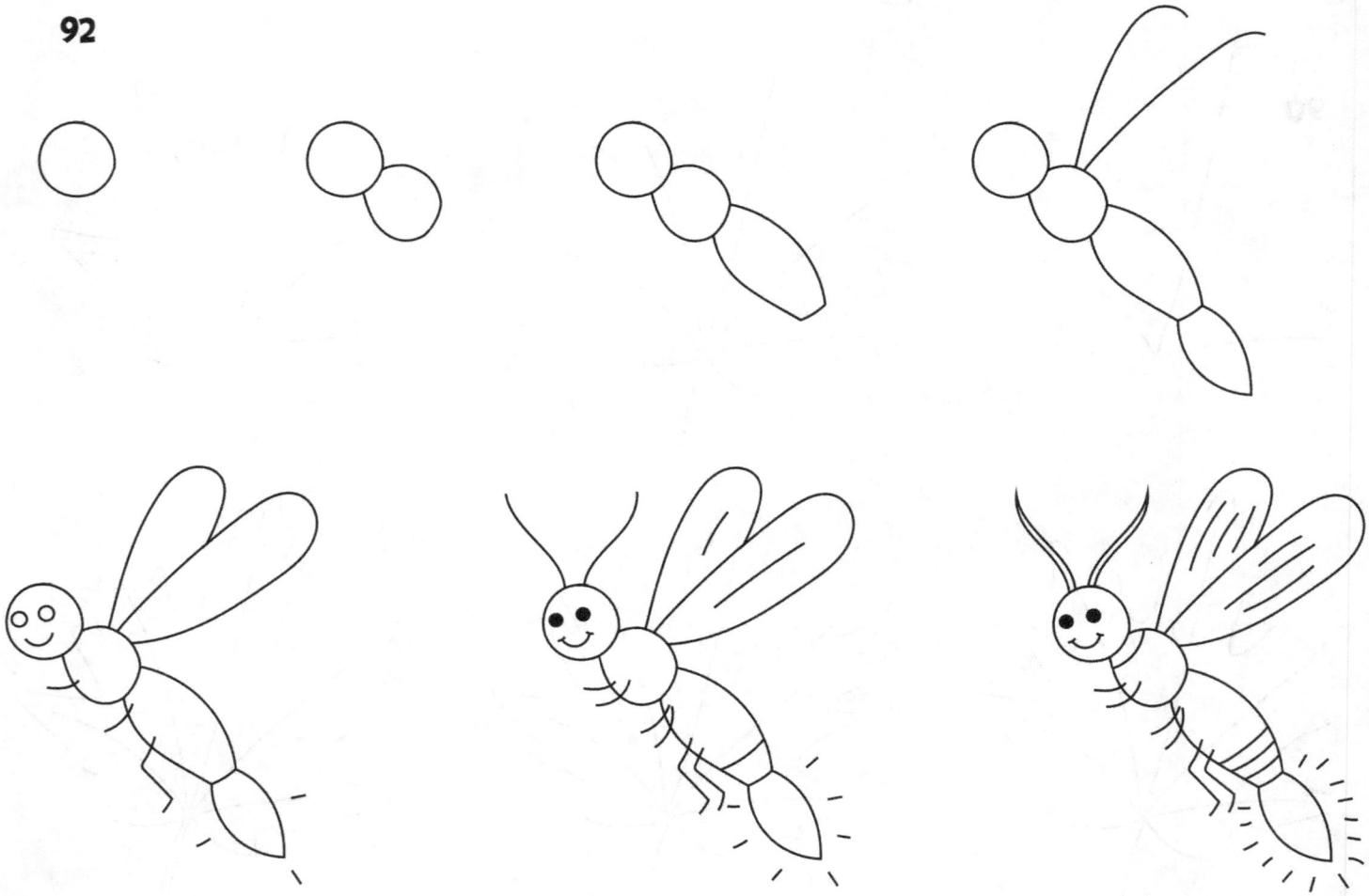

93

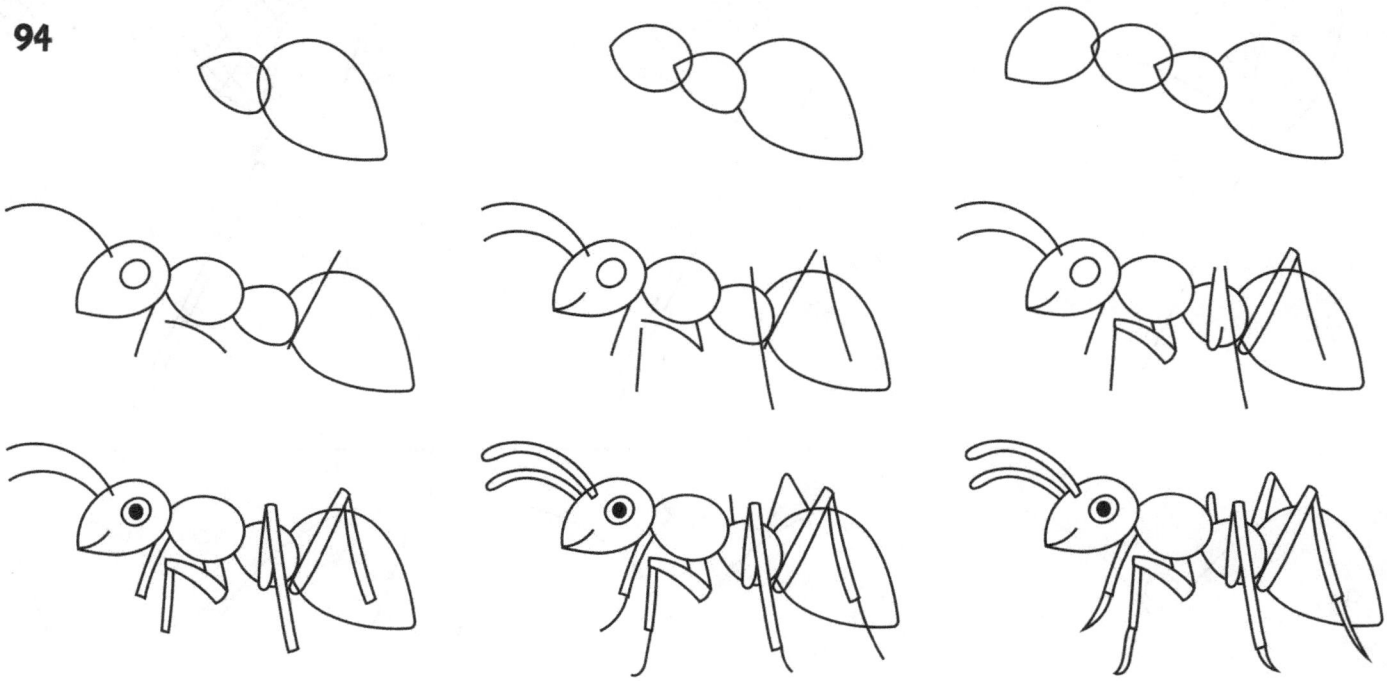
94

95

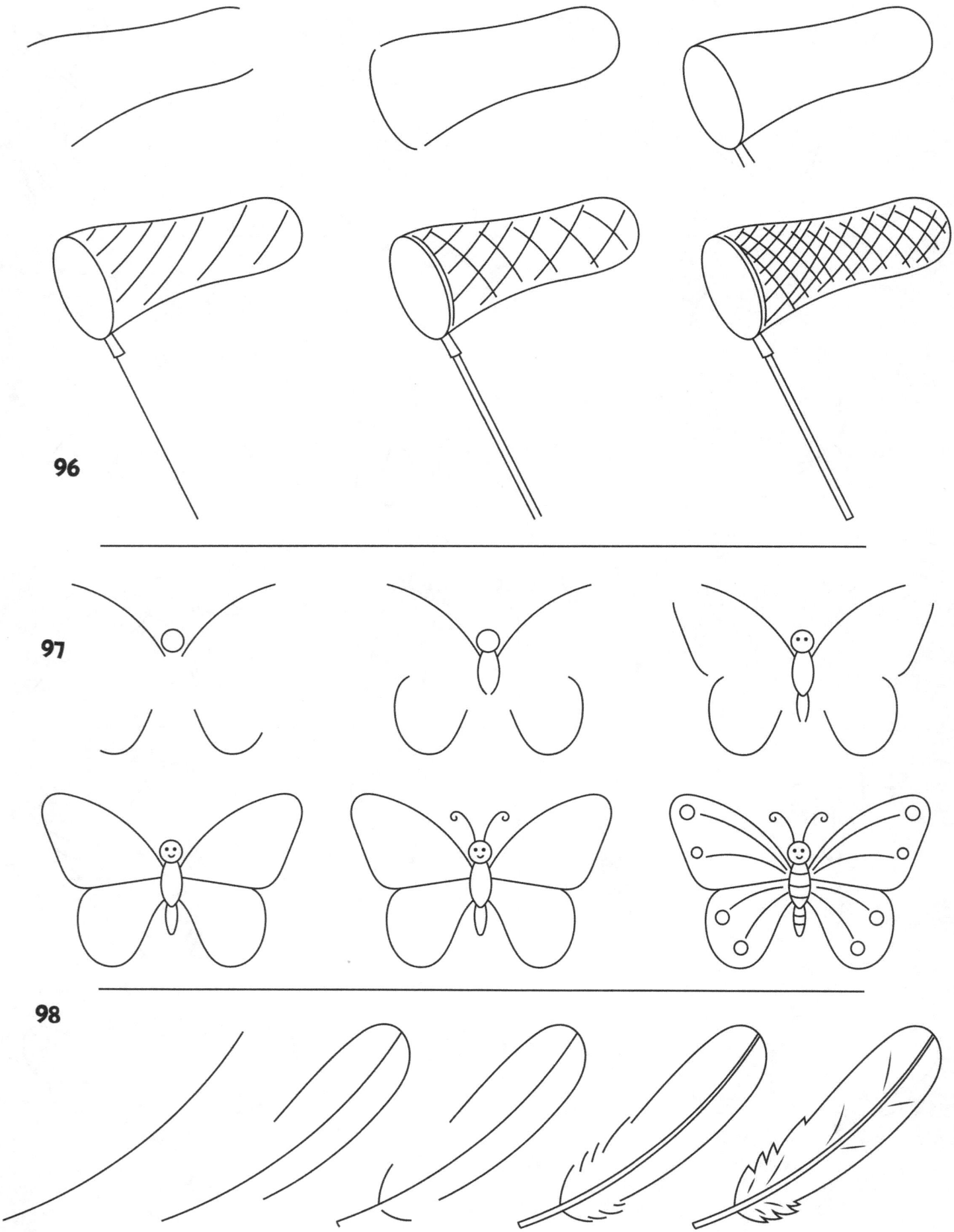
96
97
98

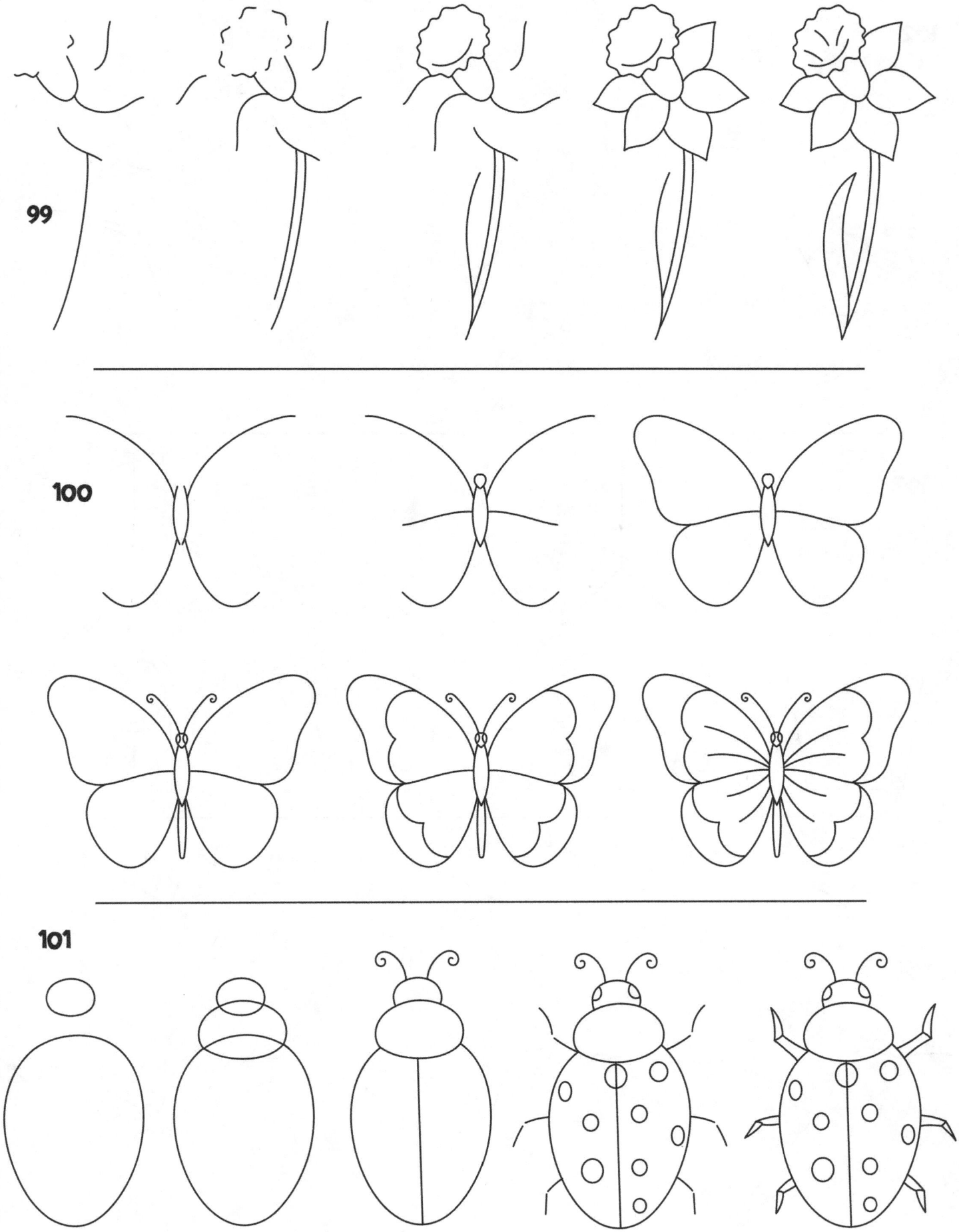
99
100
101

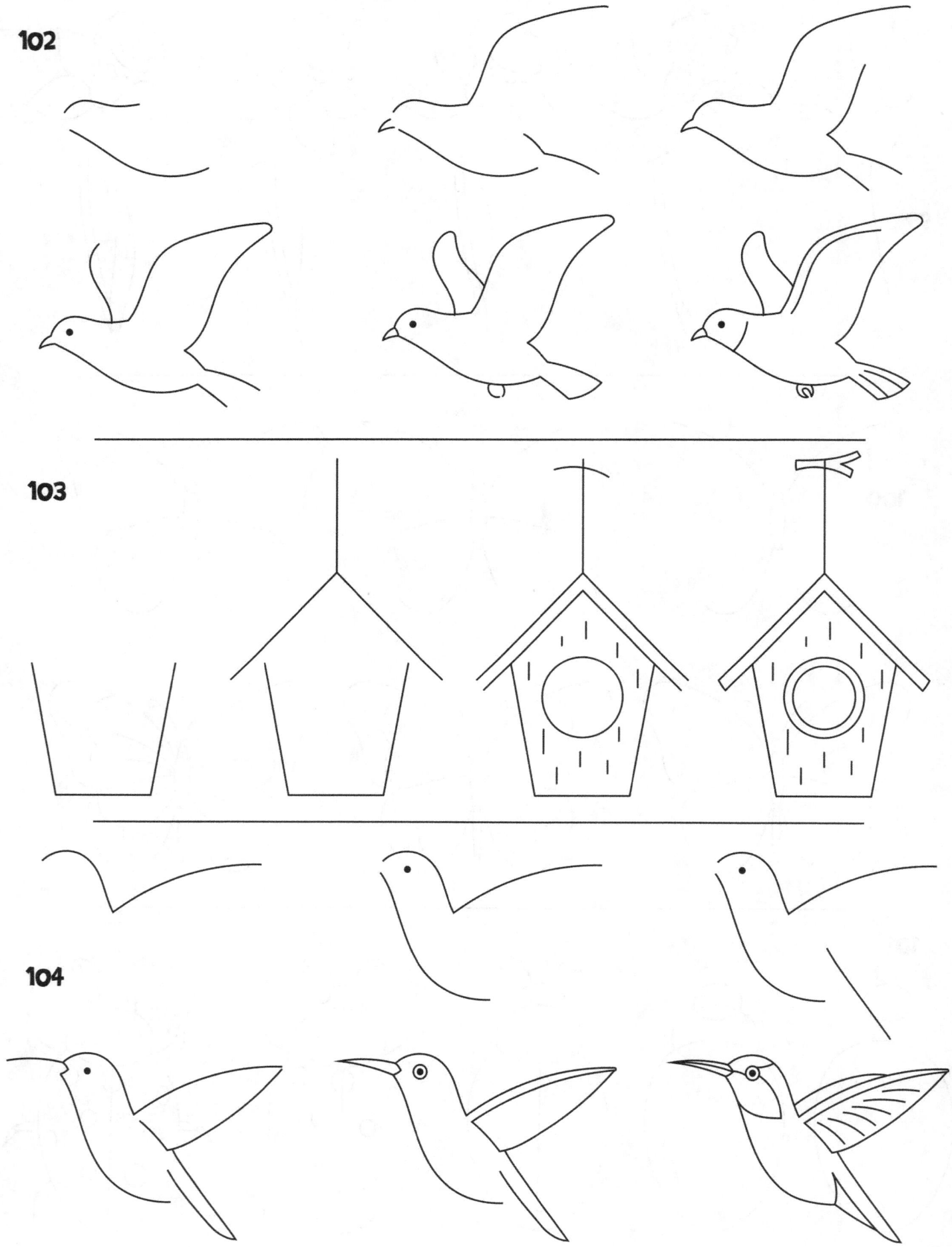
102
103
104

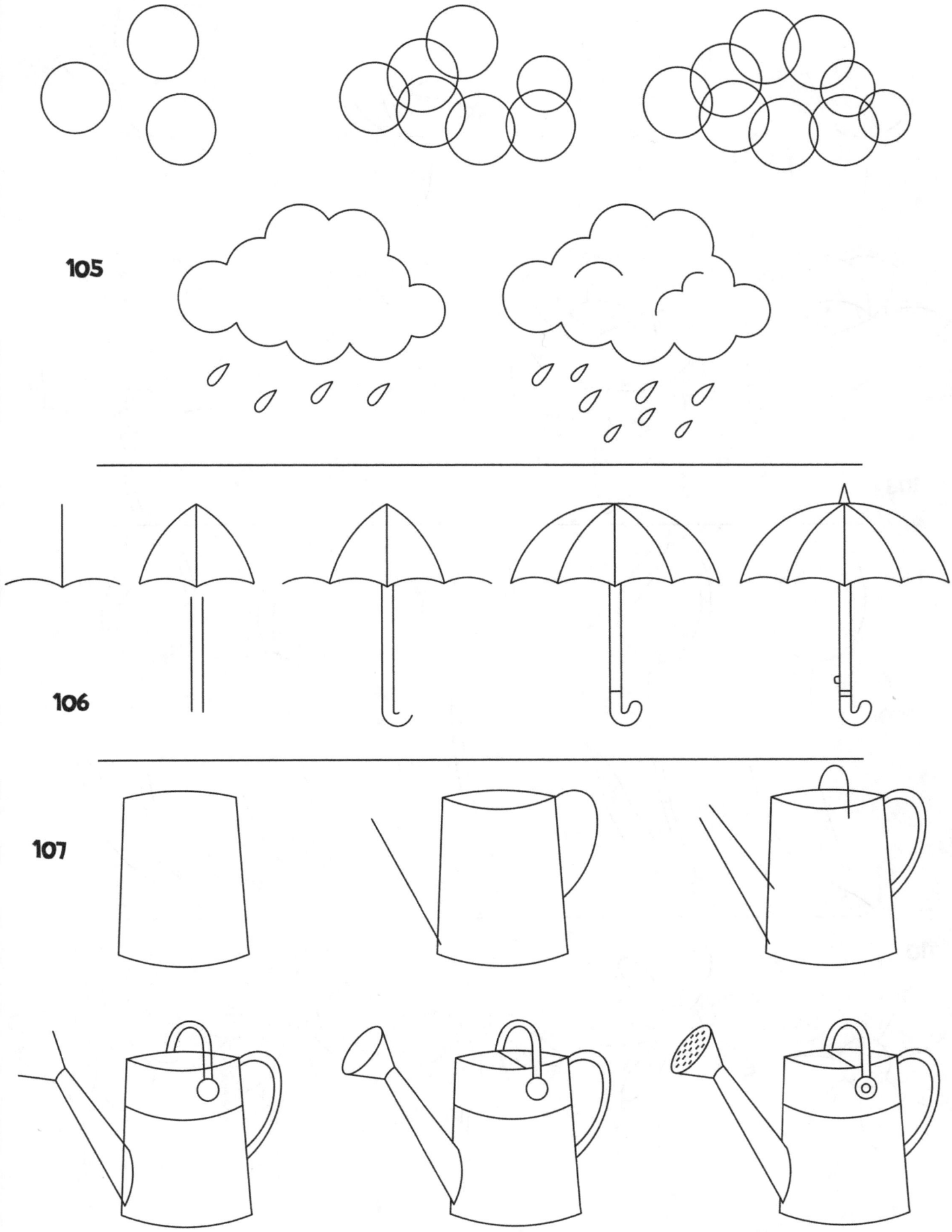
105
106
107

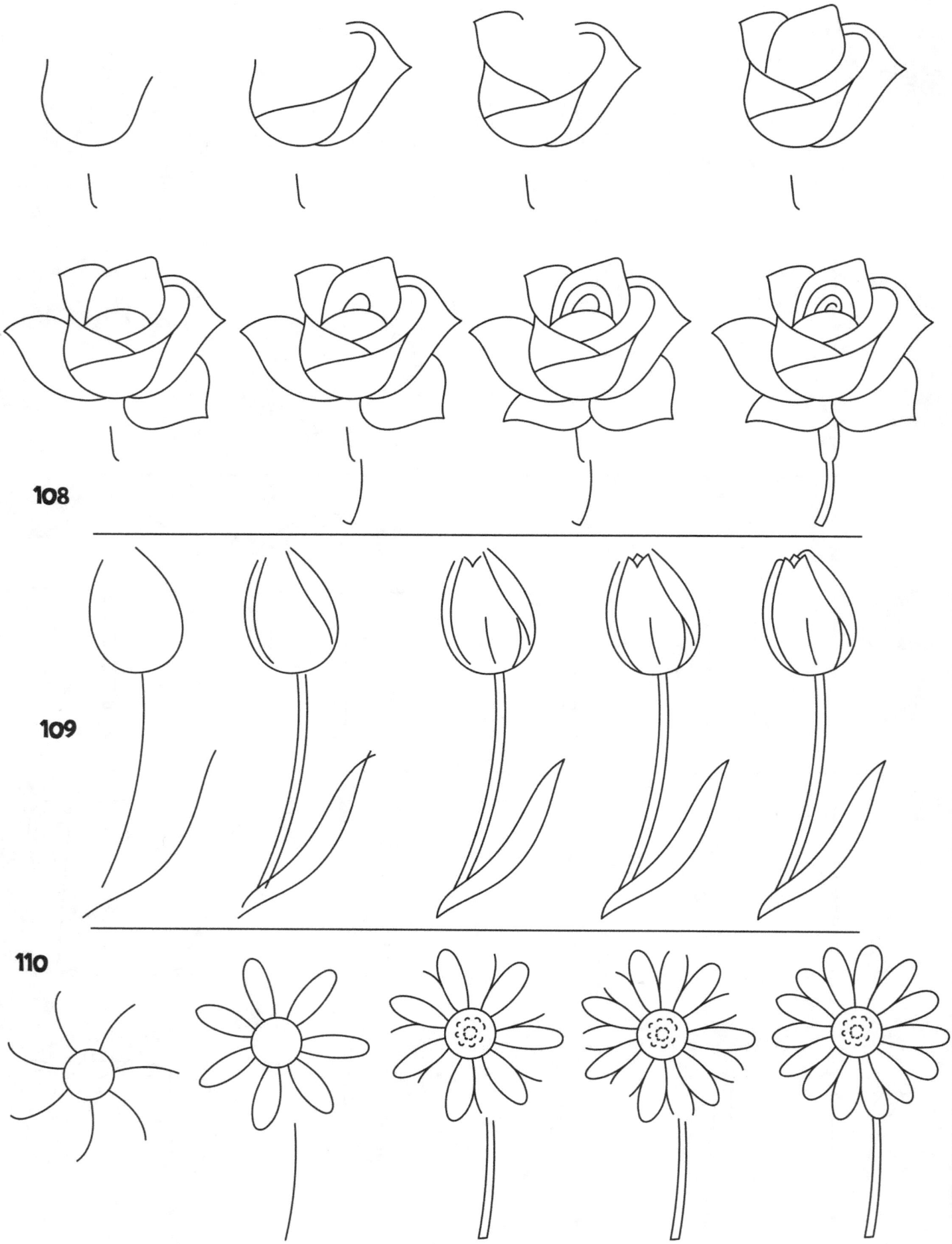
108
109
110

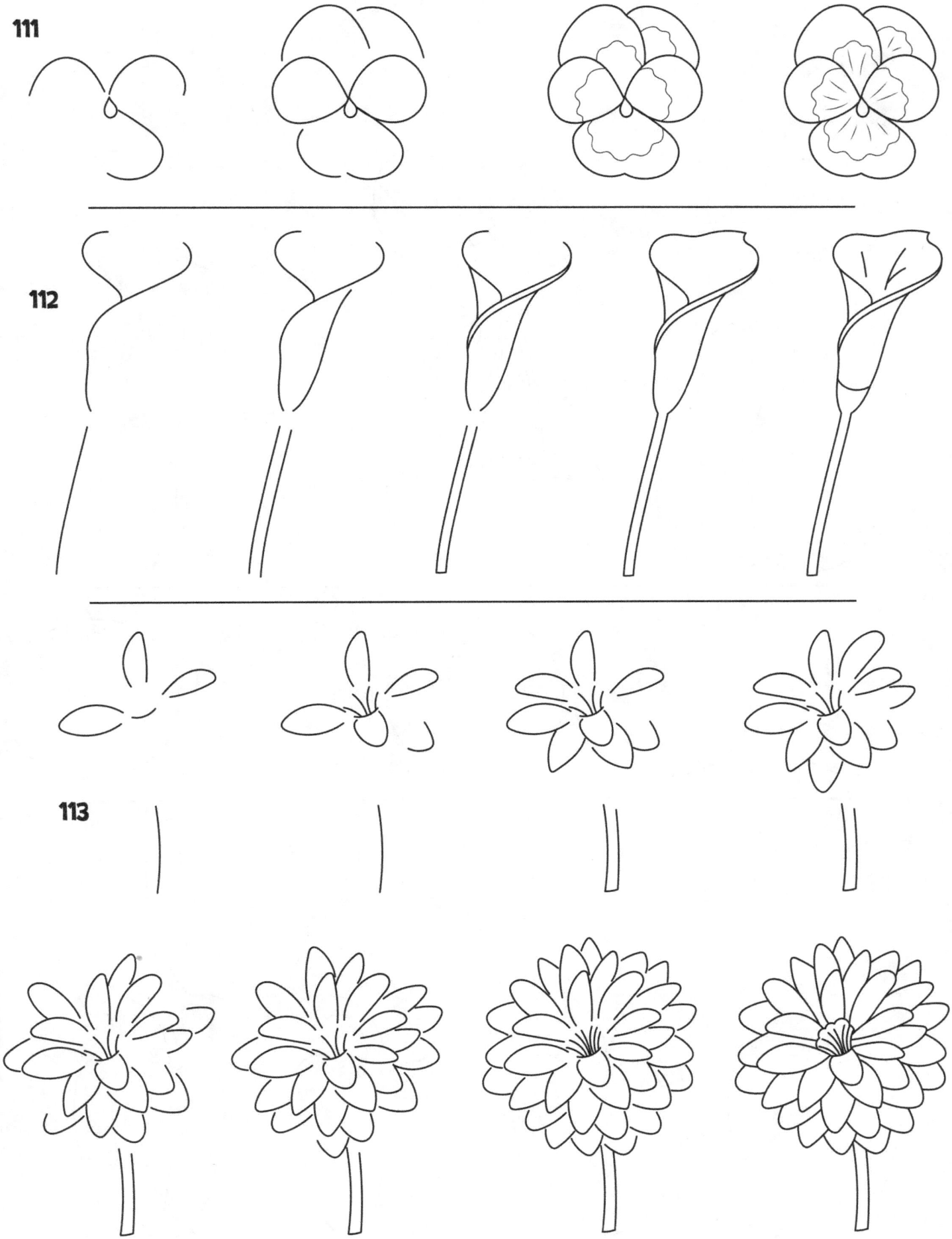
111
112
113

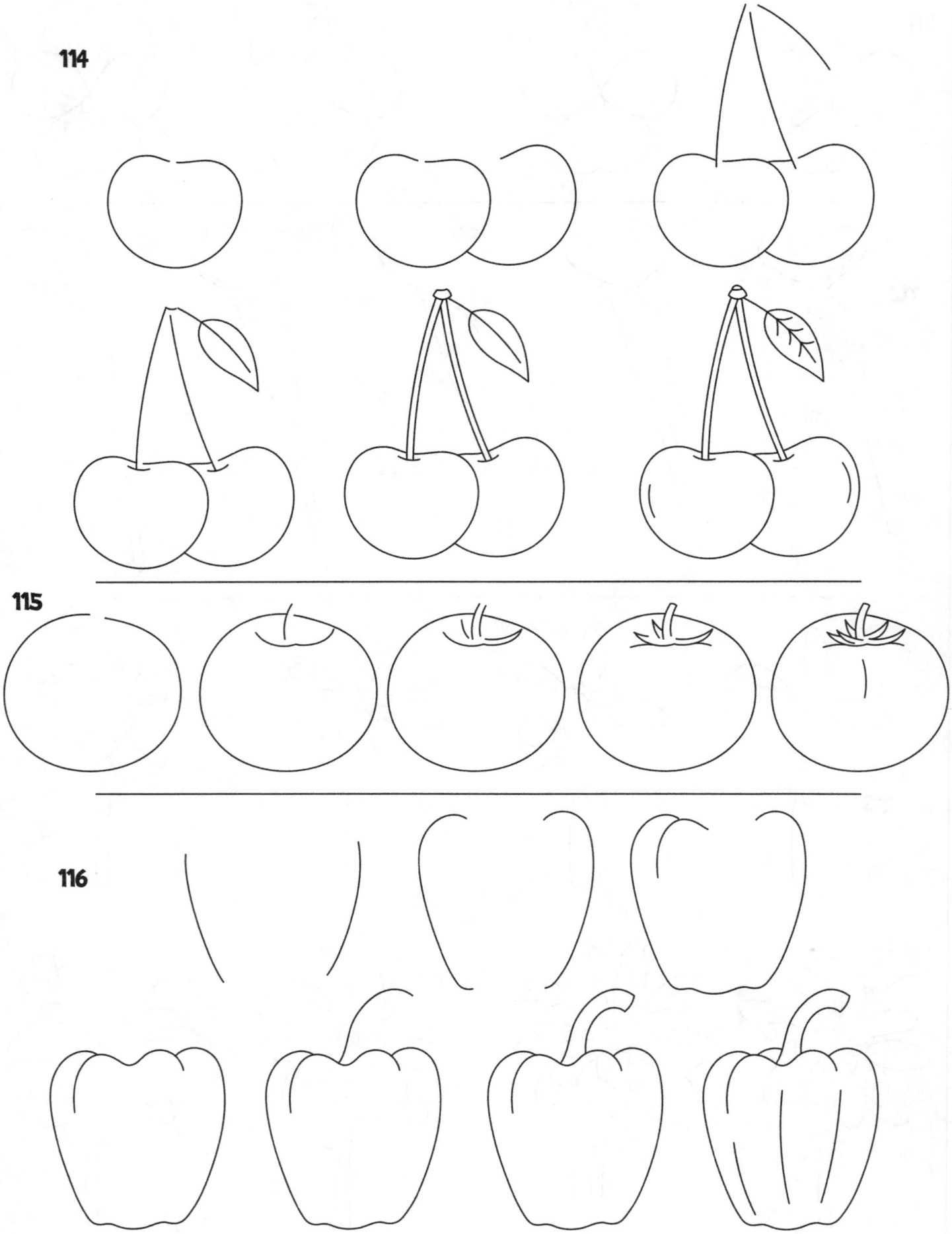
114
115
116

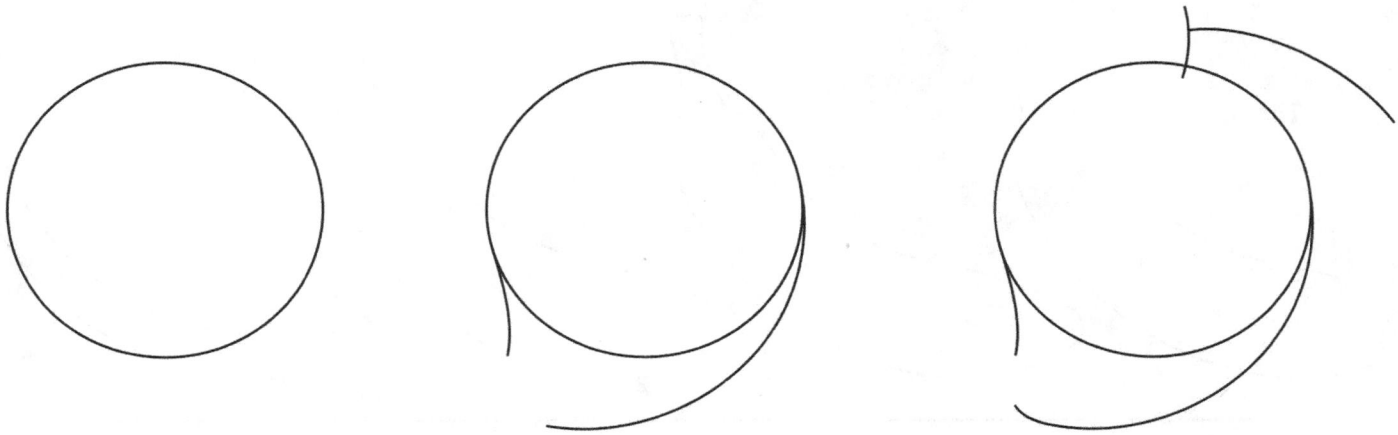

117

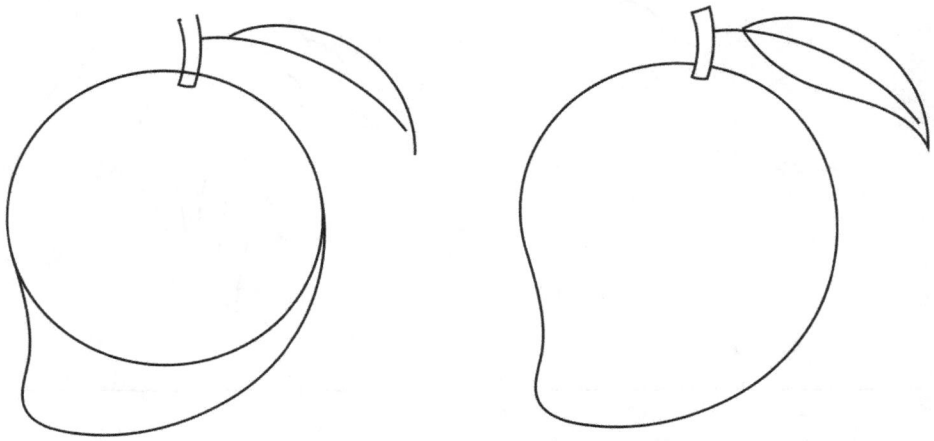

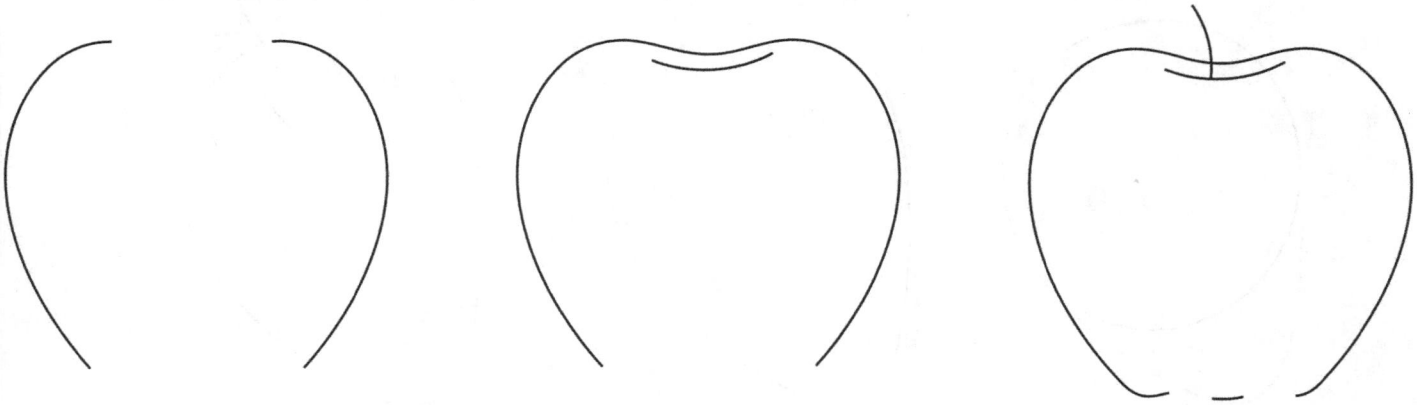

118

119

120

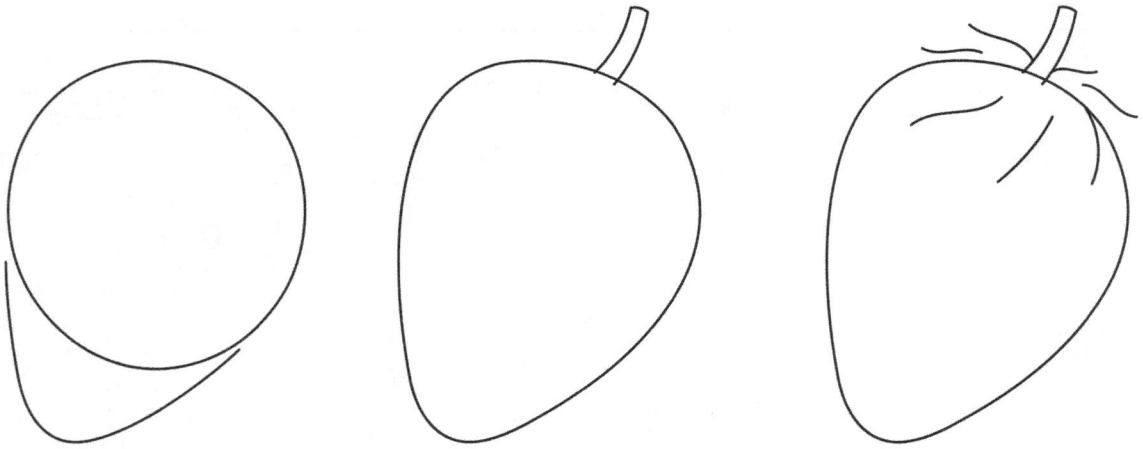

121

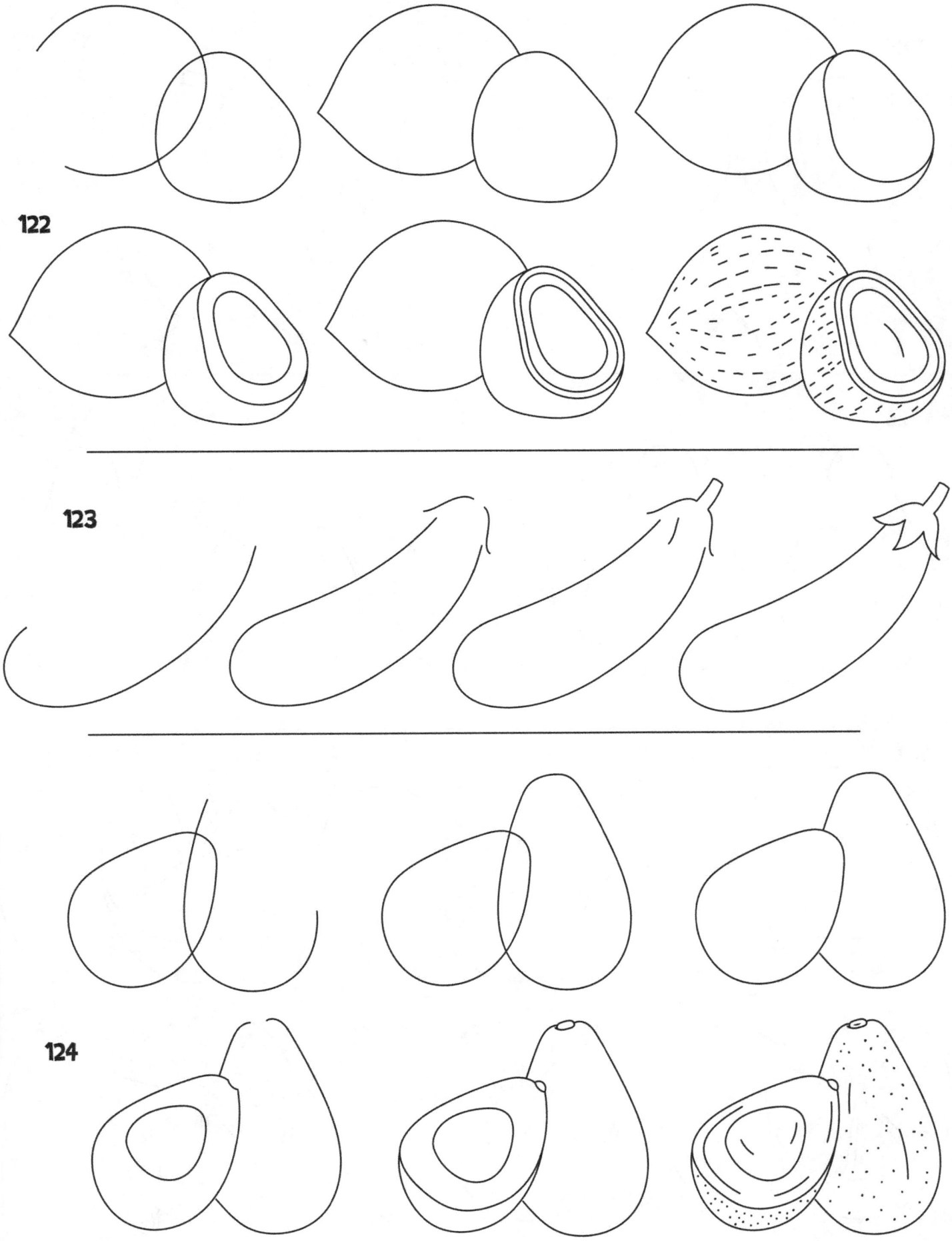
122
123
124

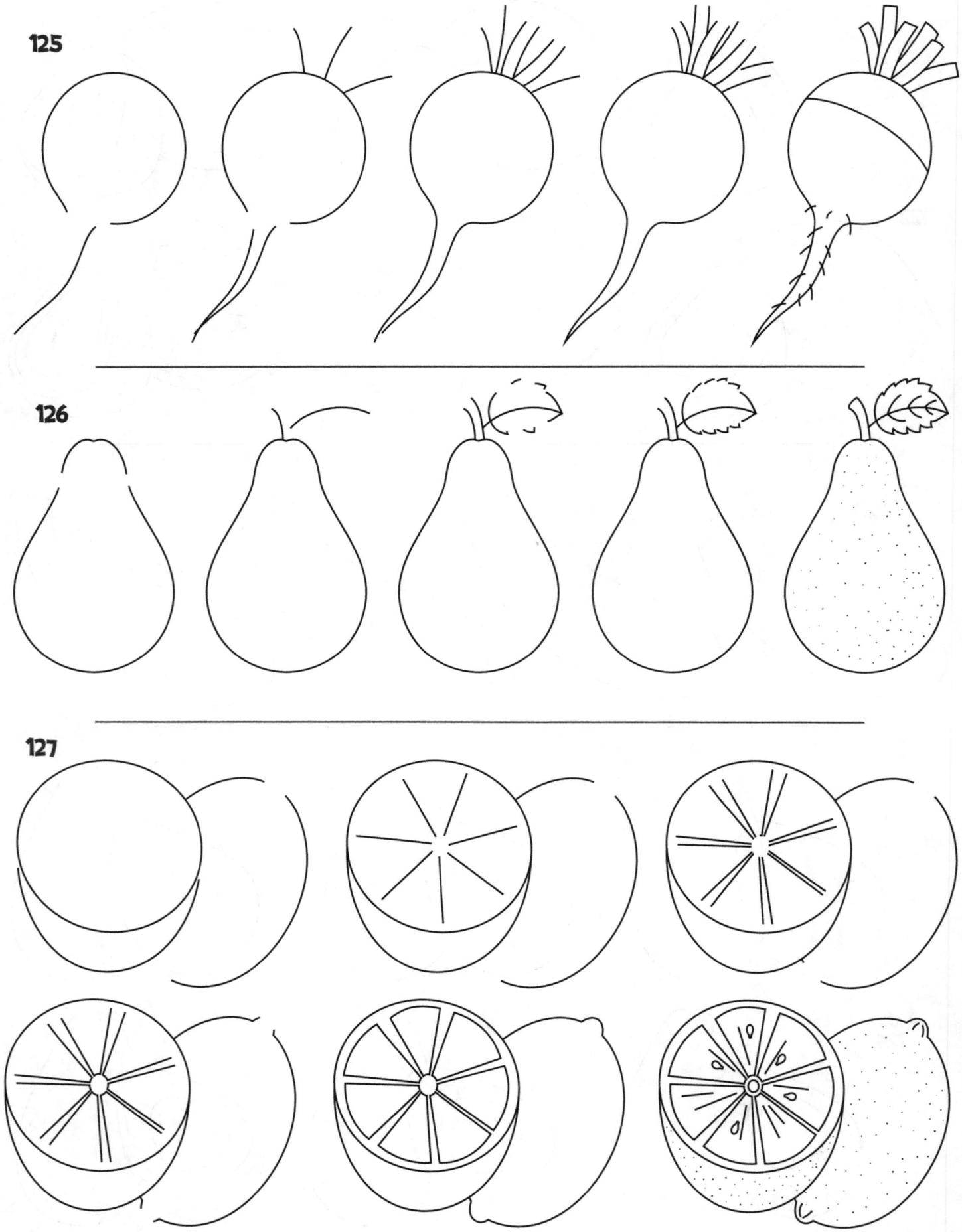
125
126
127

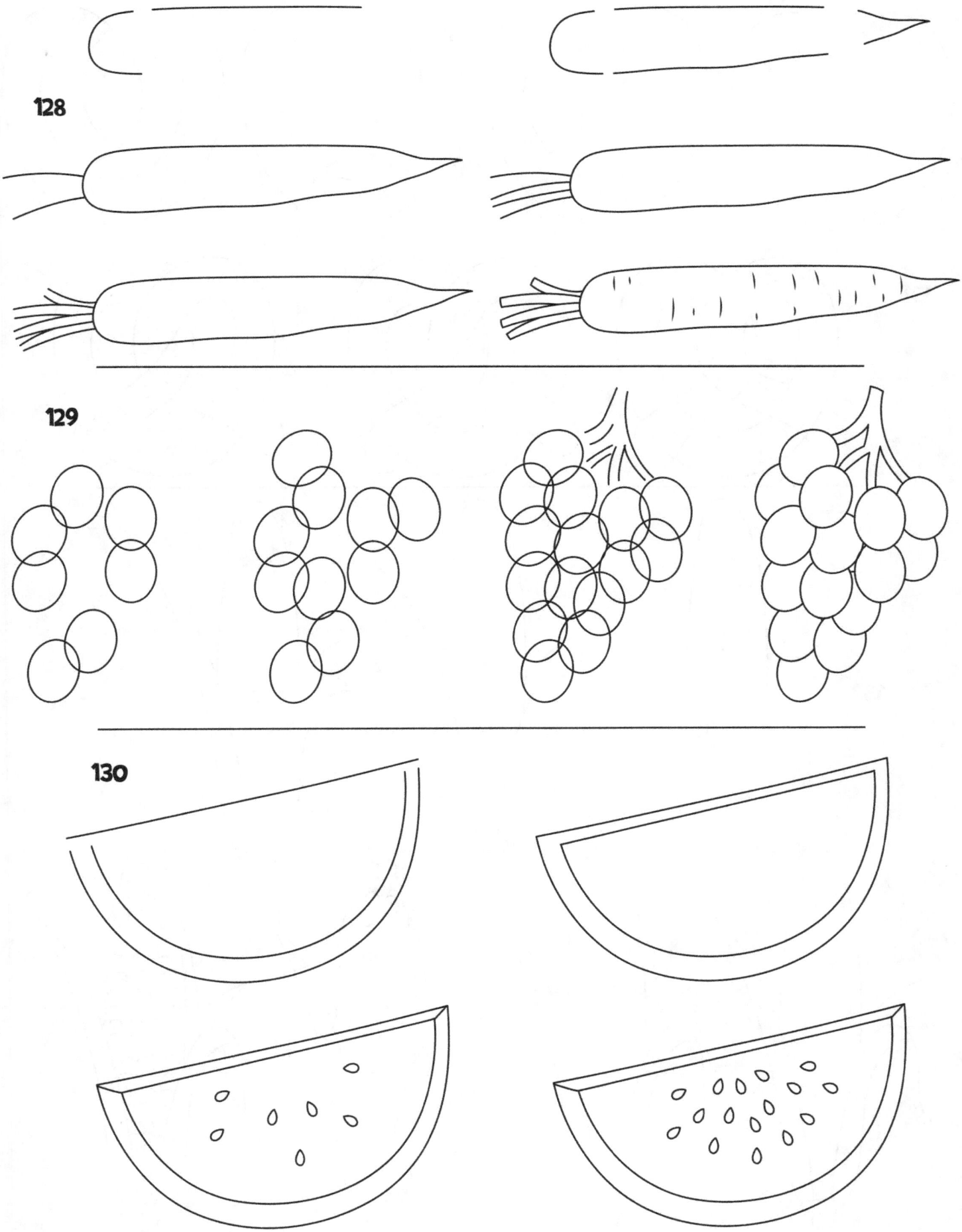
128
129
130

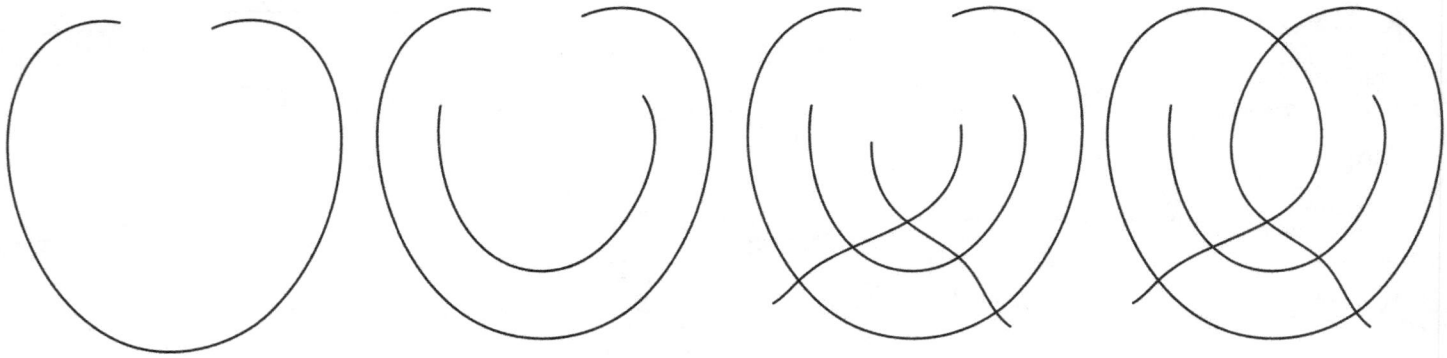

131

132

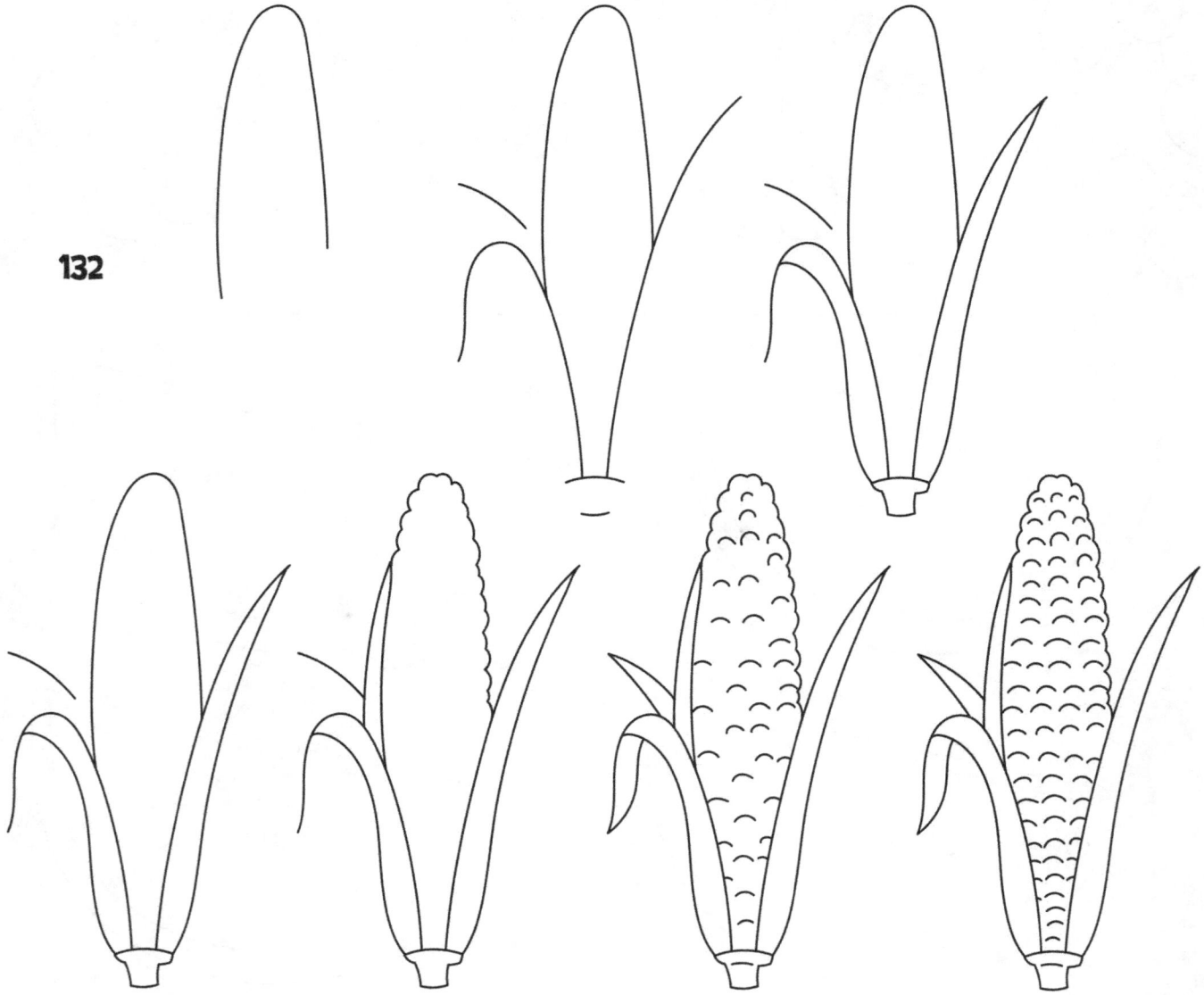

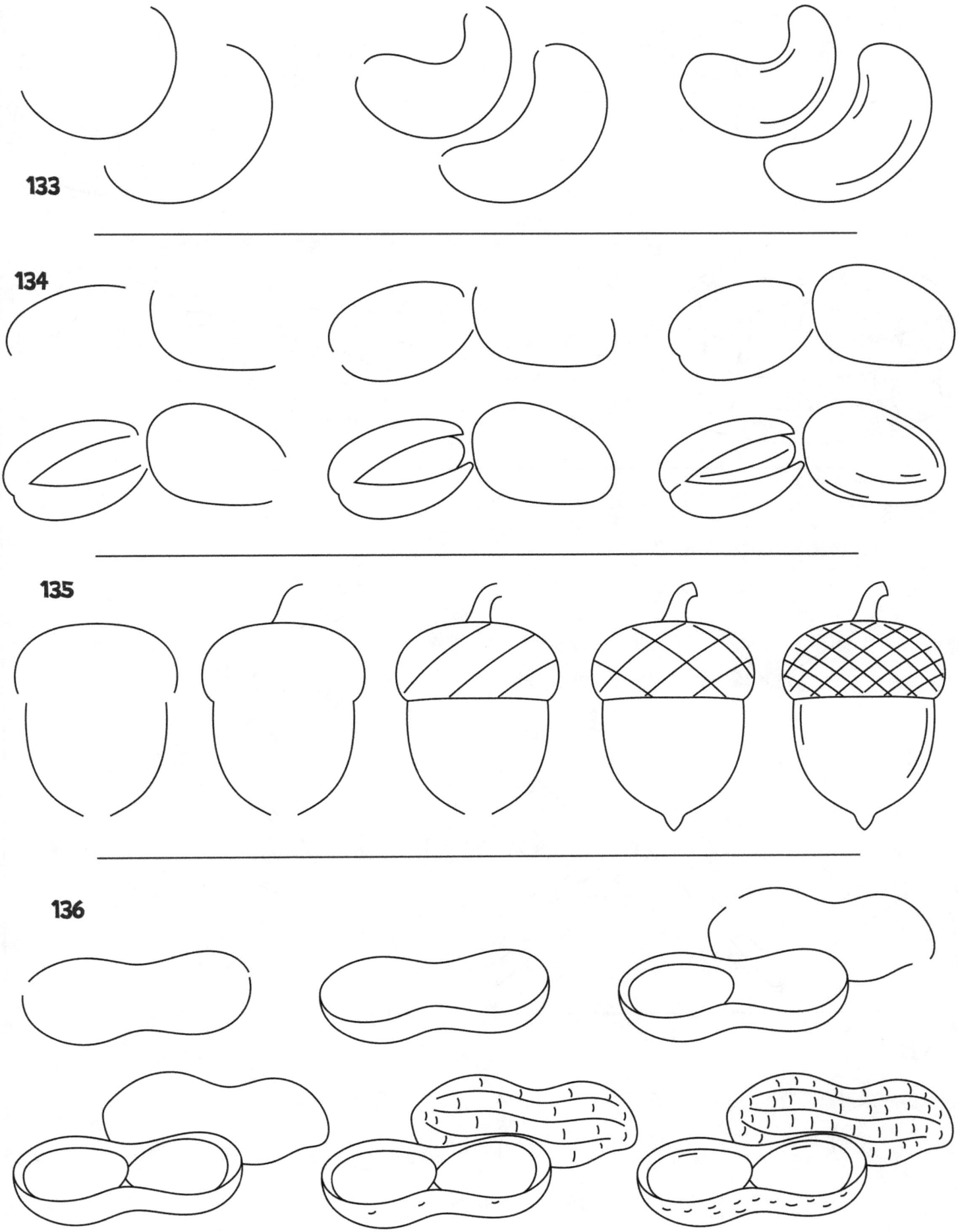
133
134
135
136

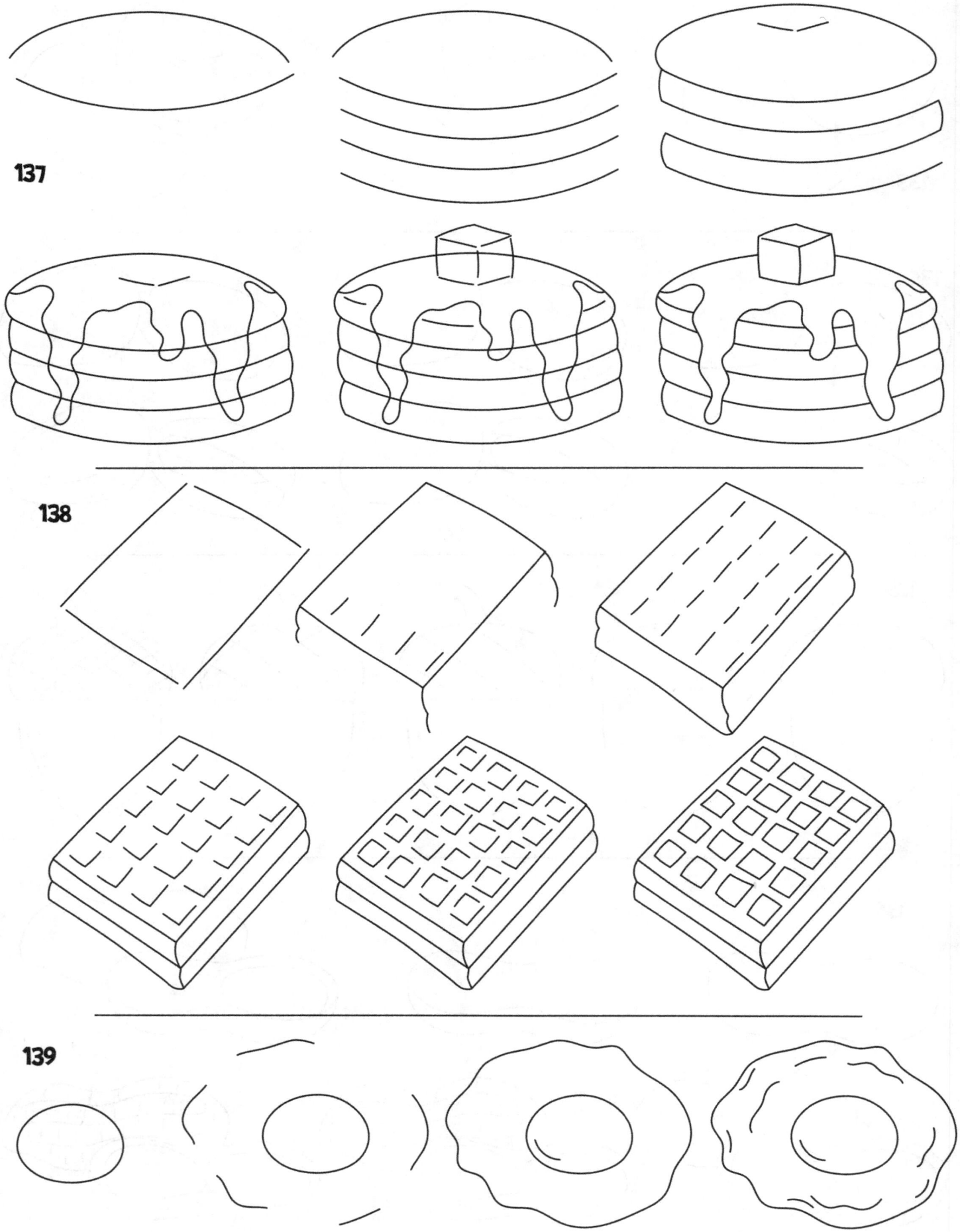
137
138
139

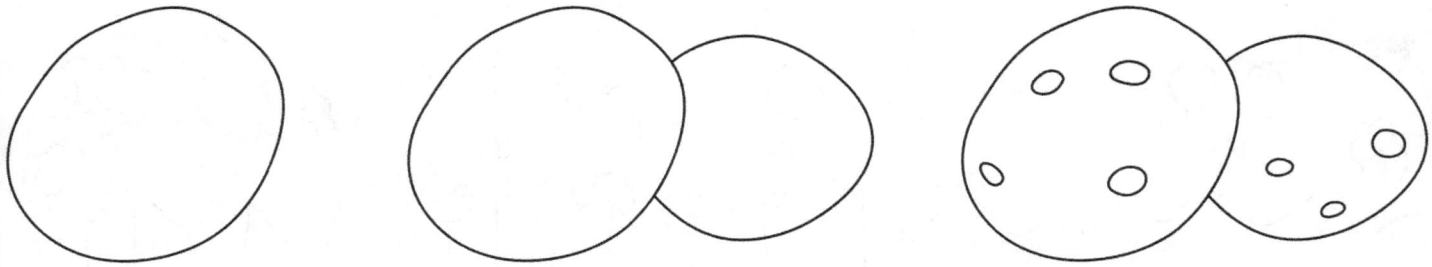

140

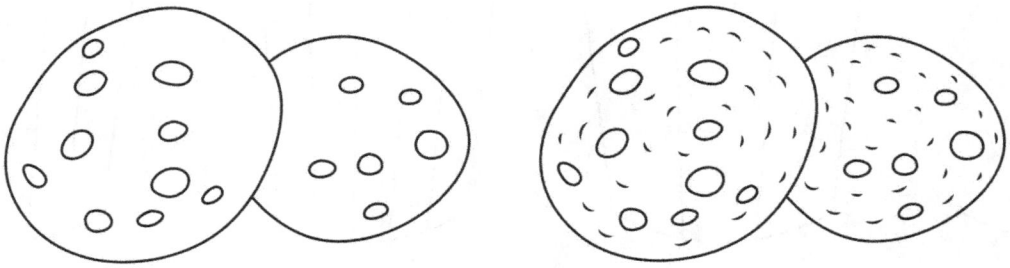

141

142

143

144

145

146

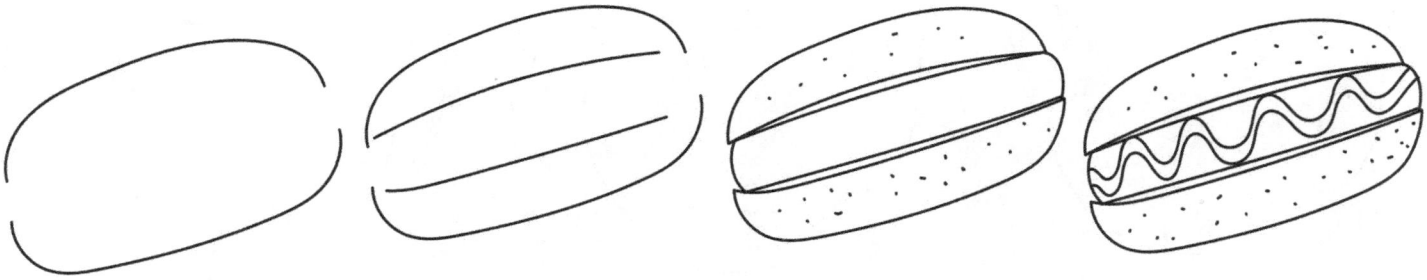

147

148

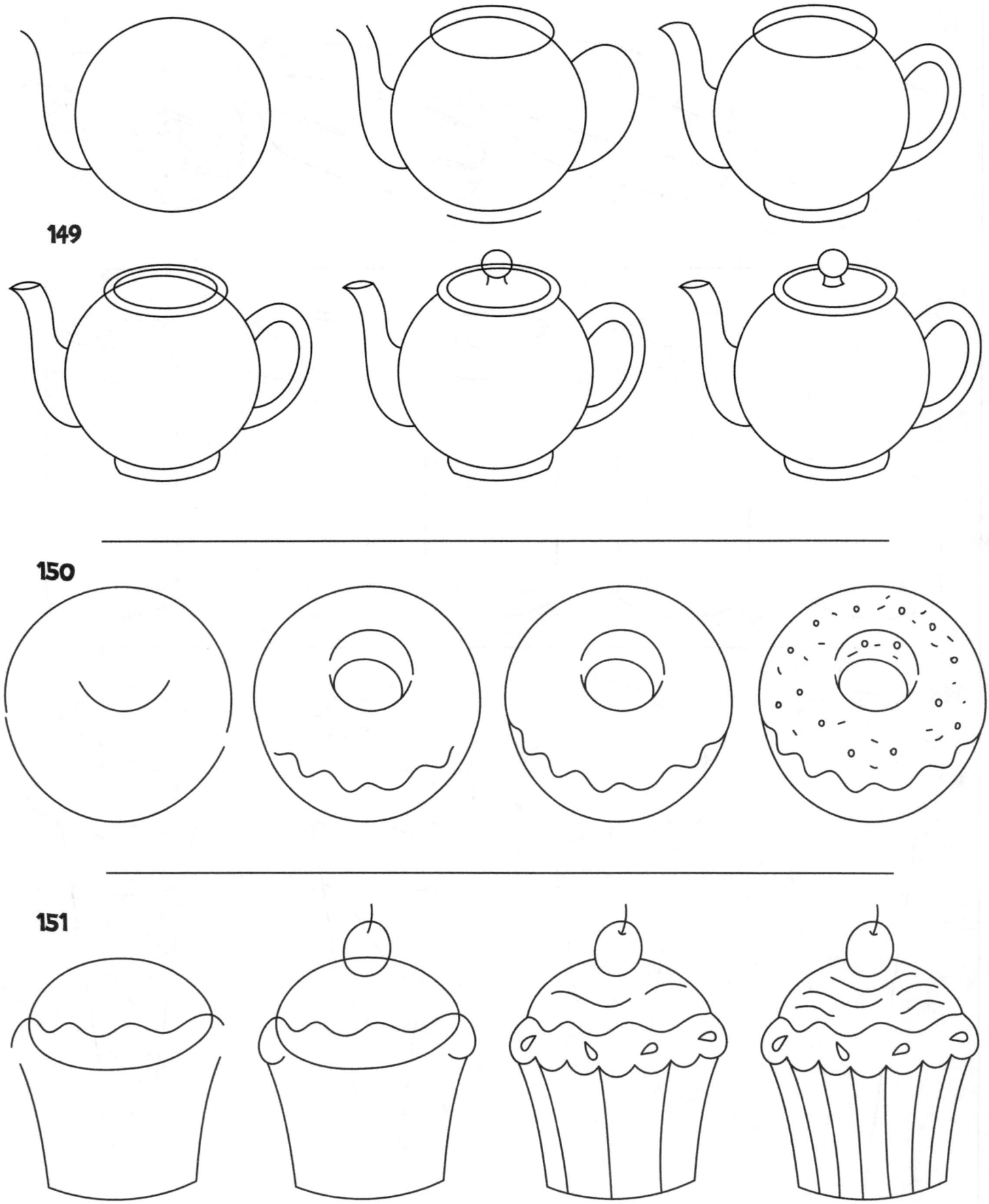
149
150
151

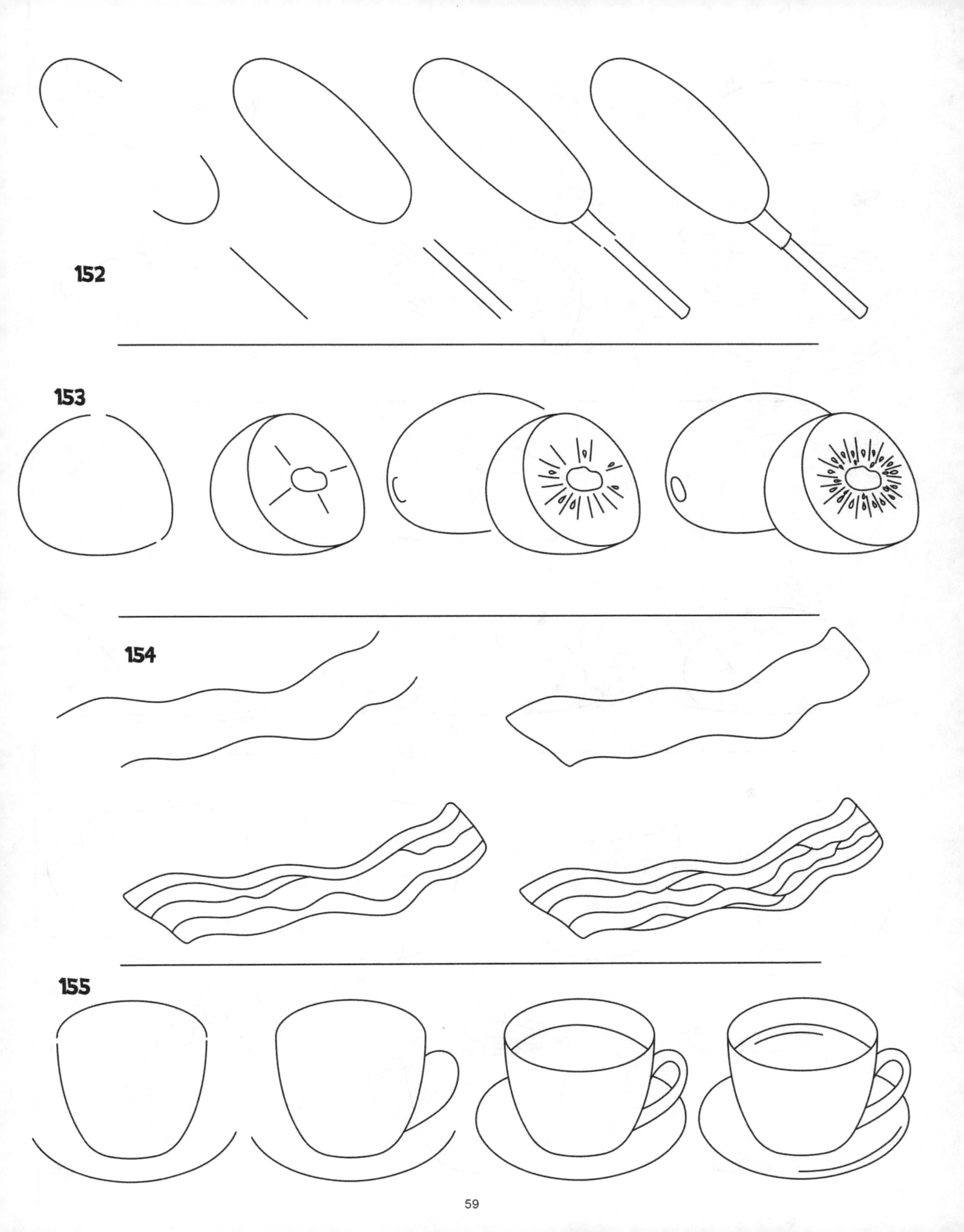
152
153
154
155

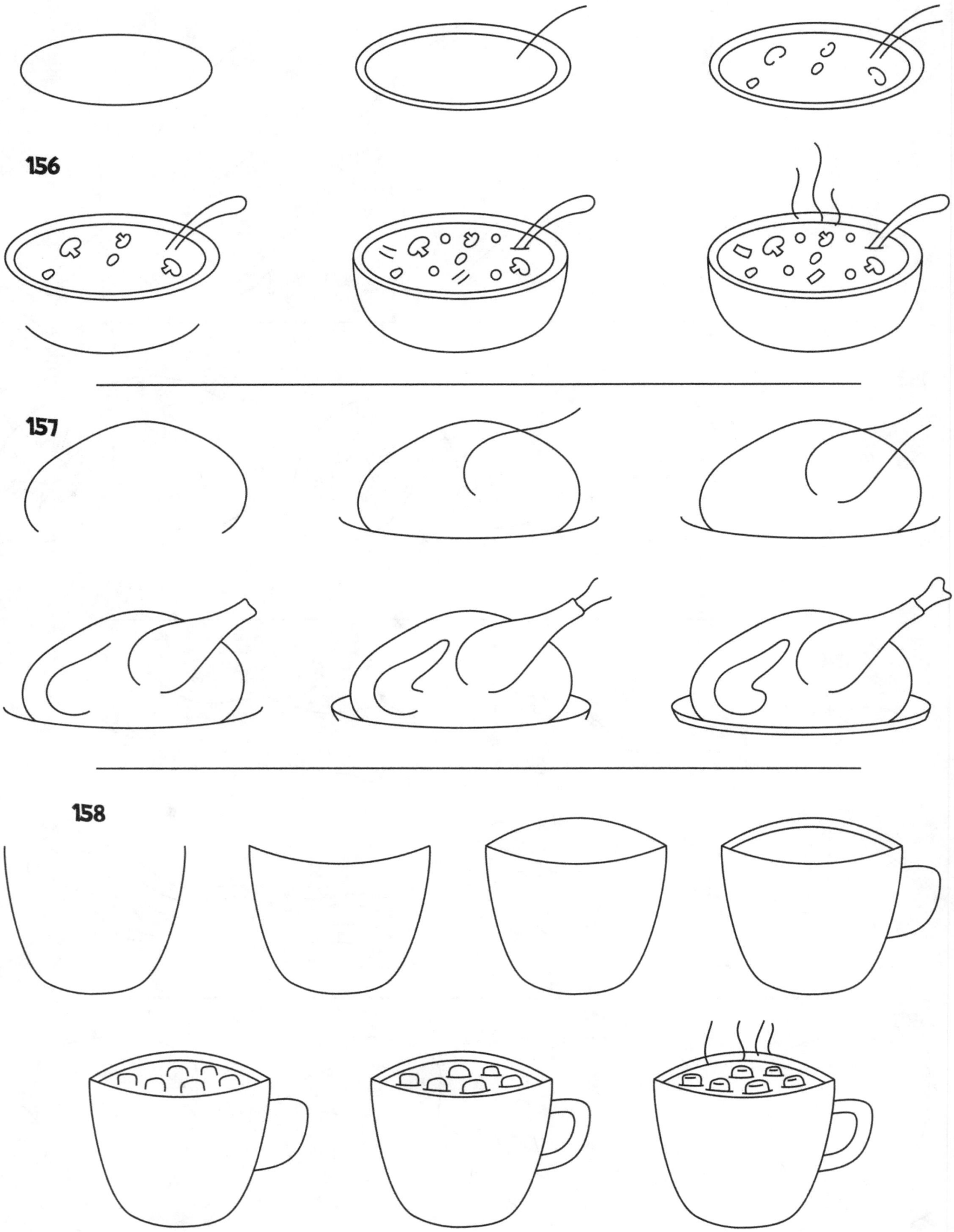
156
157
158

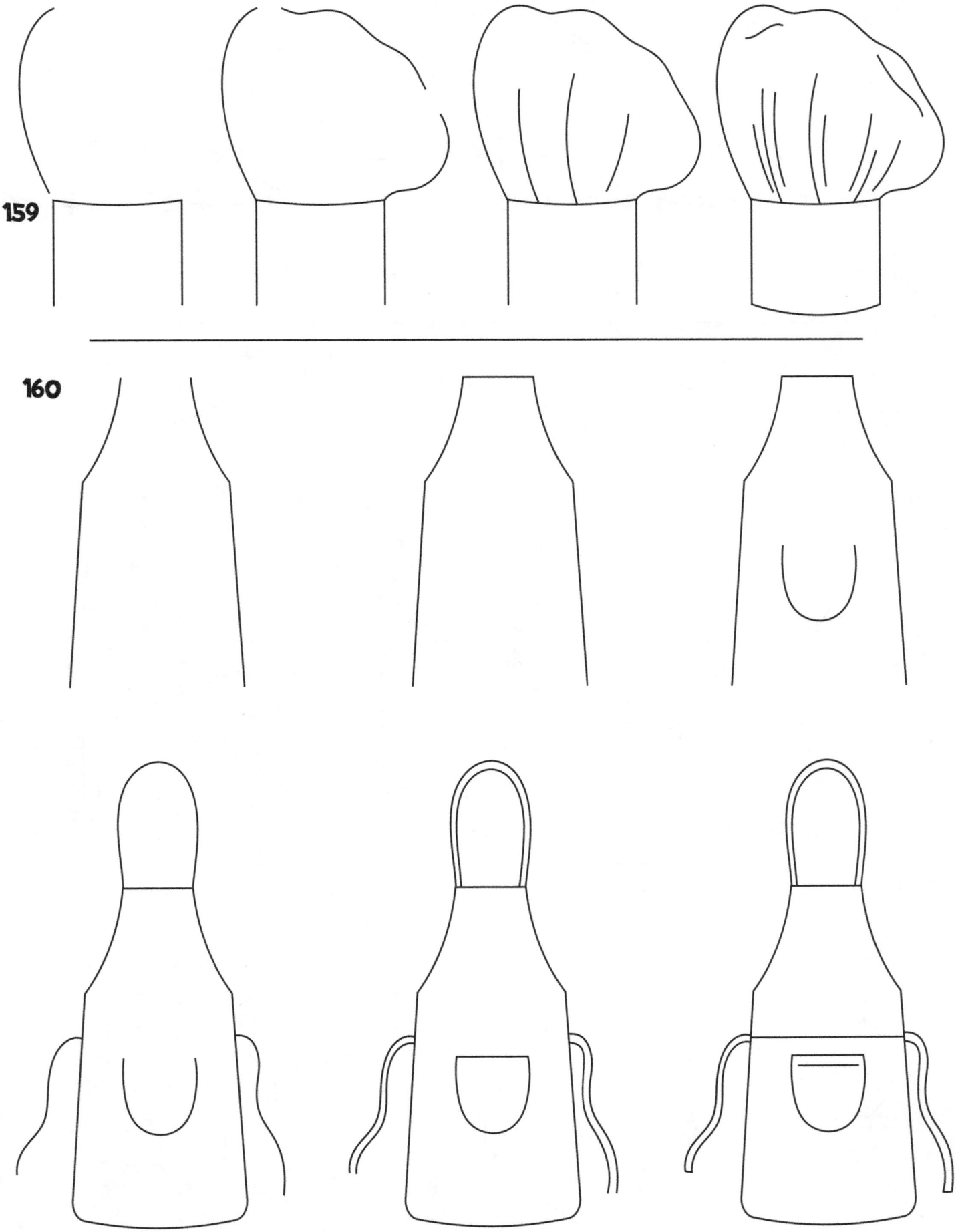
159
160

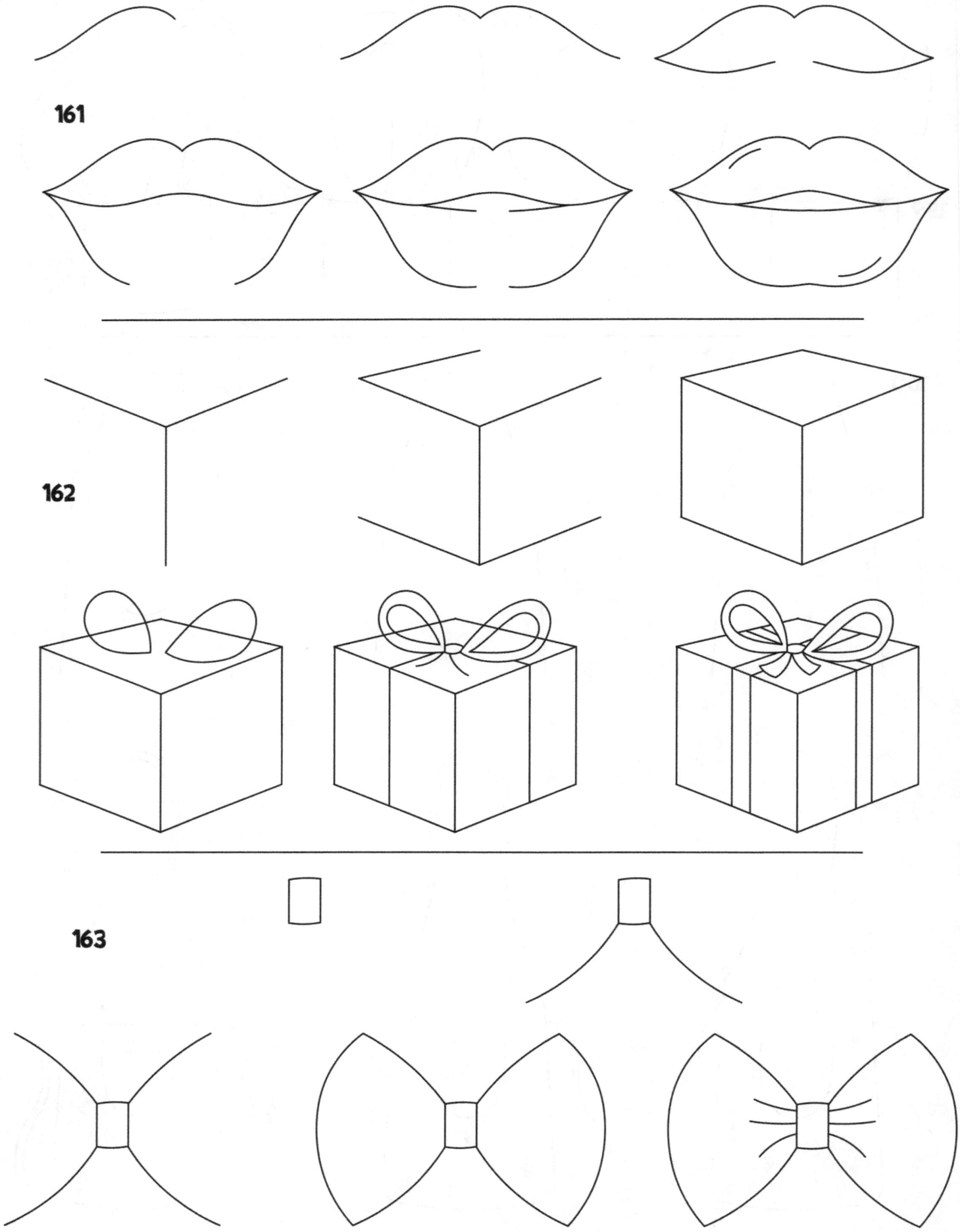
161
162
163

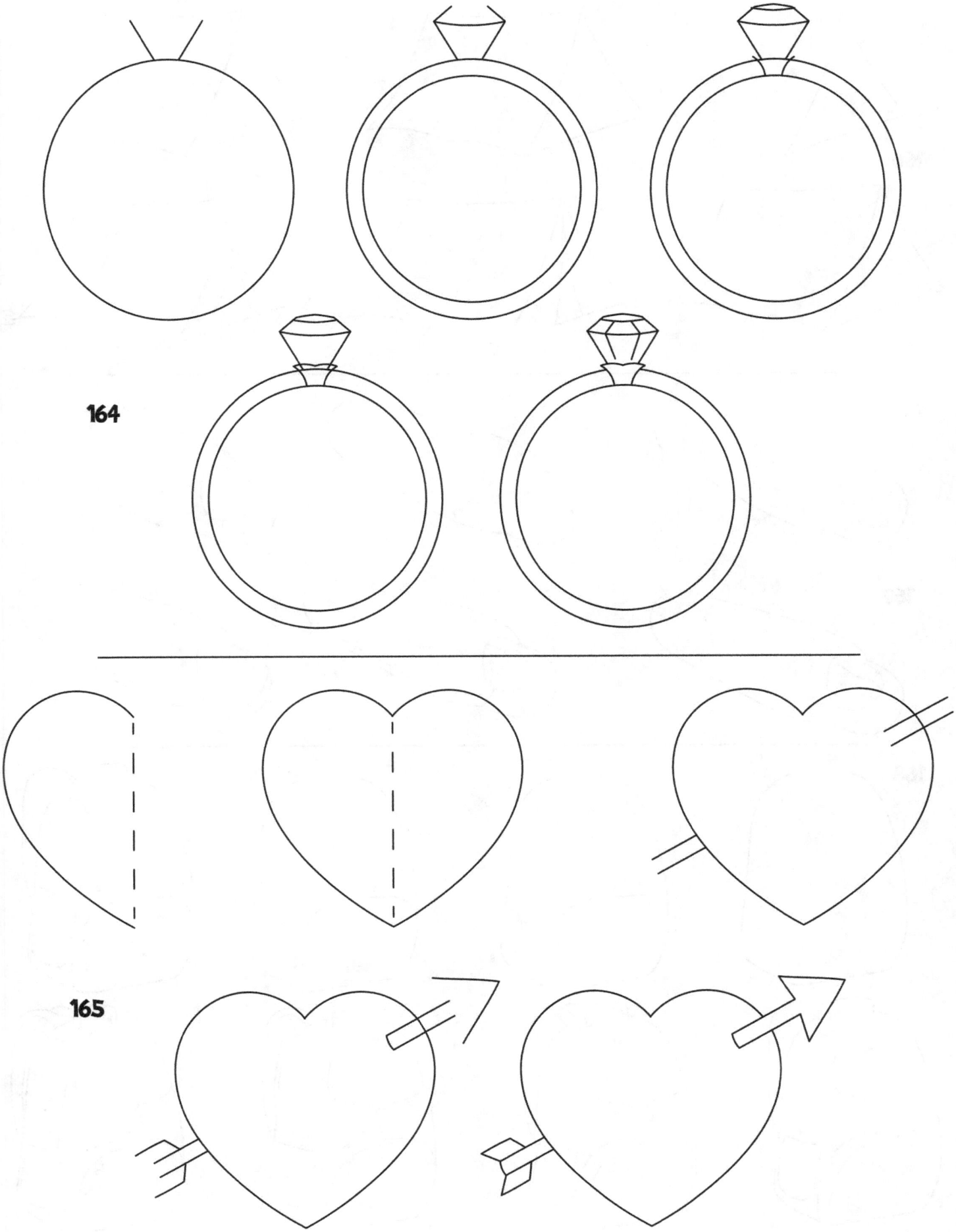
164
165

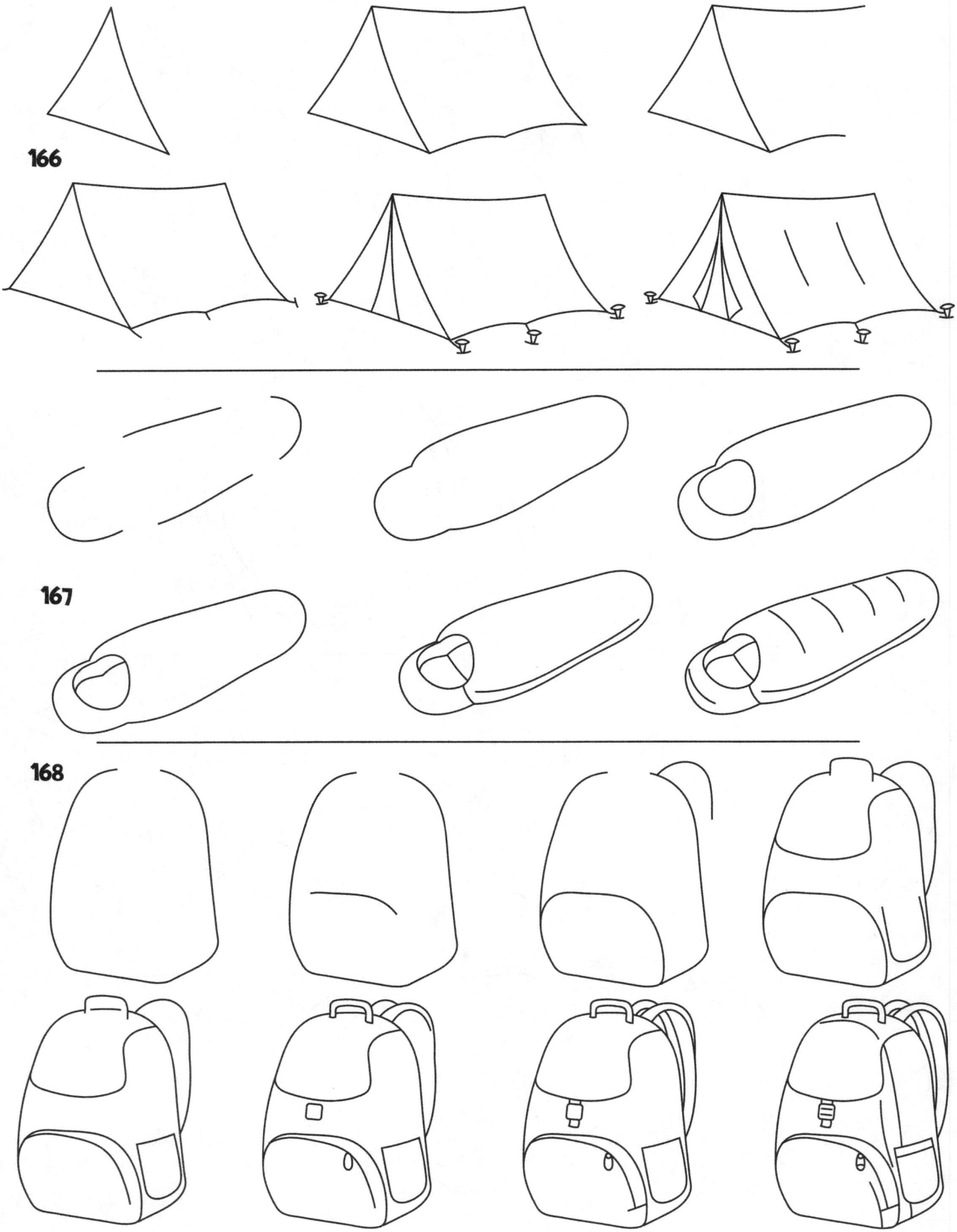
166
167
168

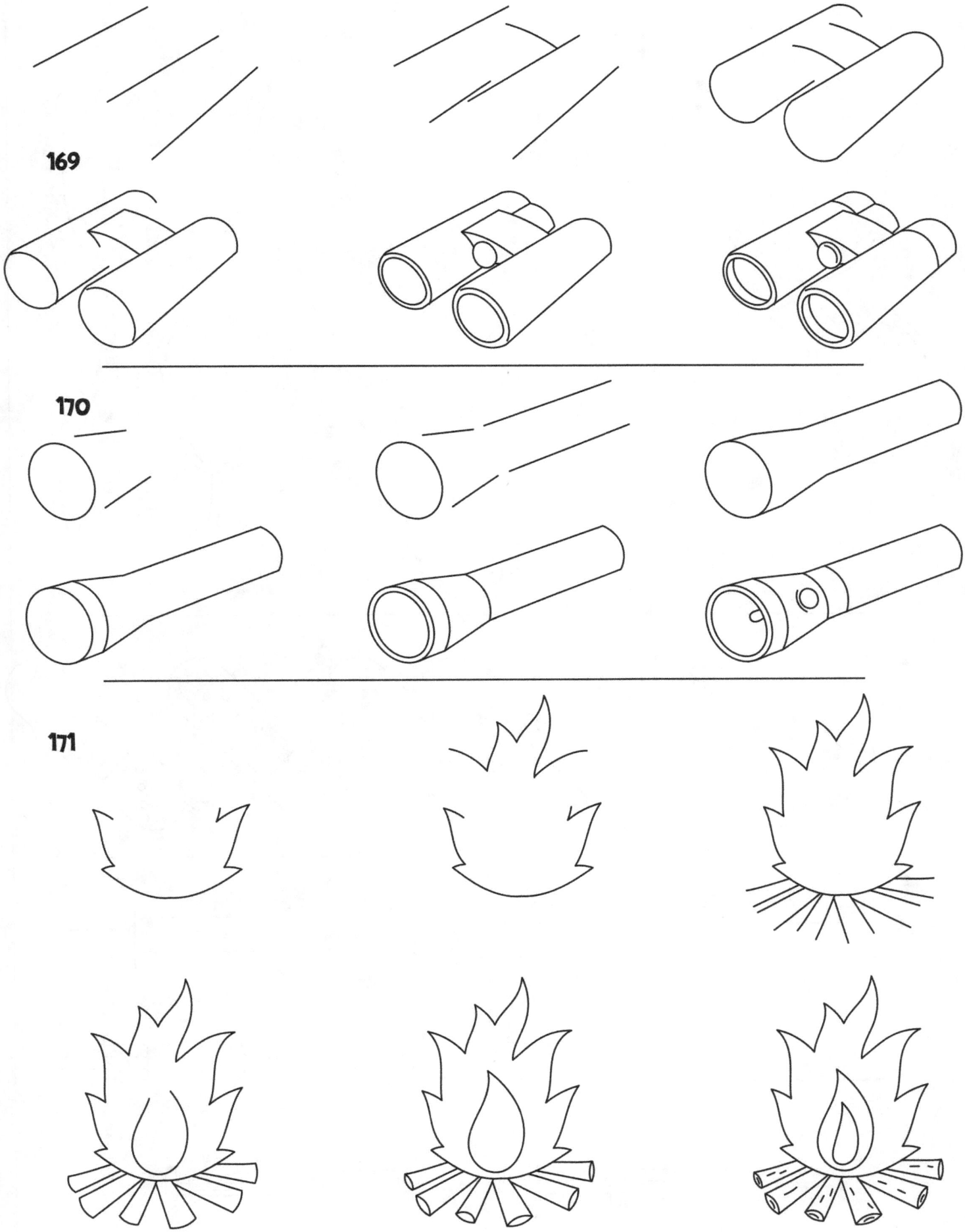
169
170
171

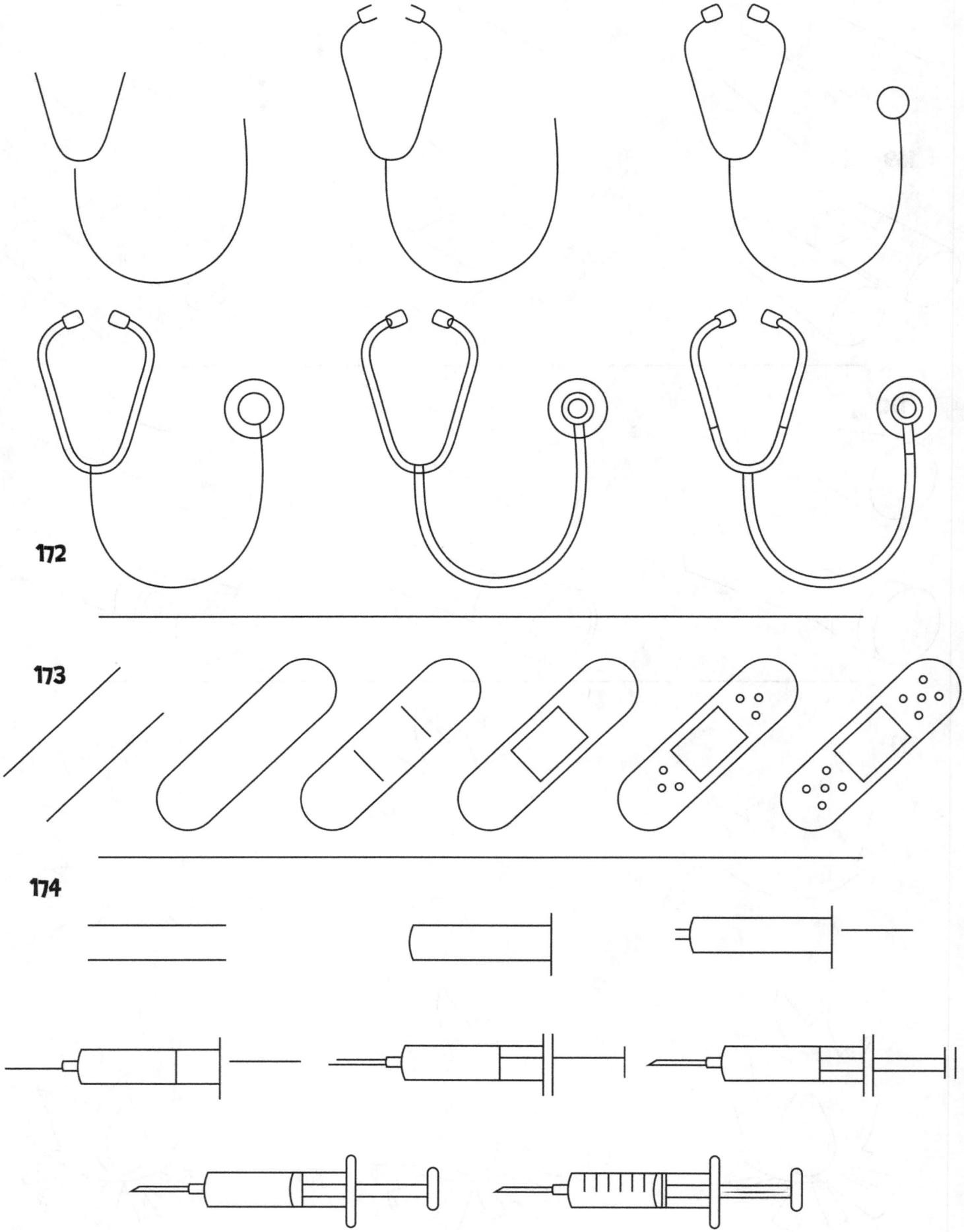
172
173
174

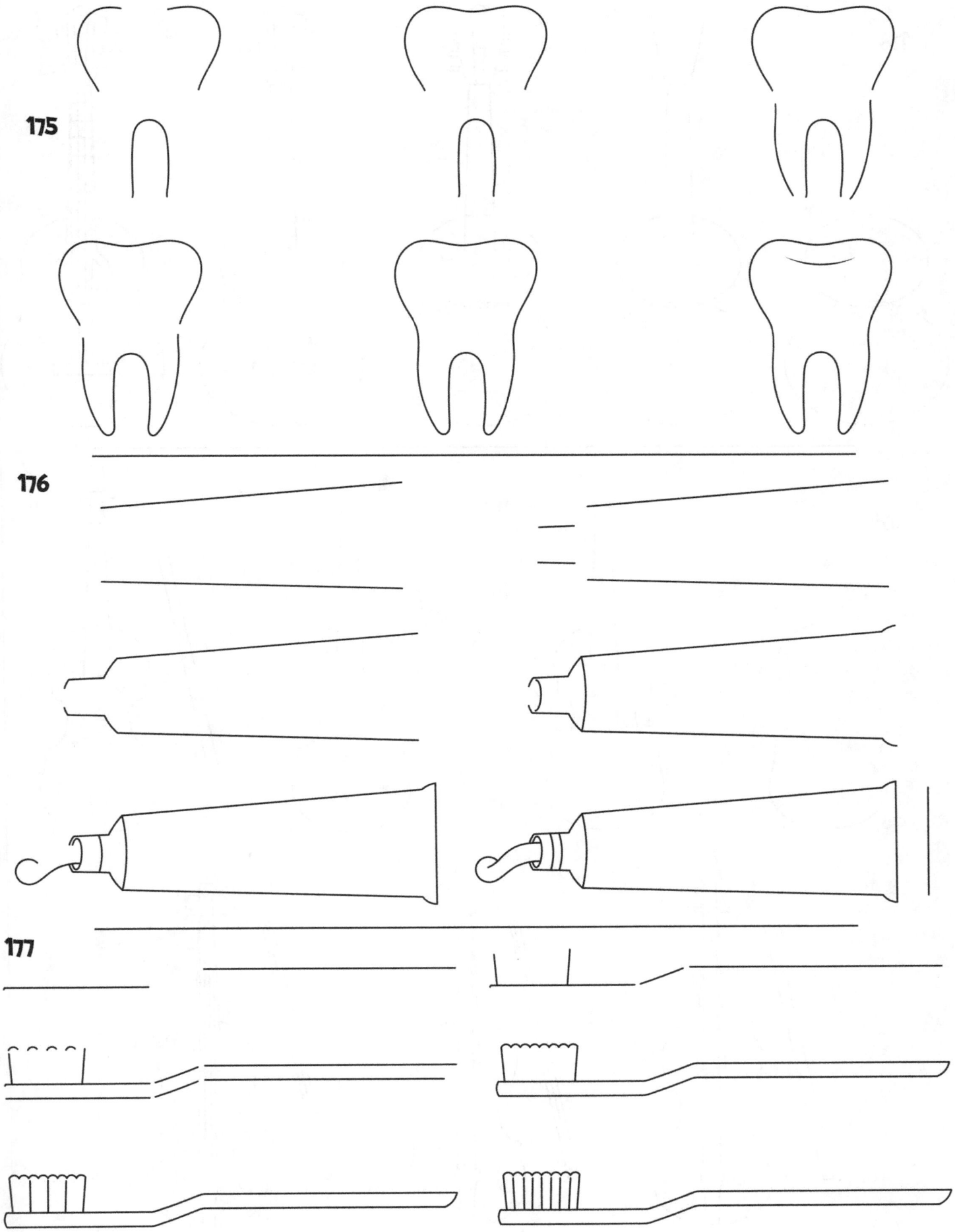
175
176
177

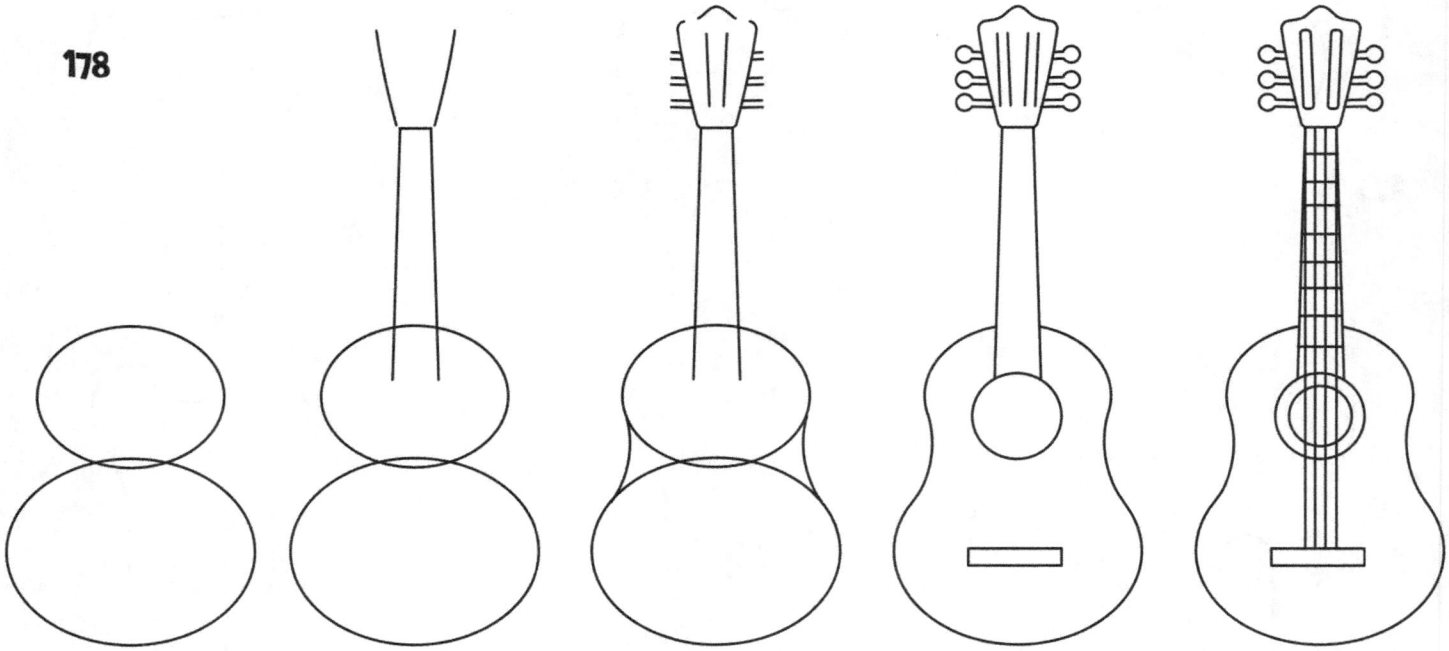
178

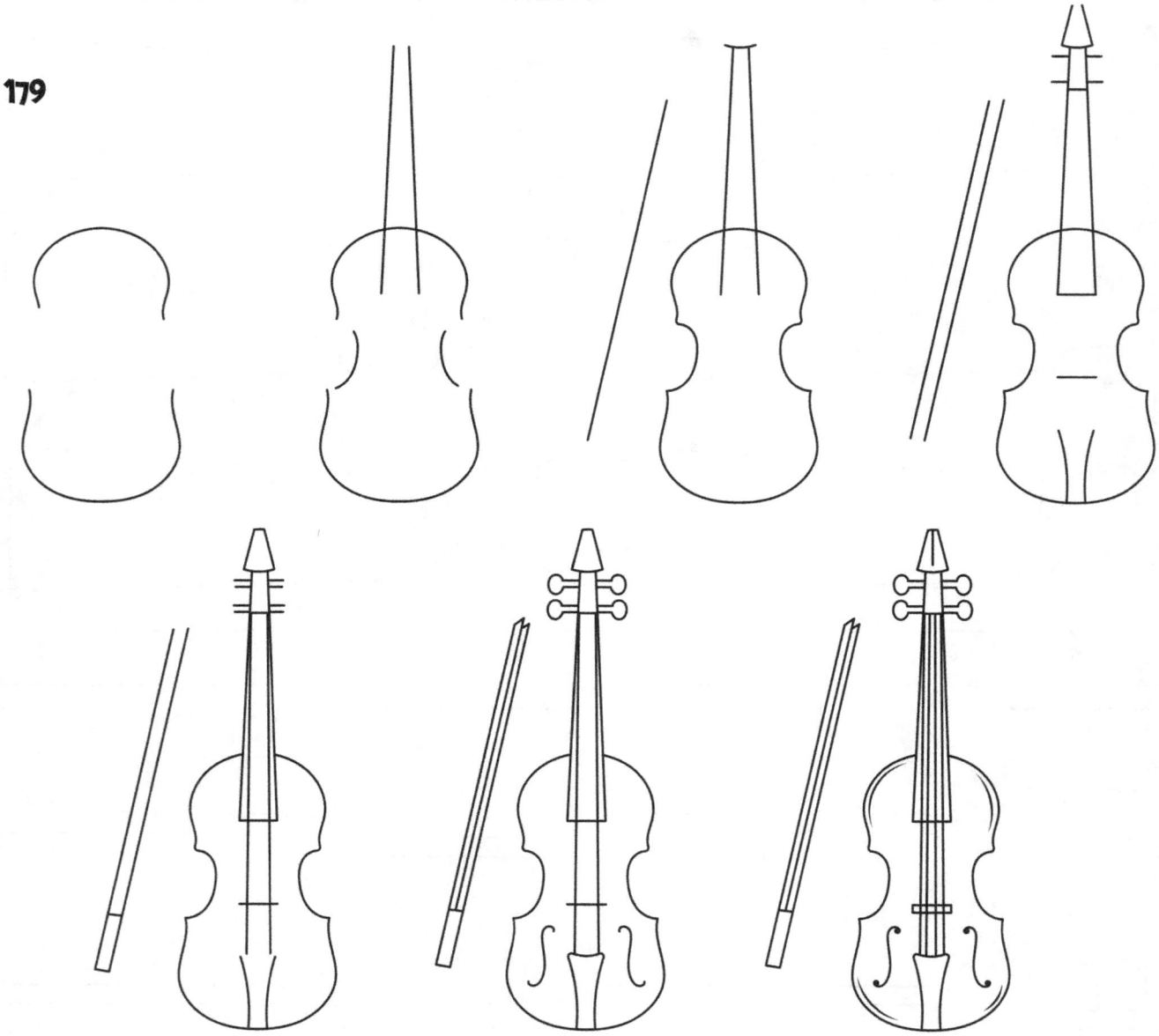
179

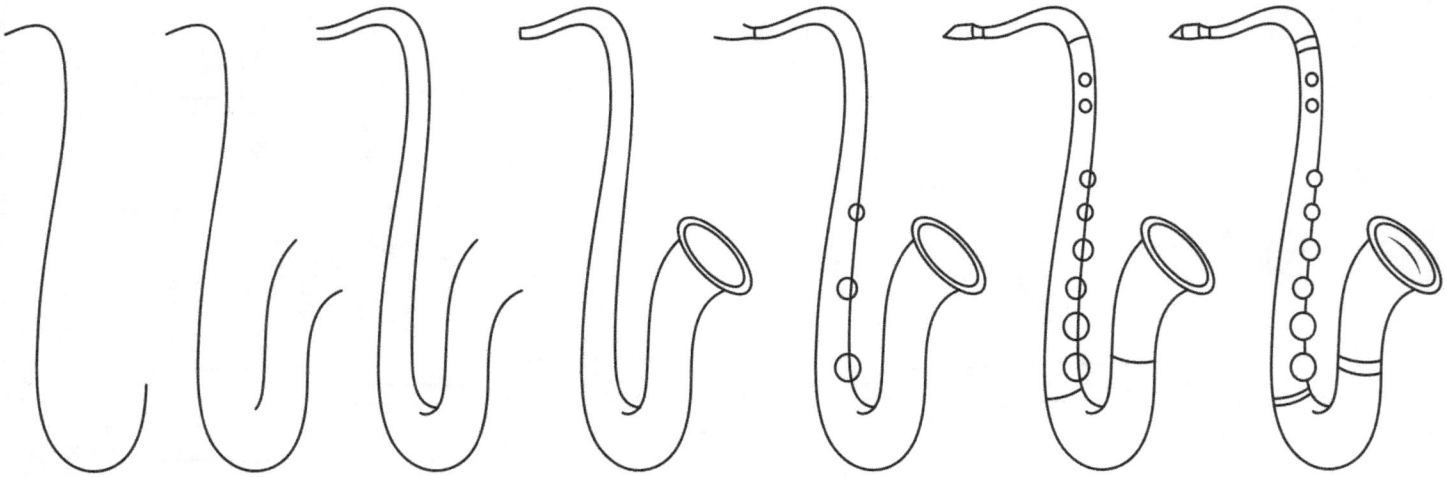

180

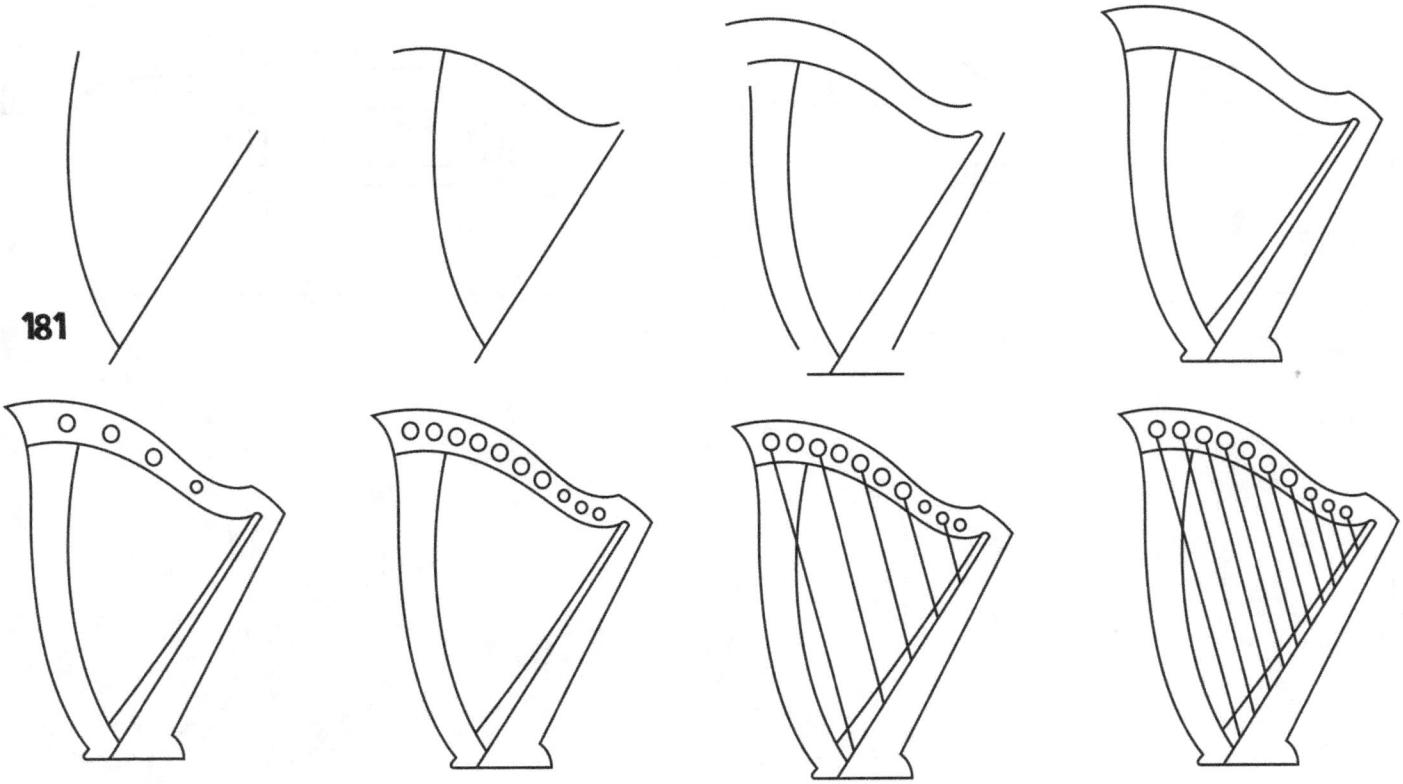

181

182

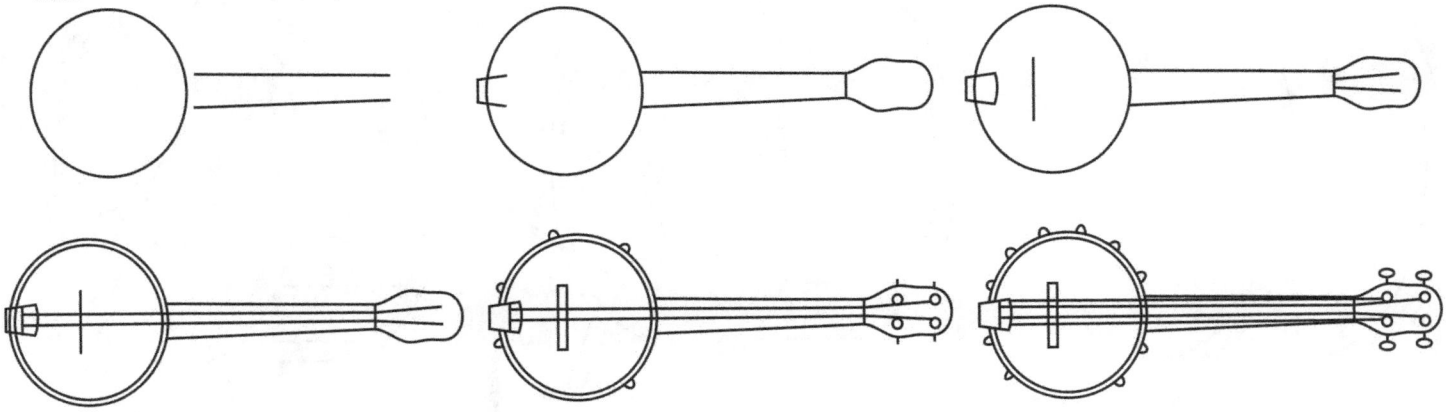

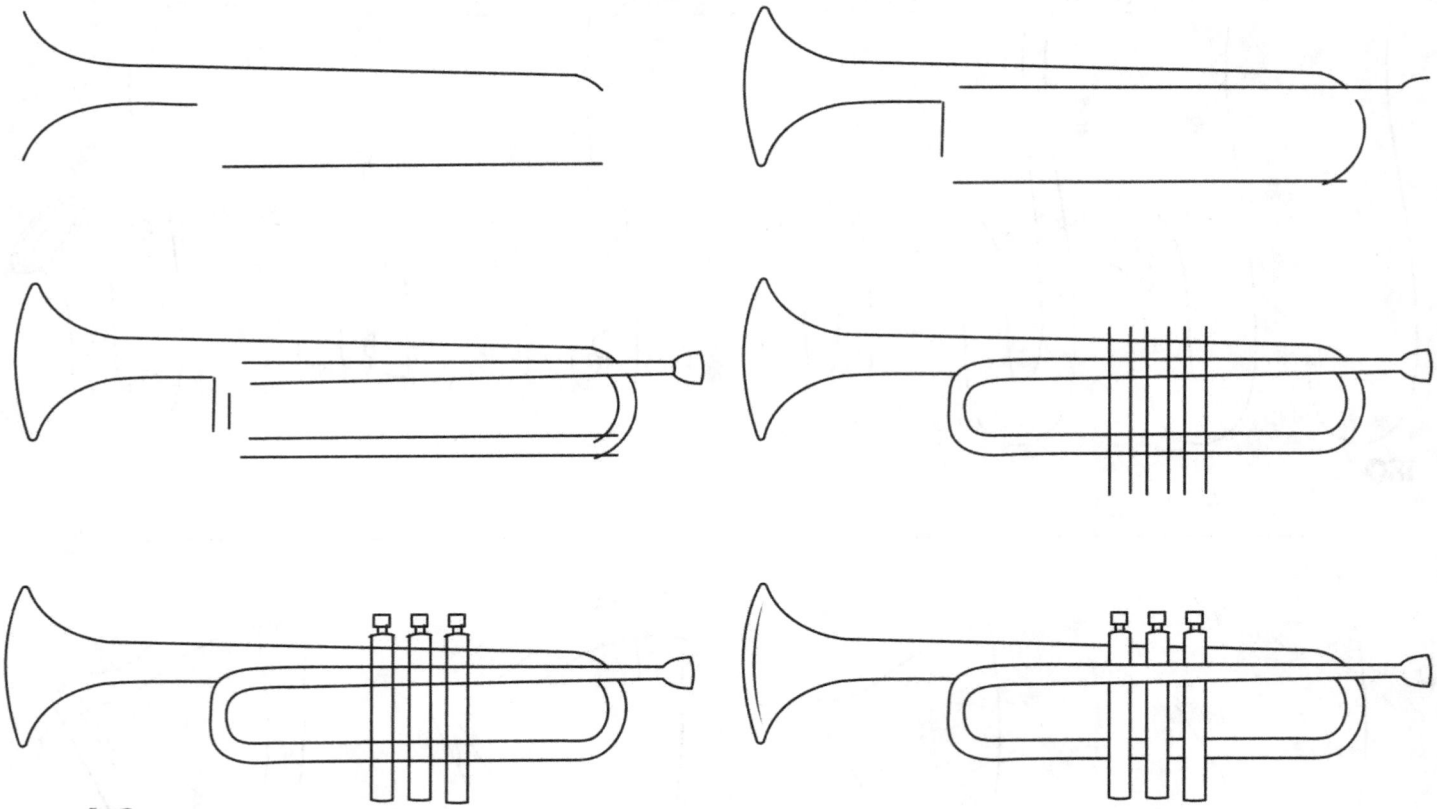

183

184

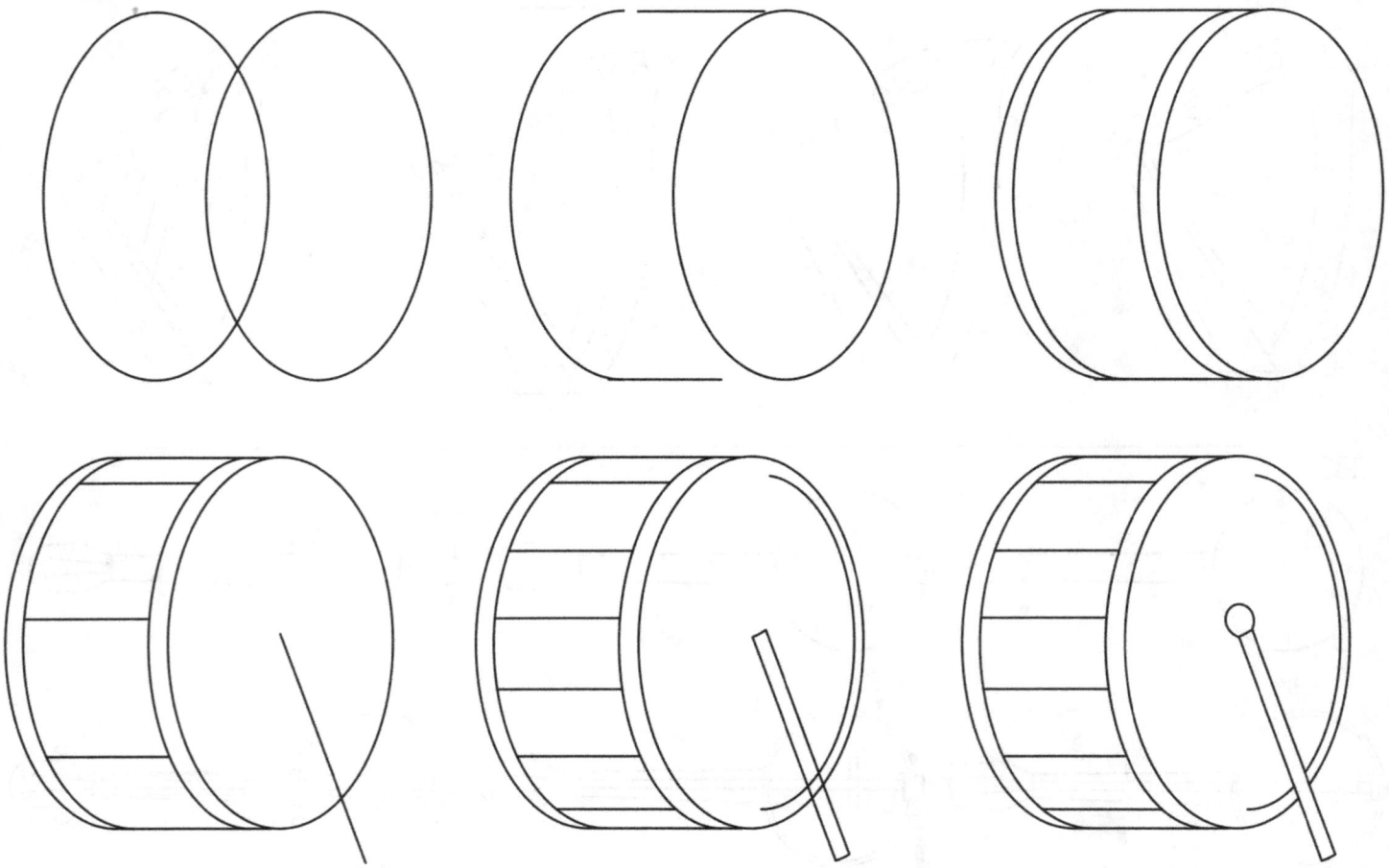

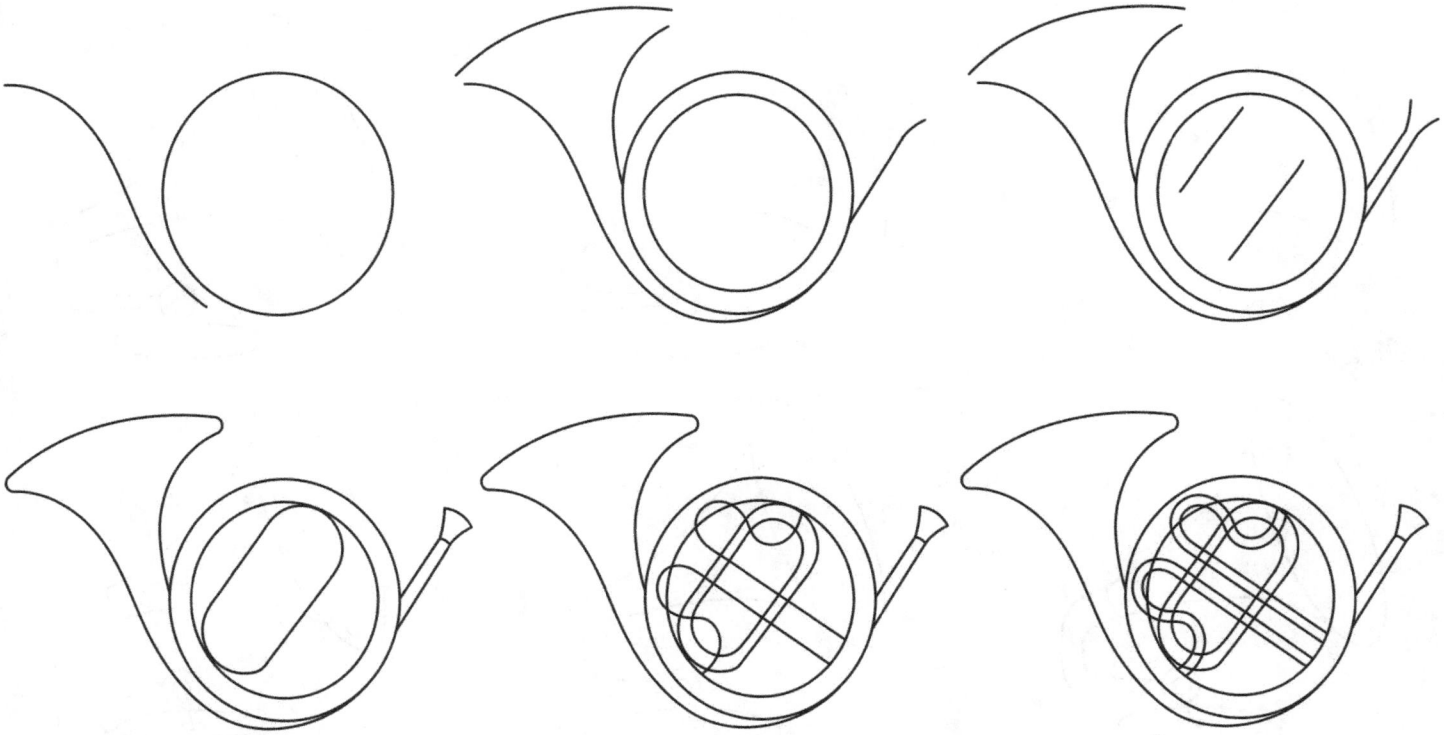

185

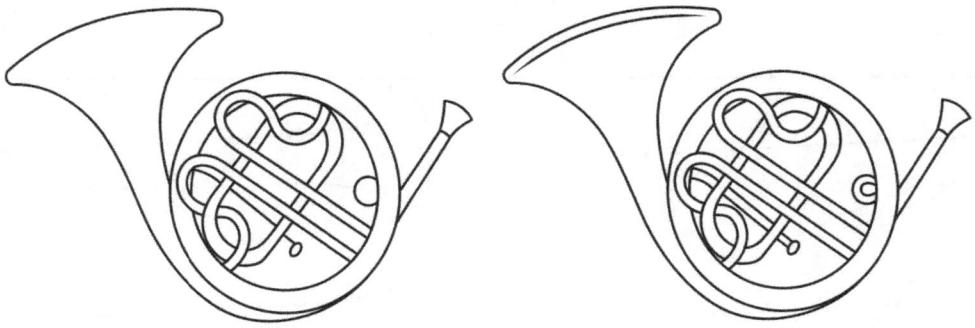

186

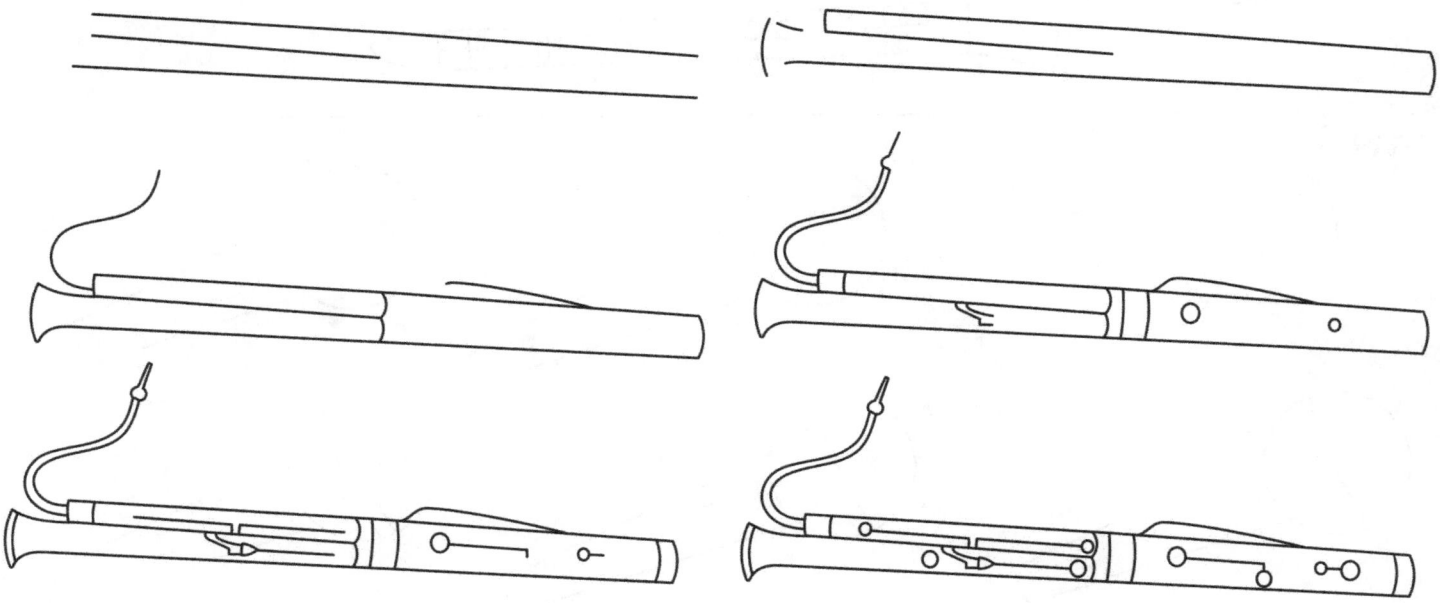

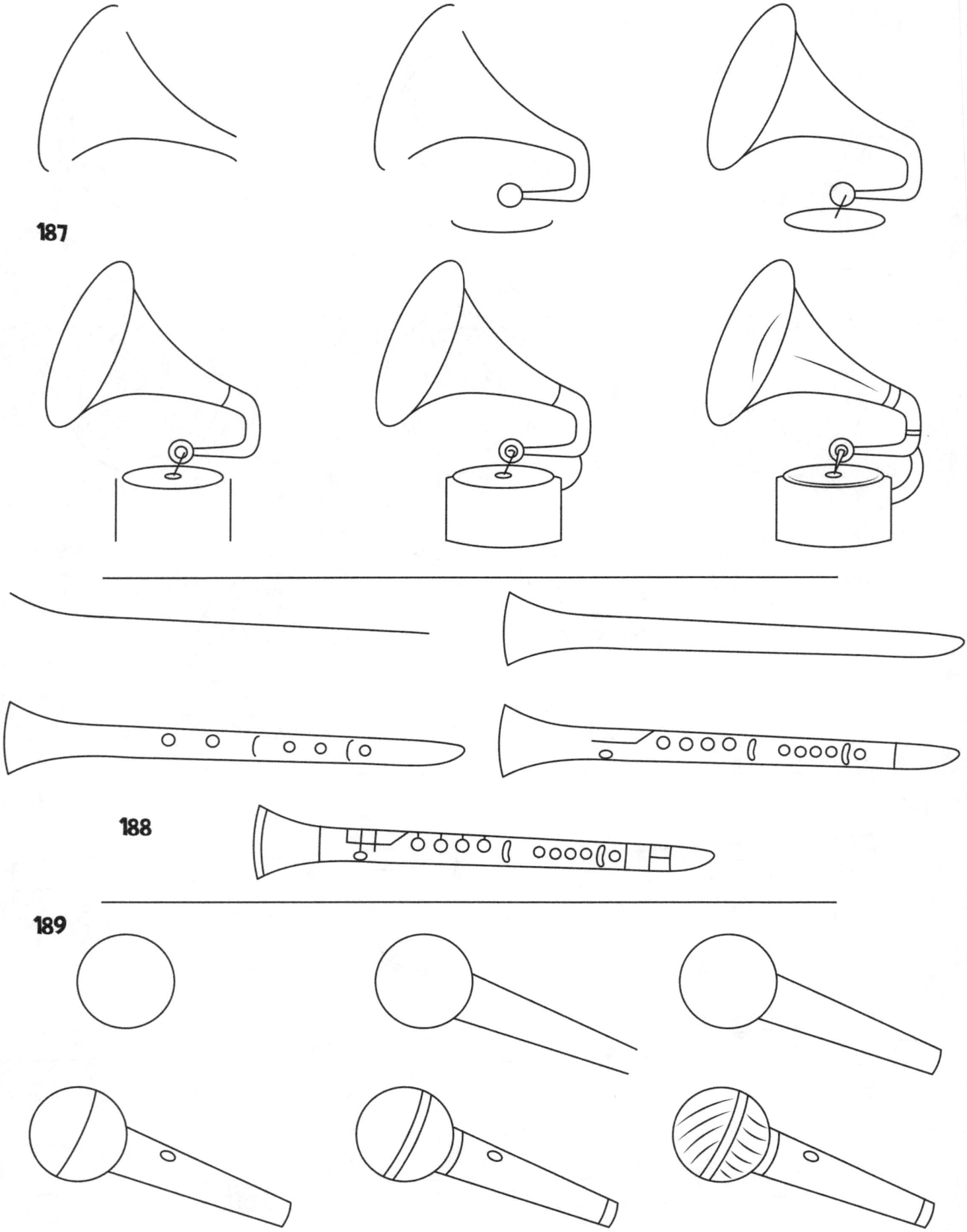
187
188
189

190

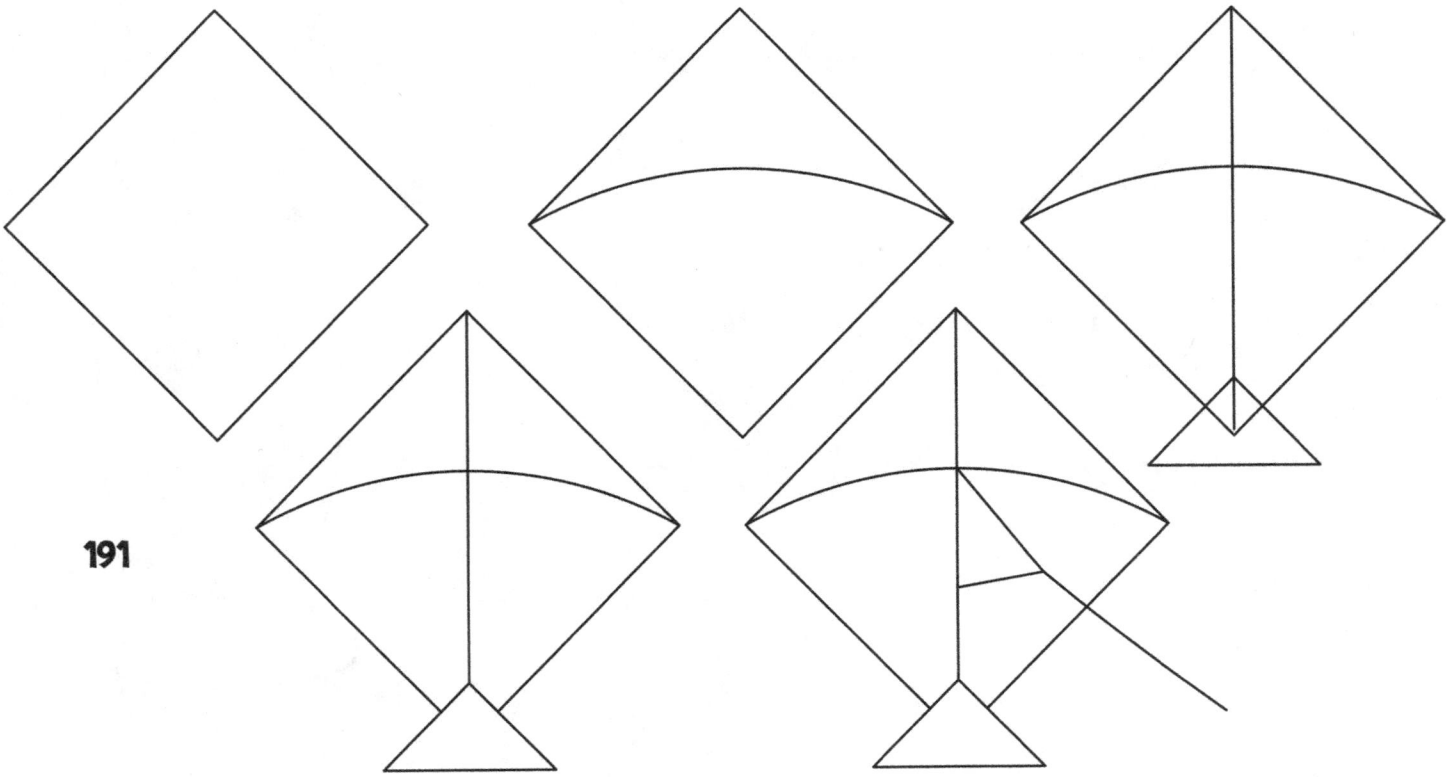

191

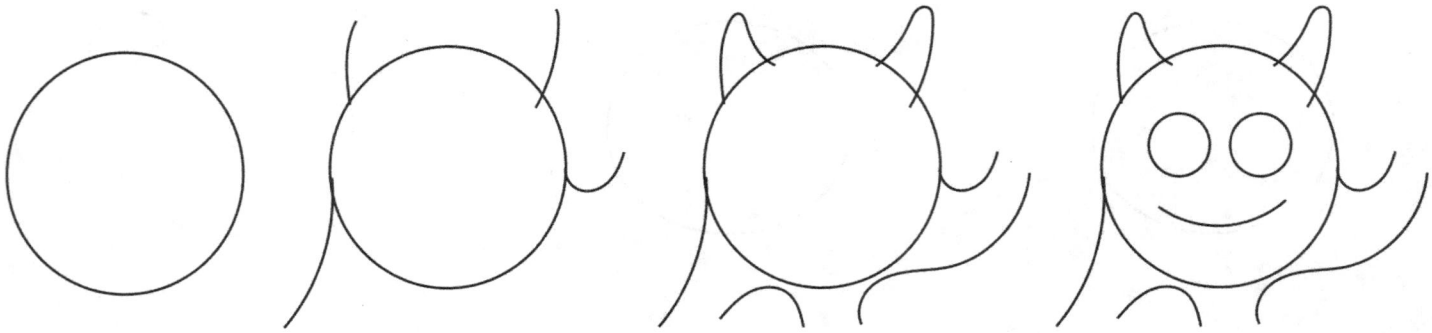

192

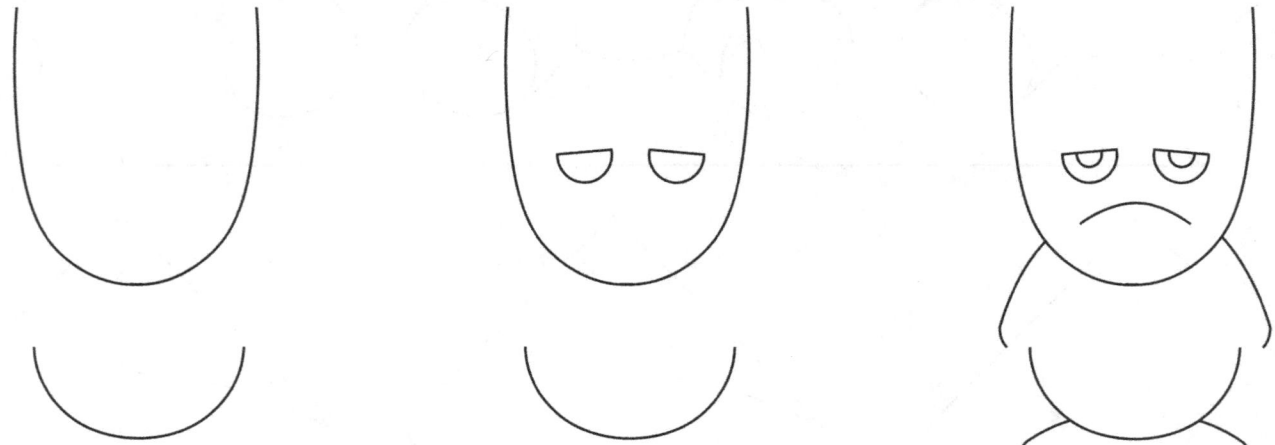

193

194

195

196

197

198

199

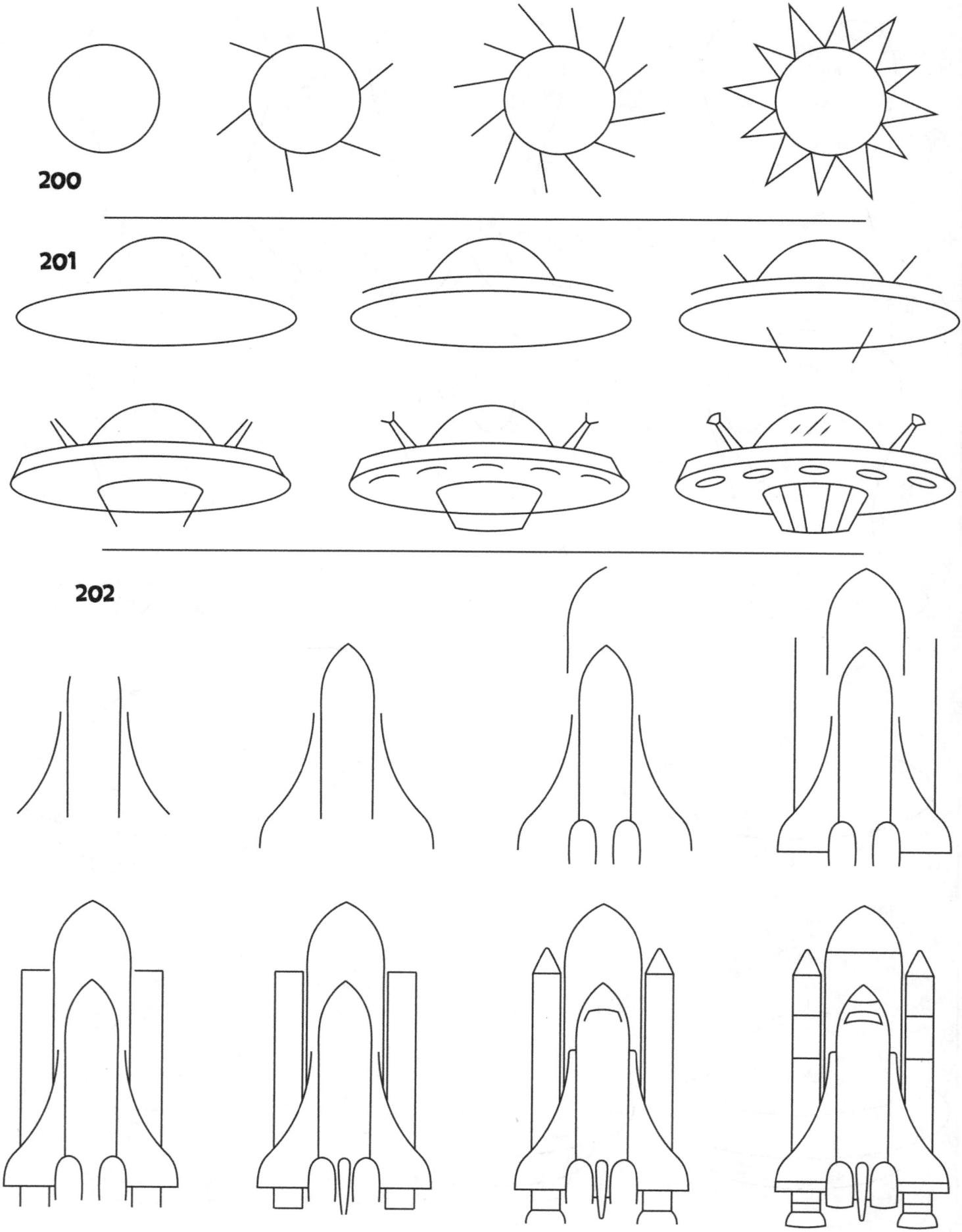
200
201
202

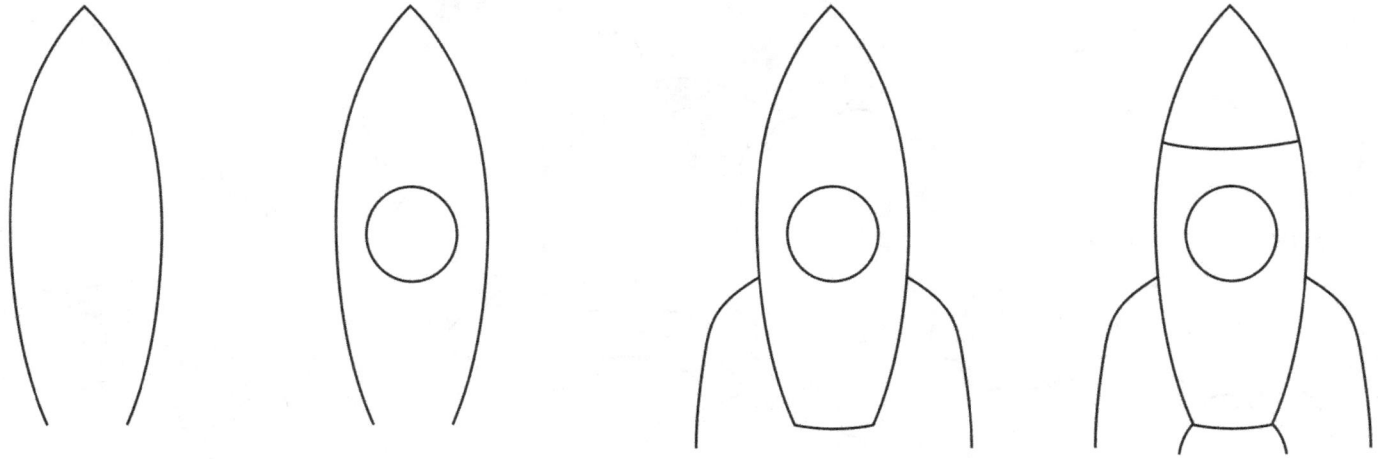

203

204

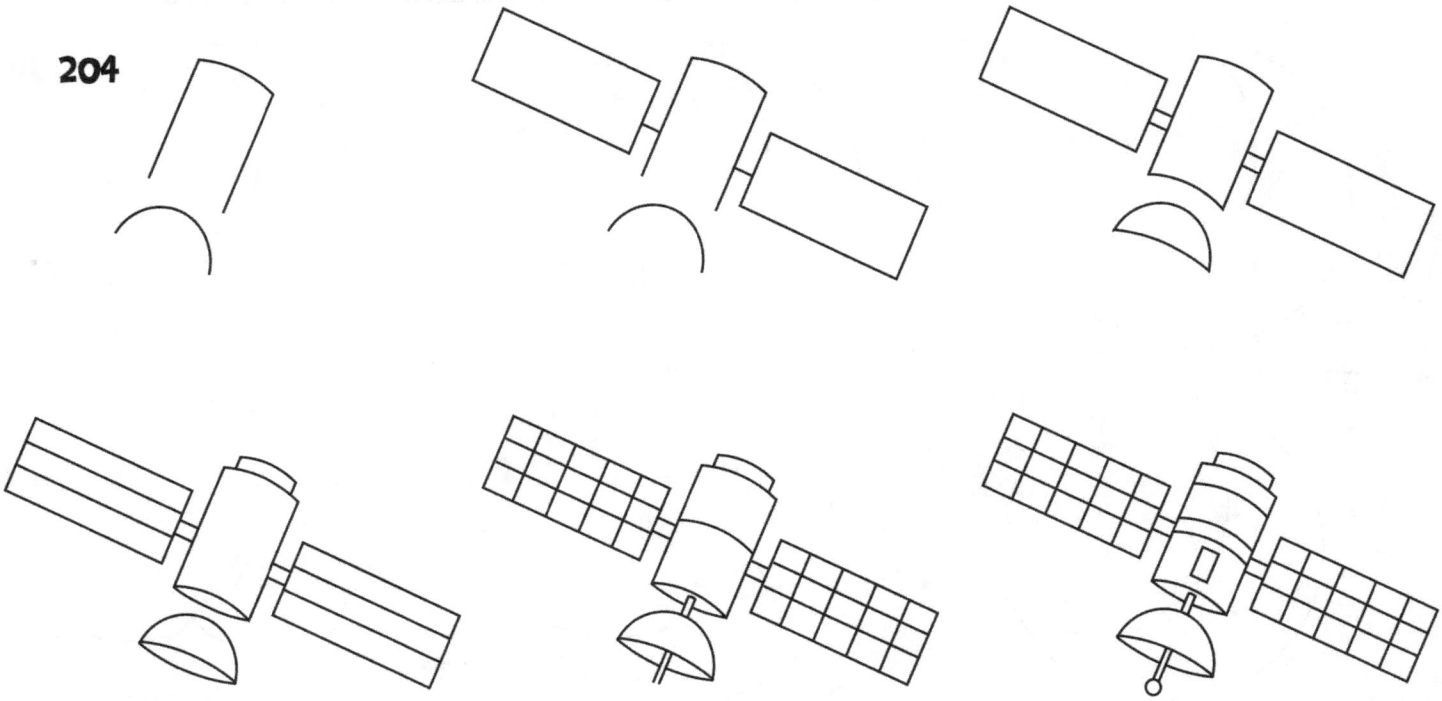

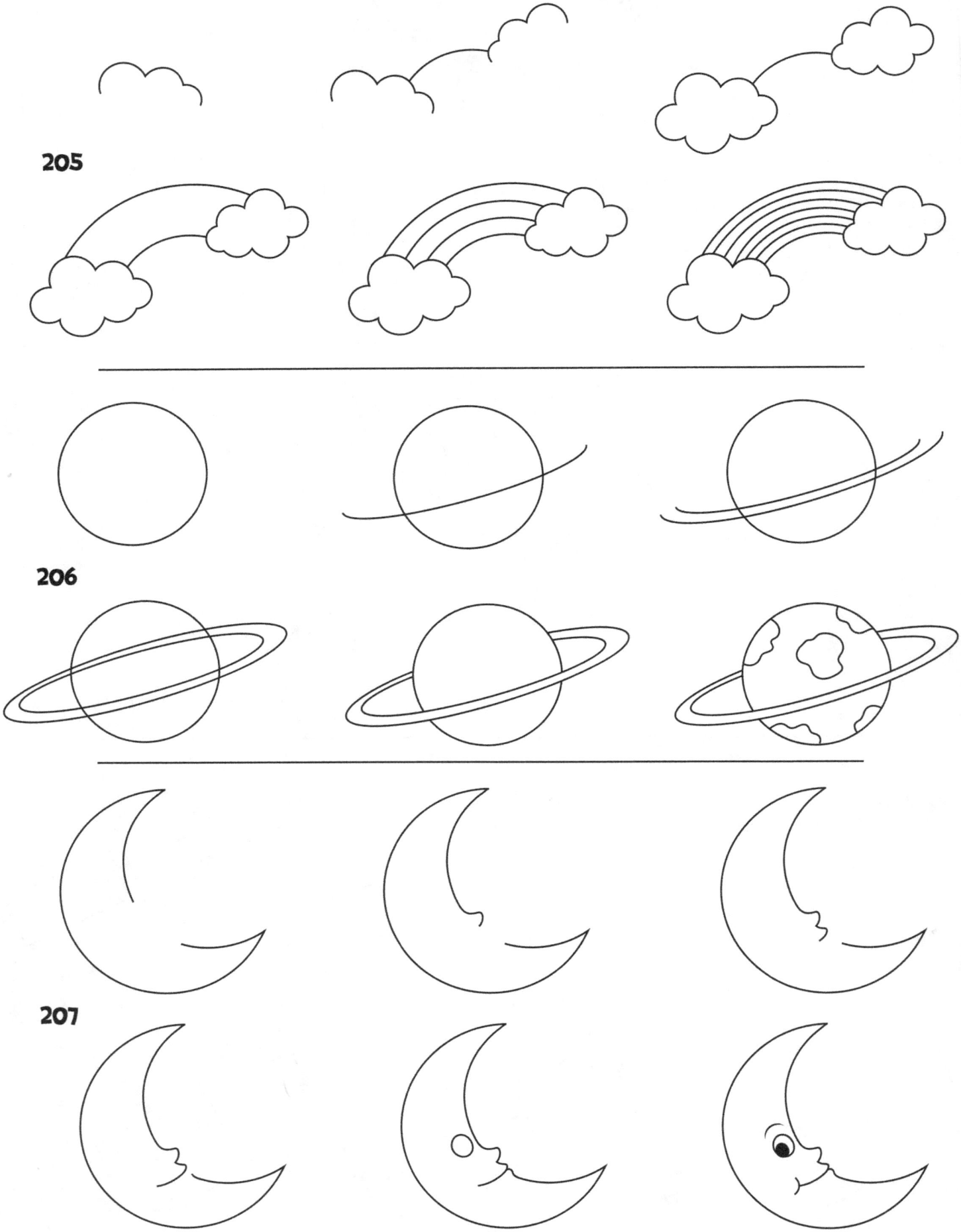
205
206
207

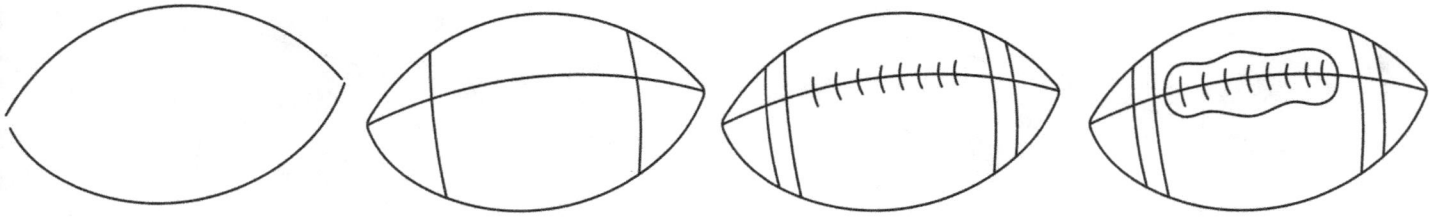

208

209

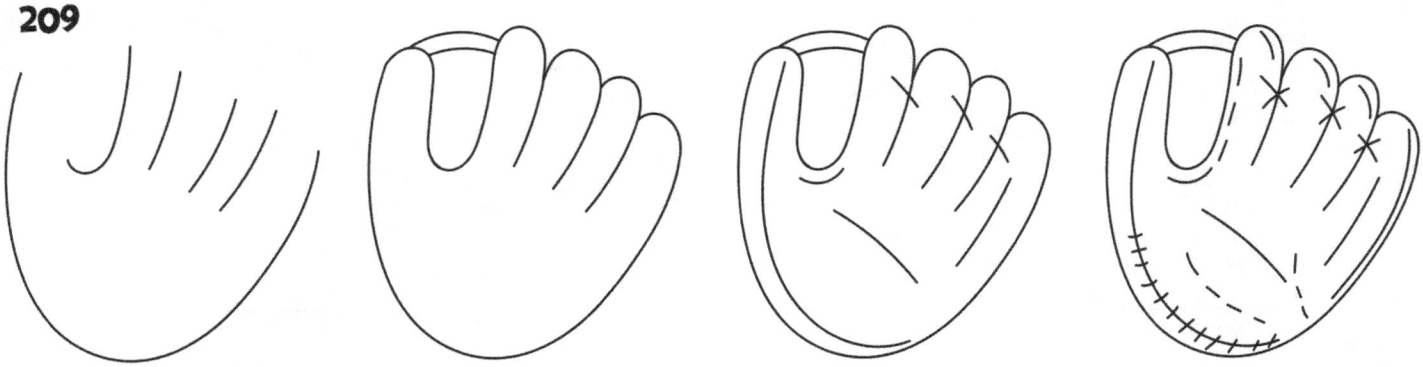

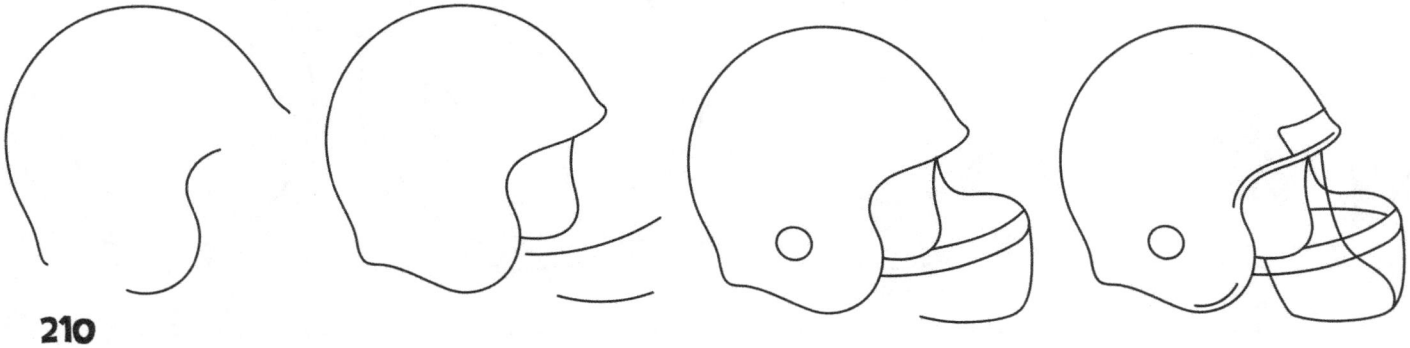

210

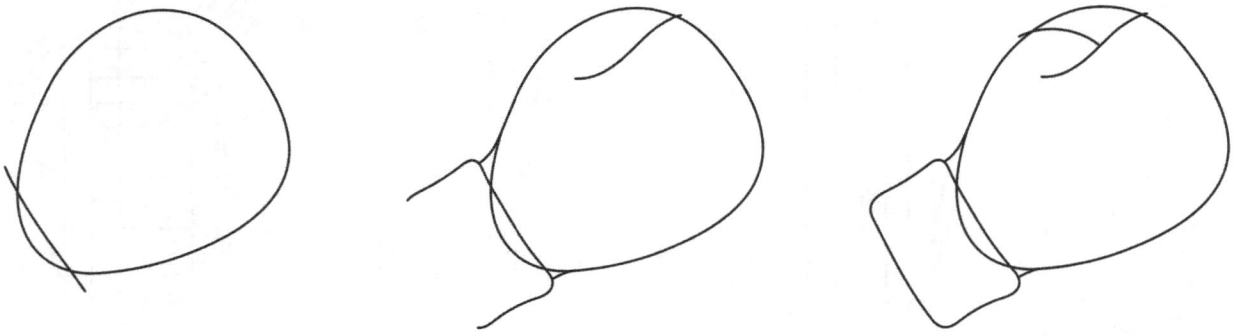

211

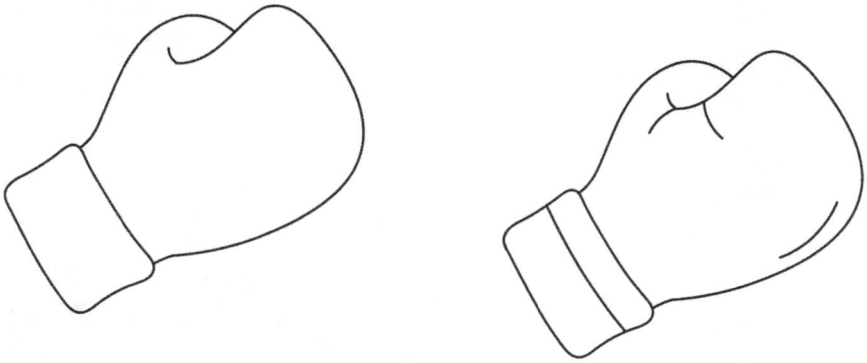

212

213

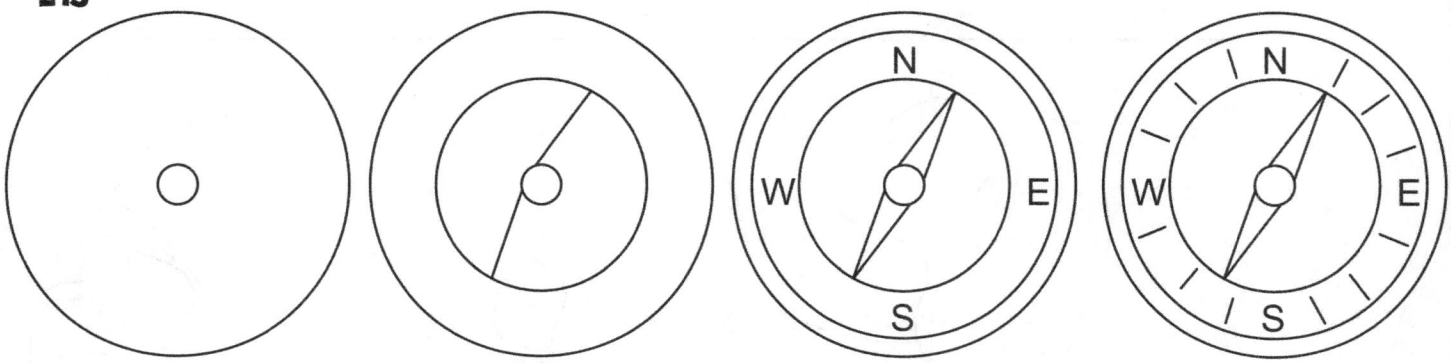

214

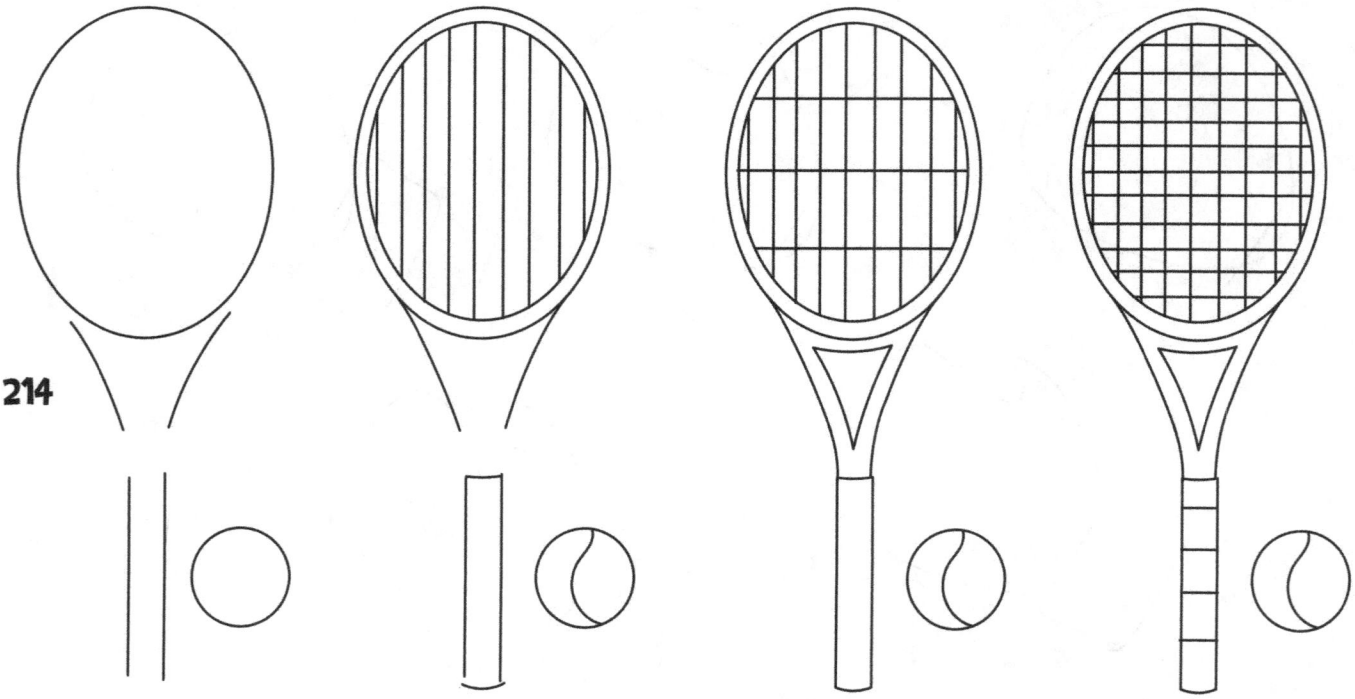

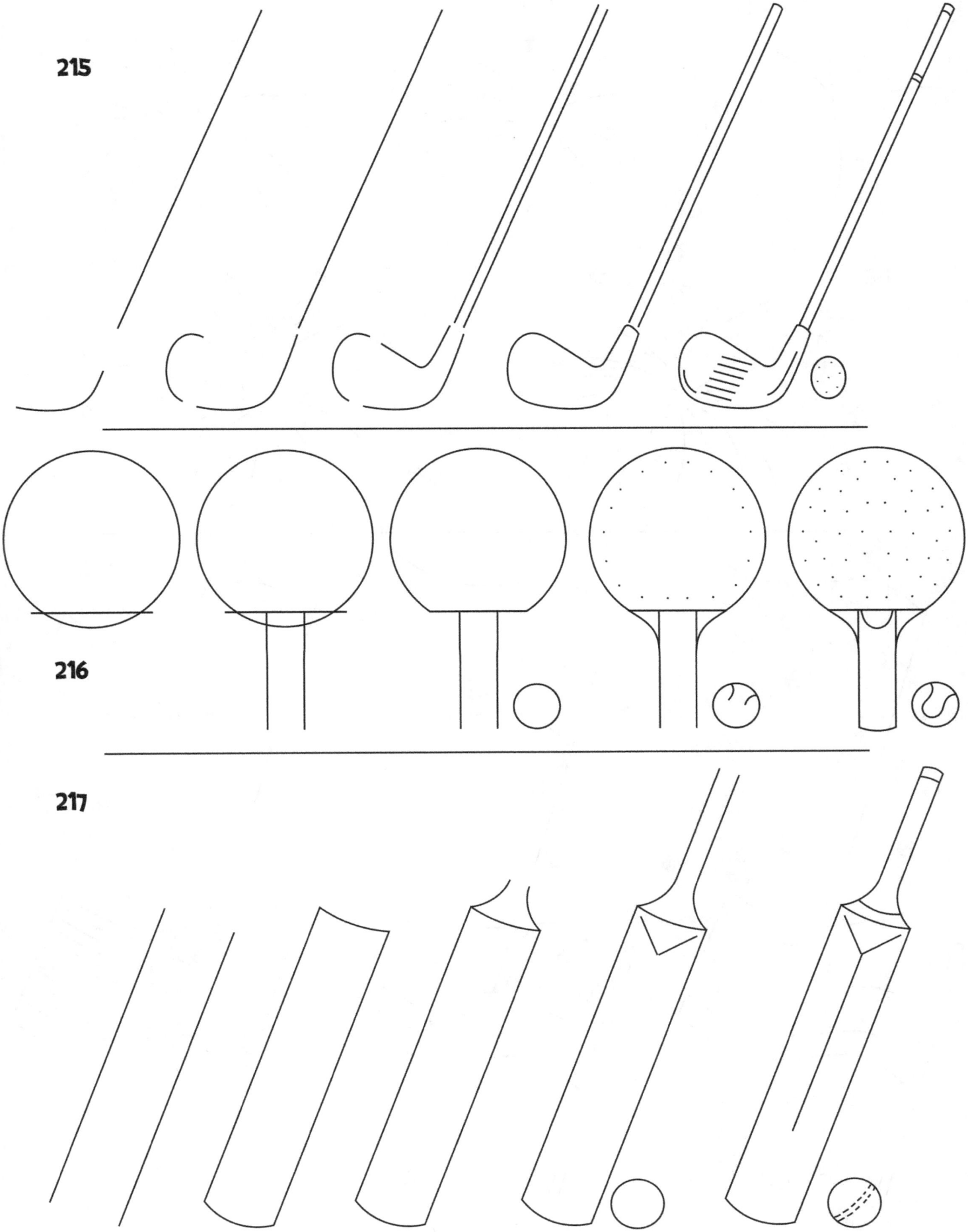
215
216
217

218
219

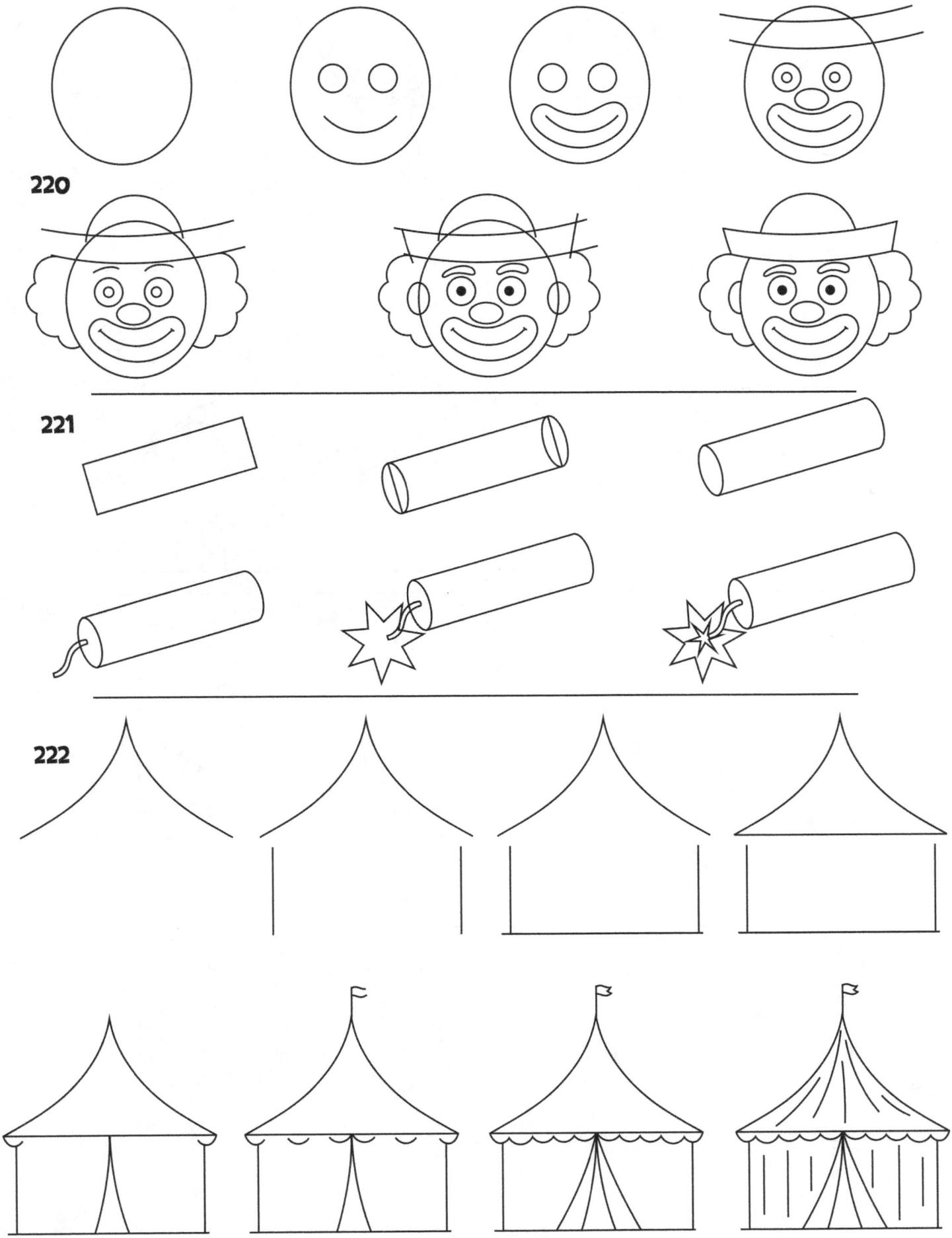
220
221
222

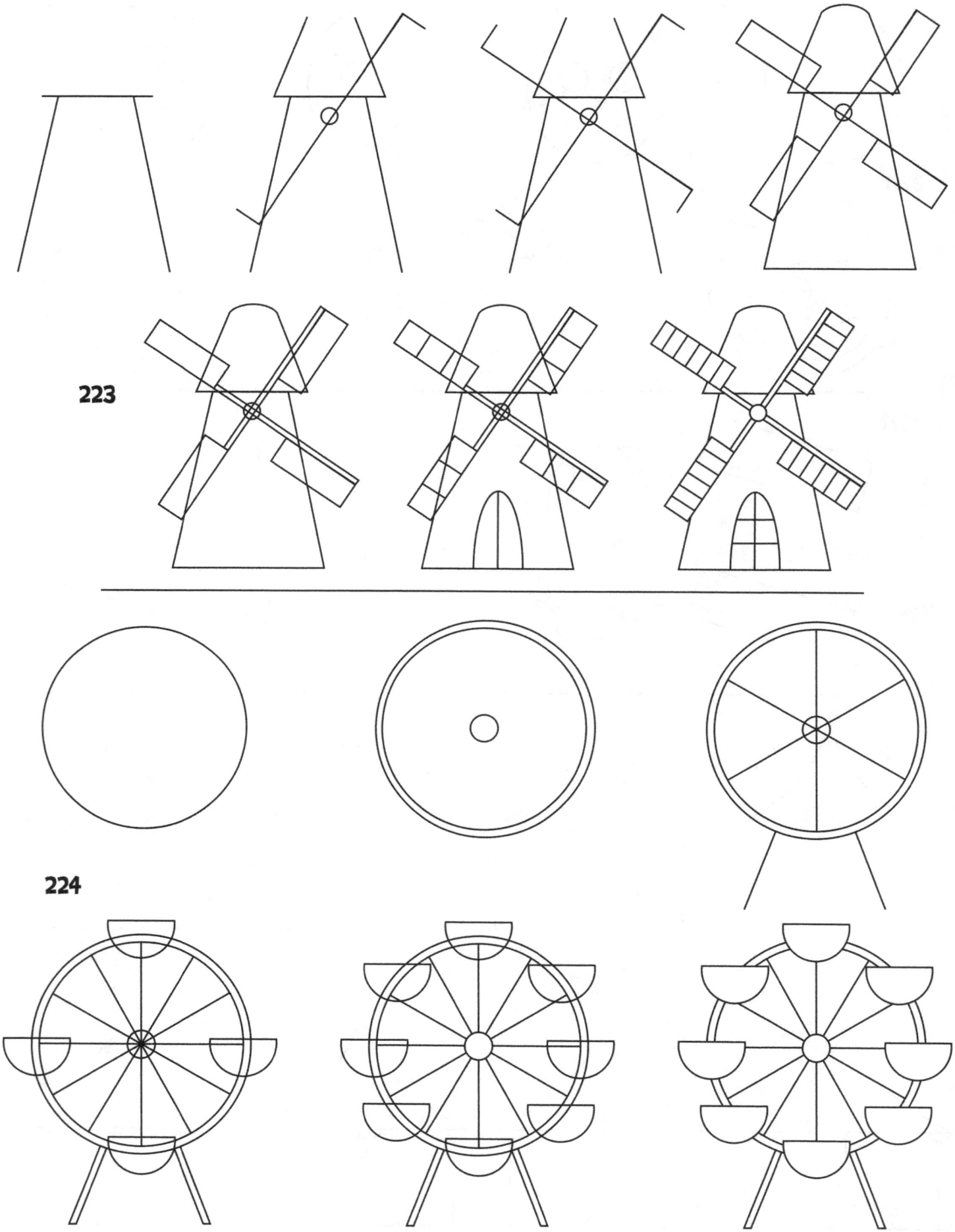
223
224

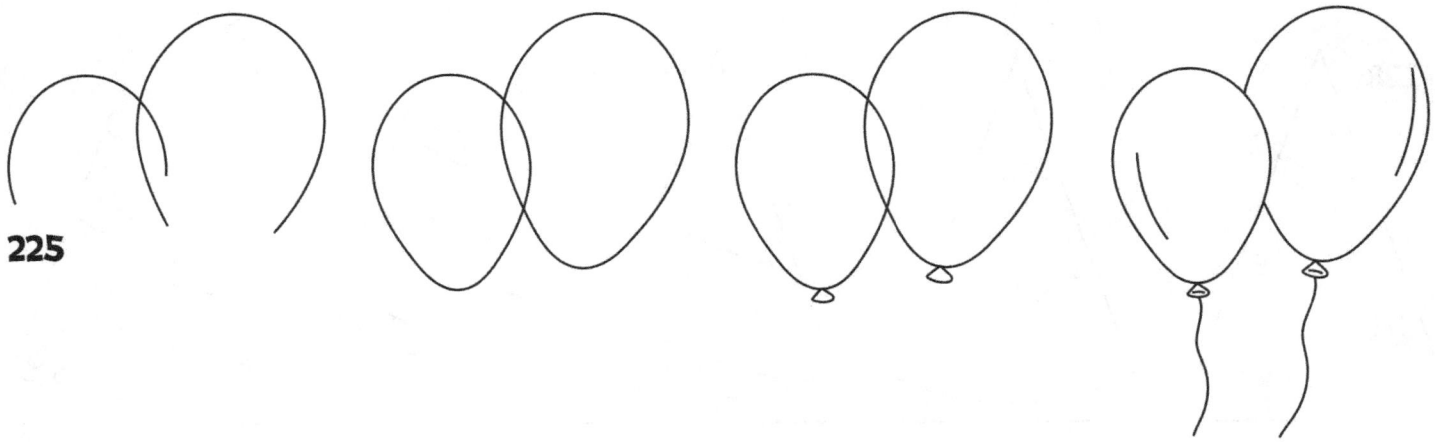

225

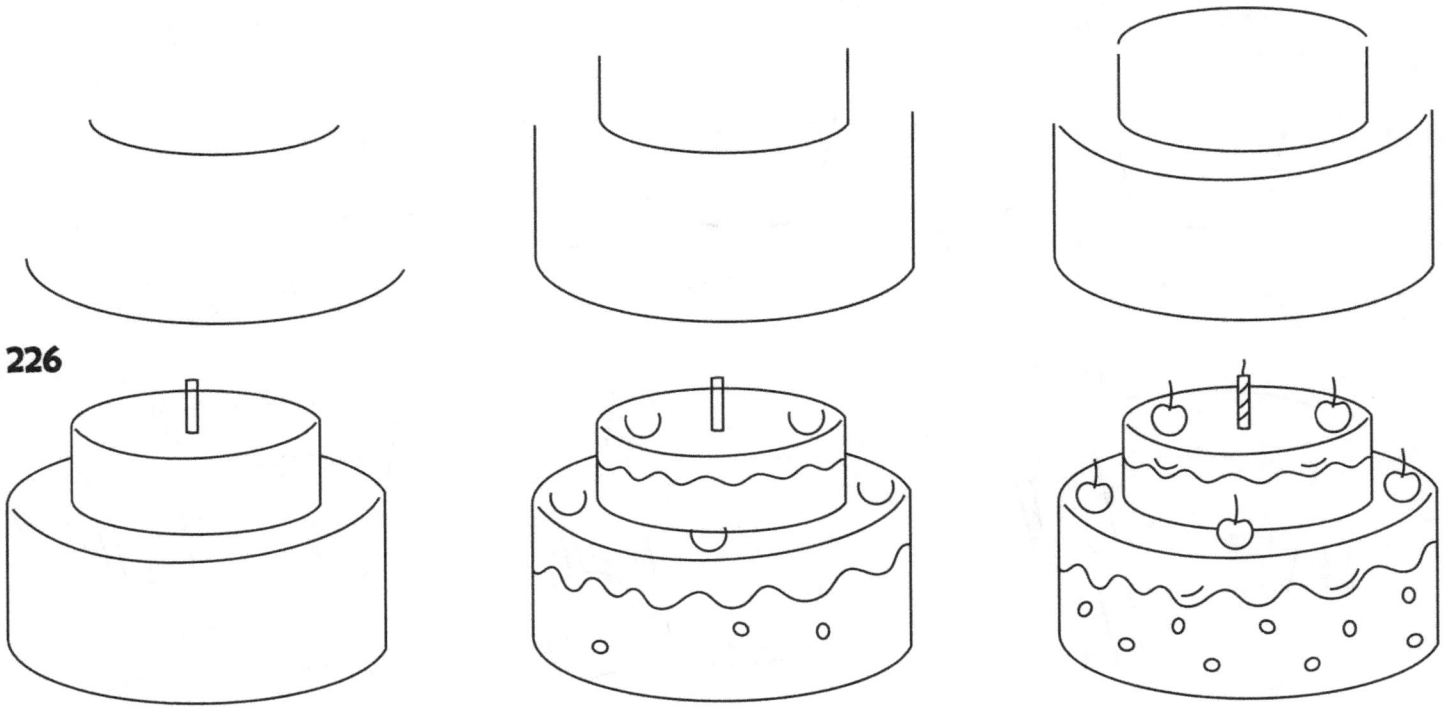

226

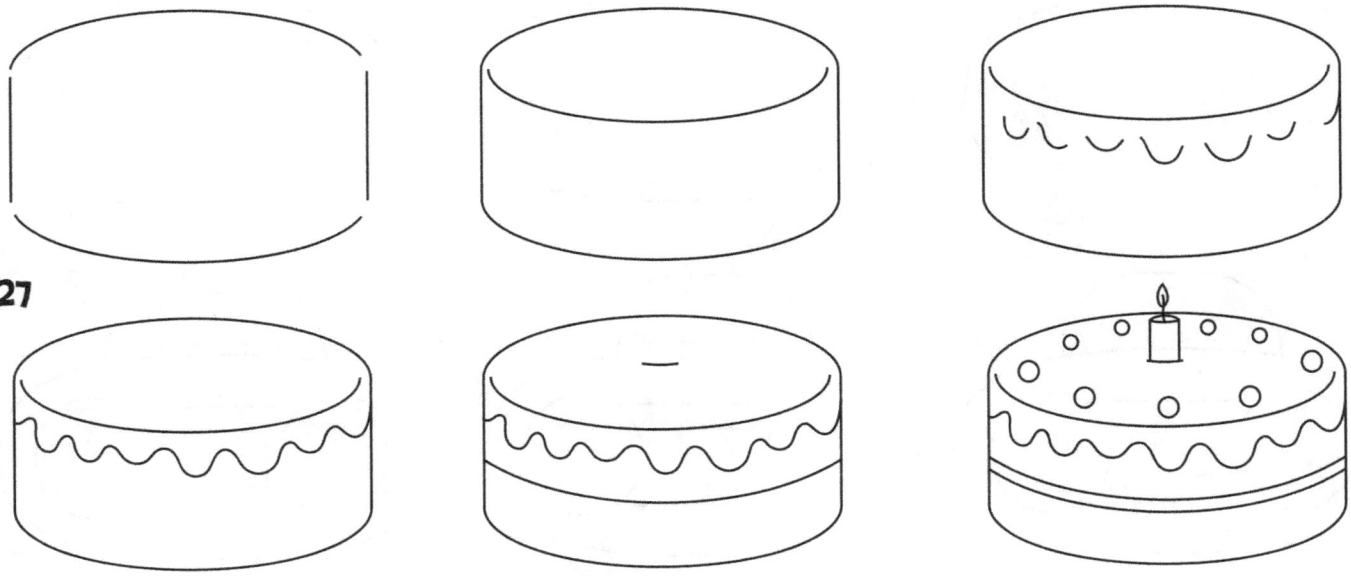

227

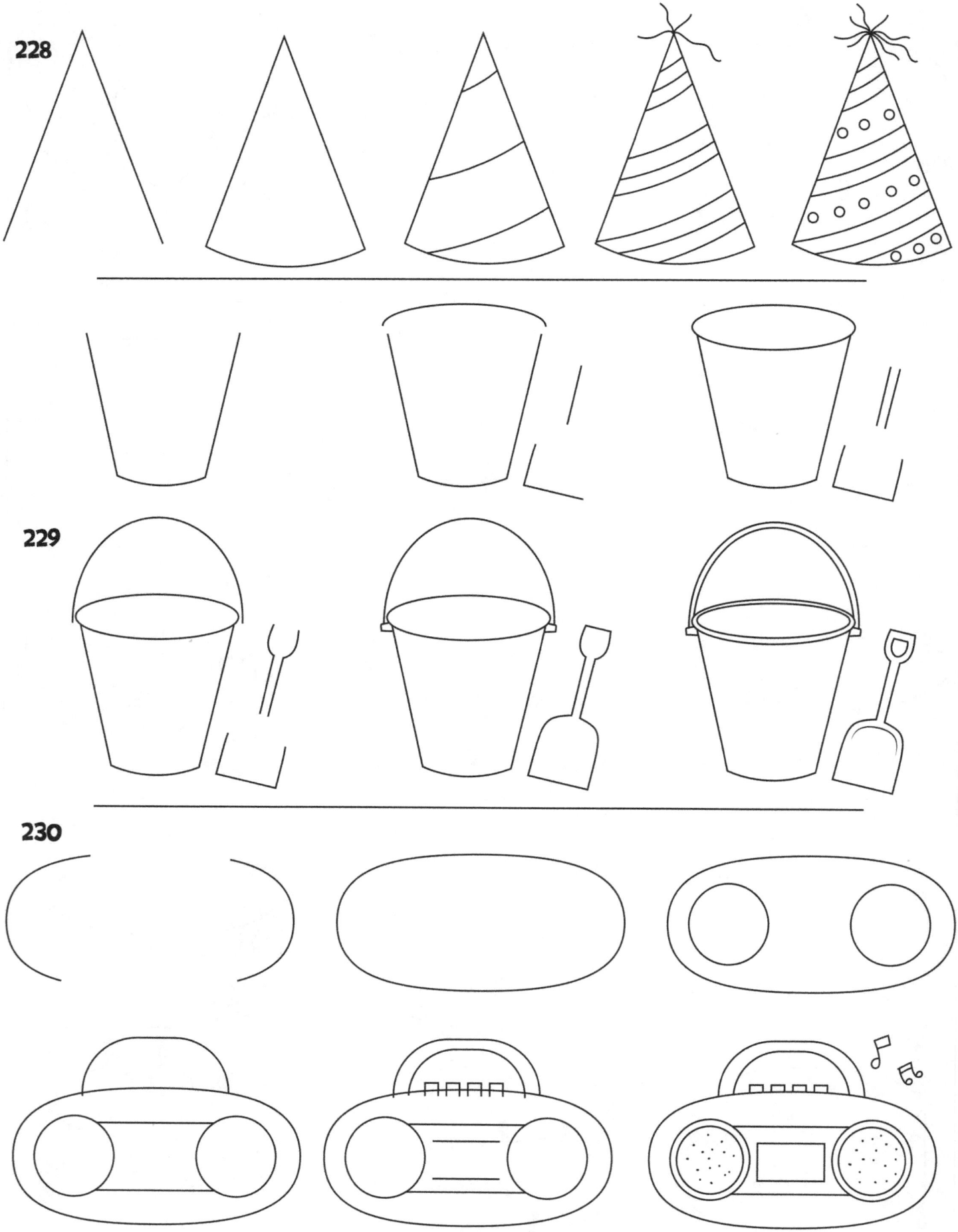
228
229
230

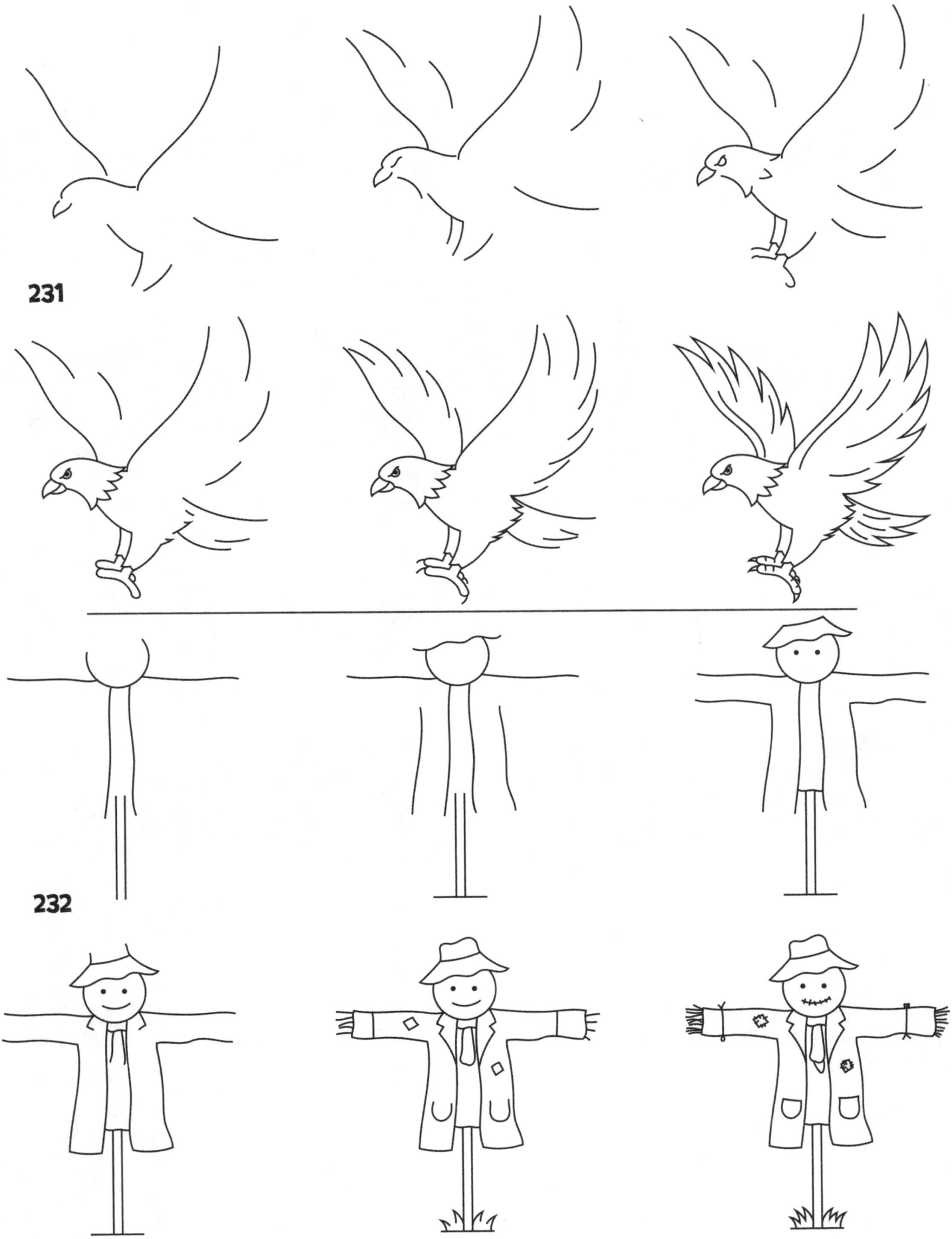
231
232

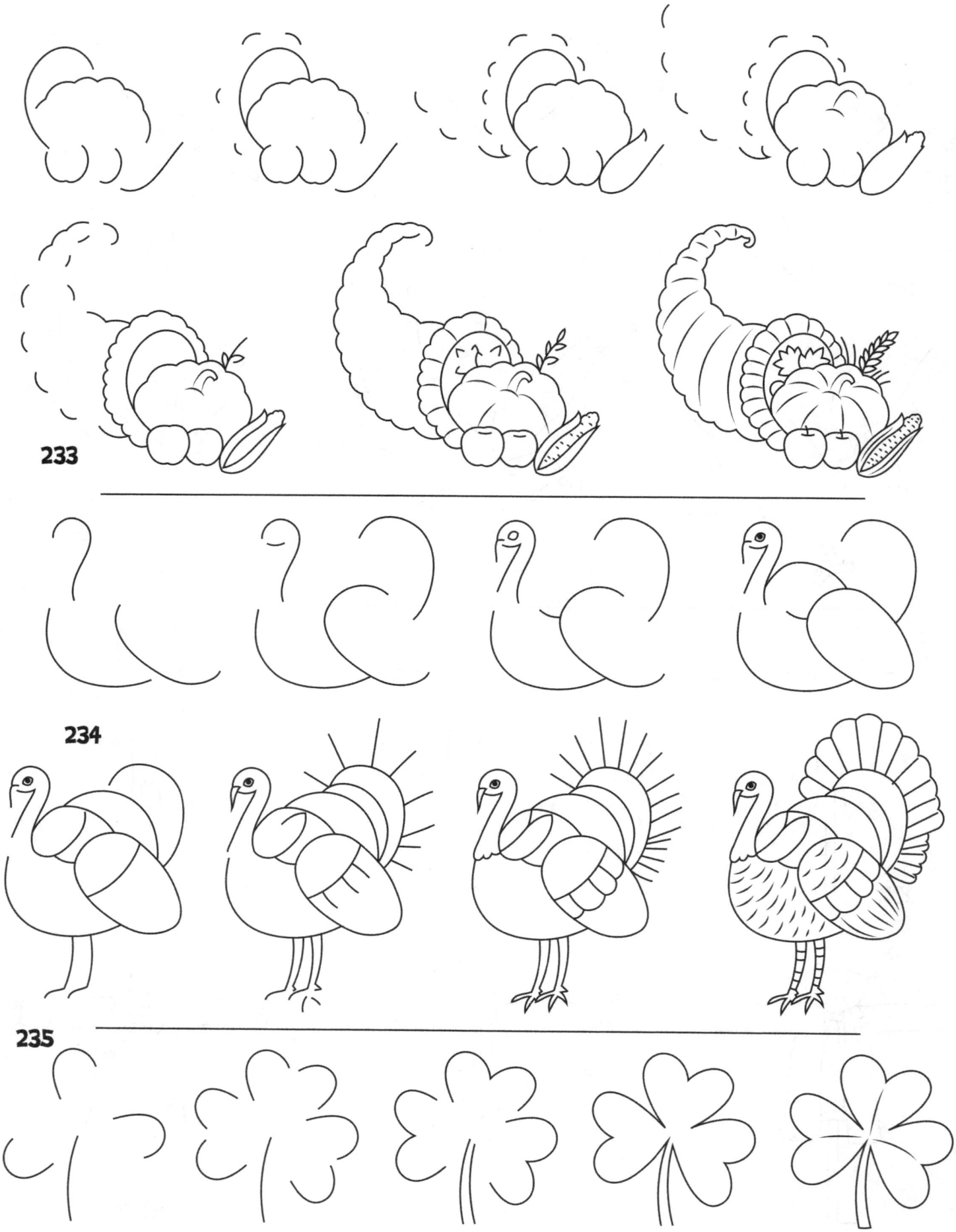
233
234
235

236
237
Happy
Happy Valentine's Day

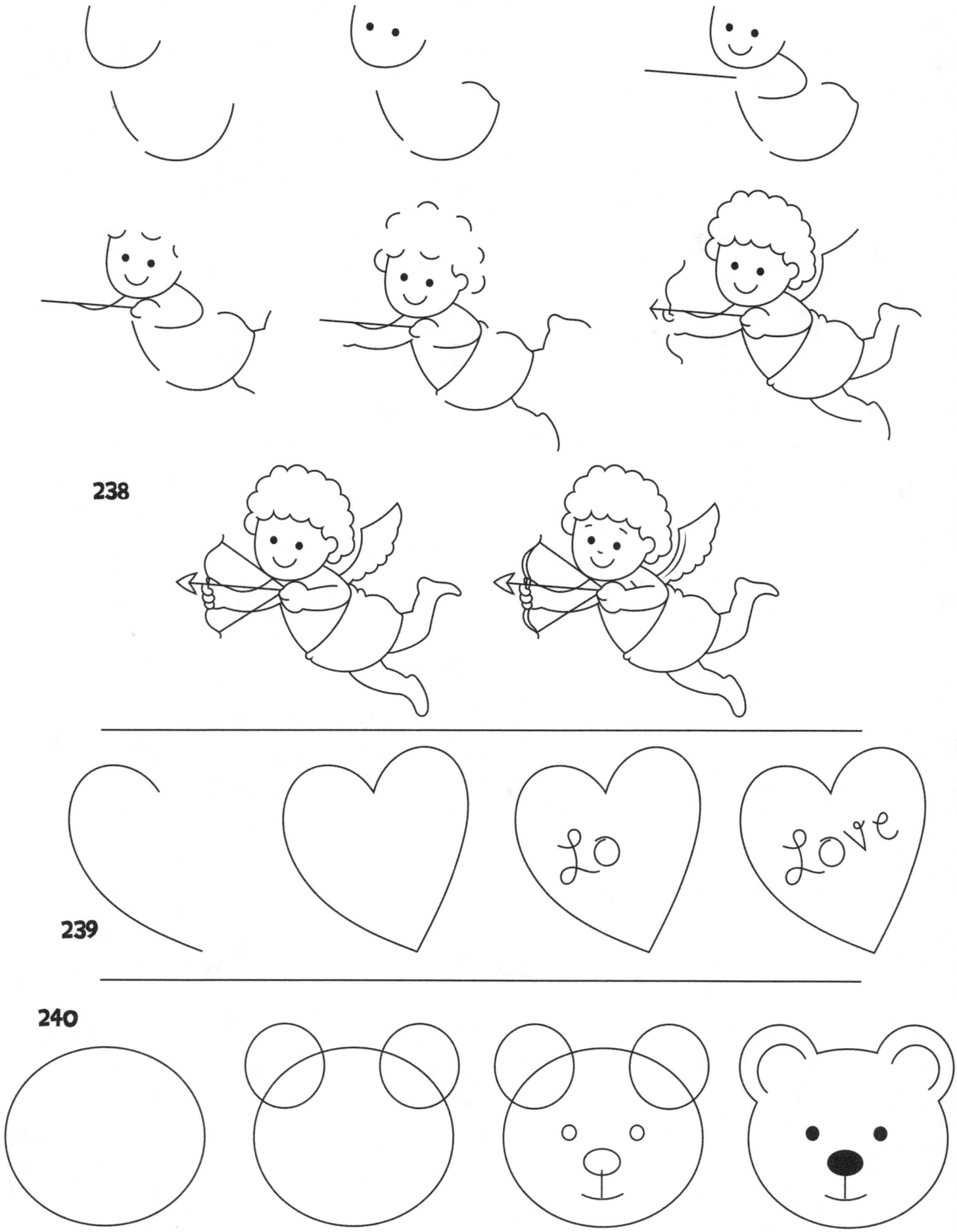
238
239
Lo
Love
240

241
242

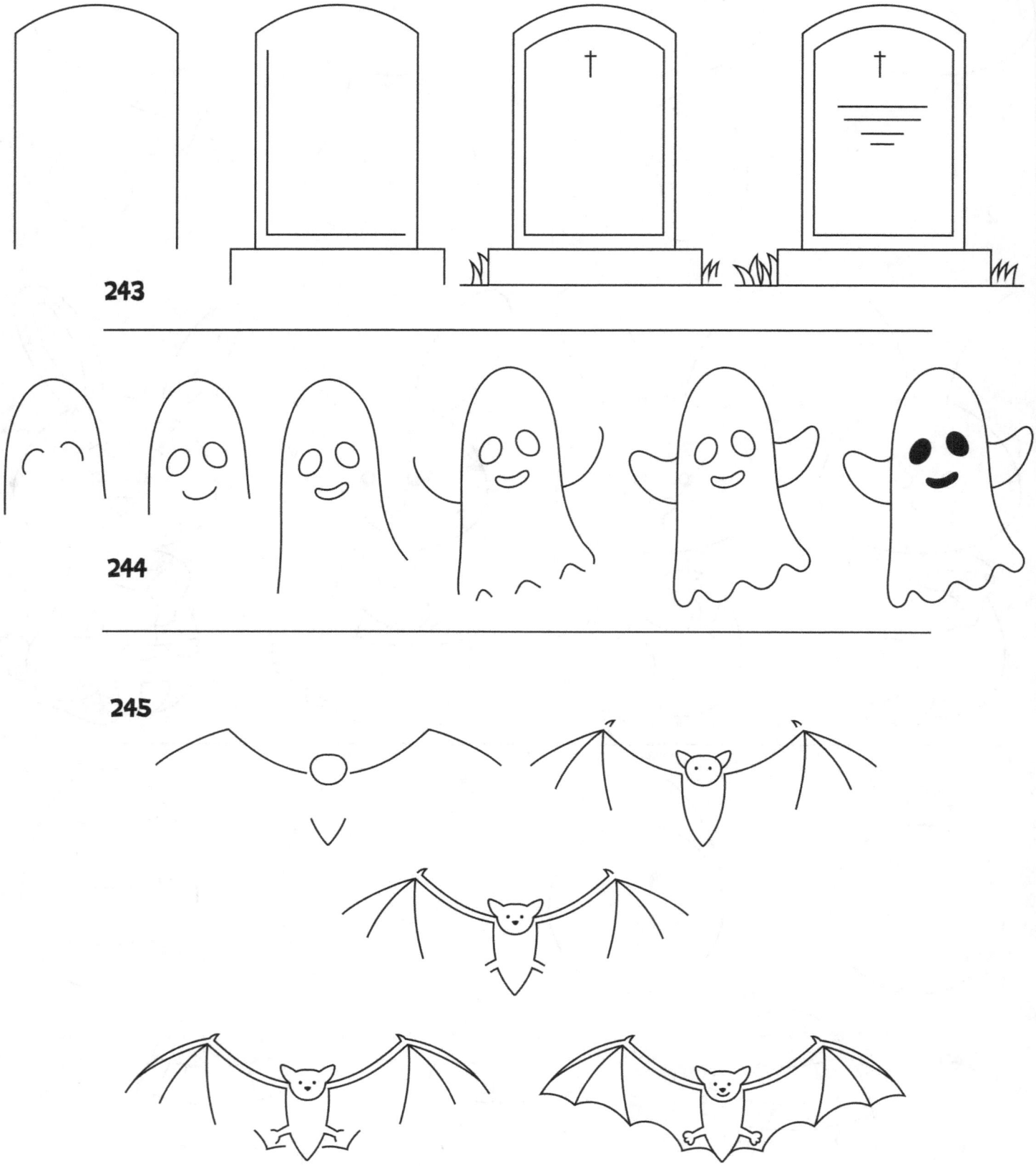
243
244
245

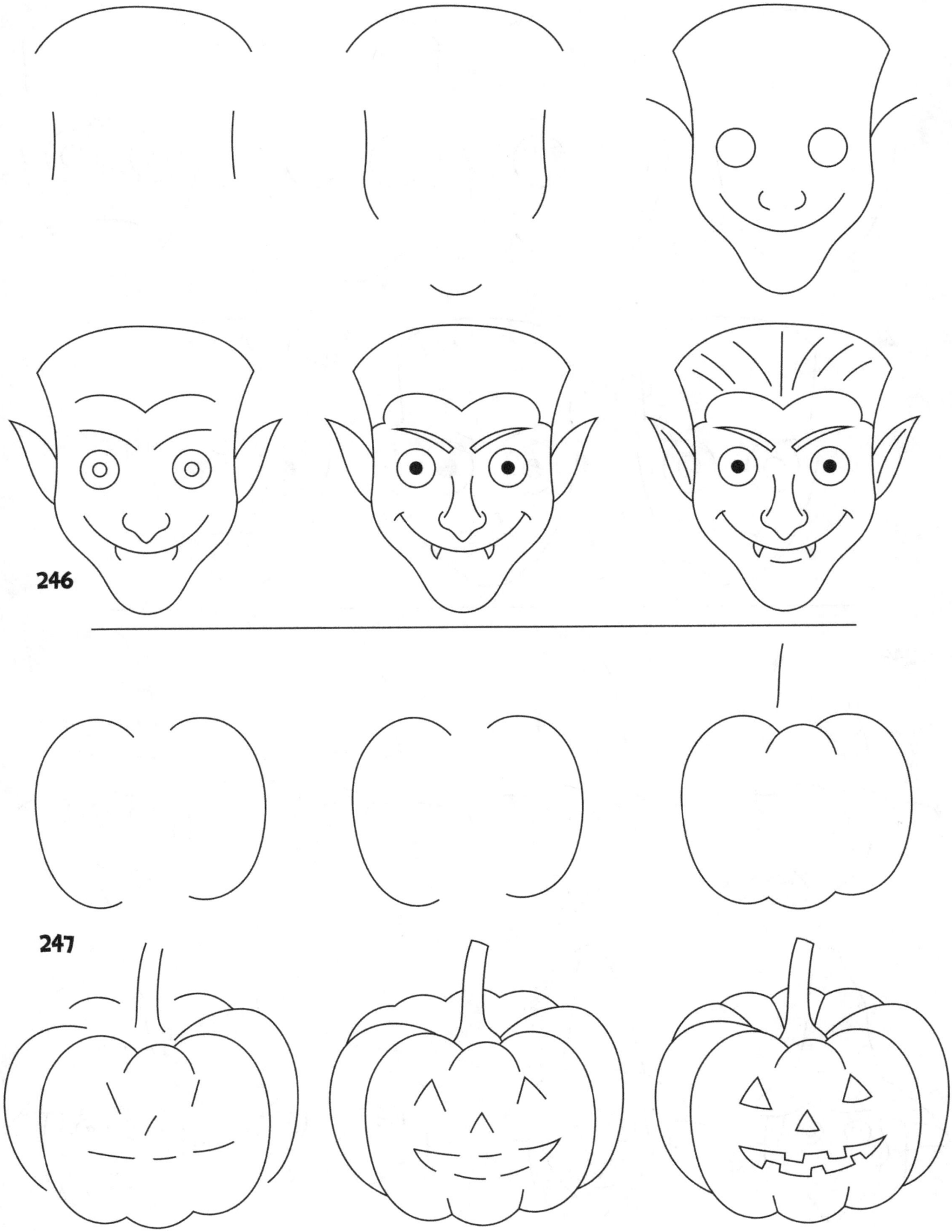
246
247

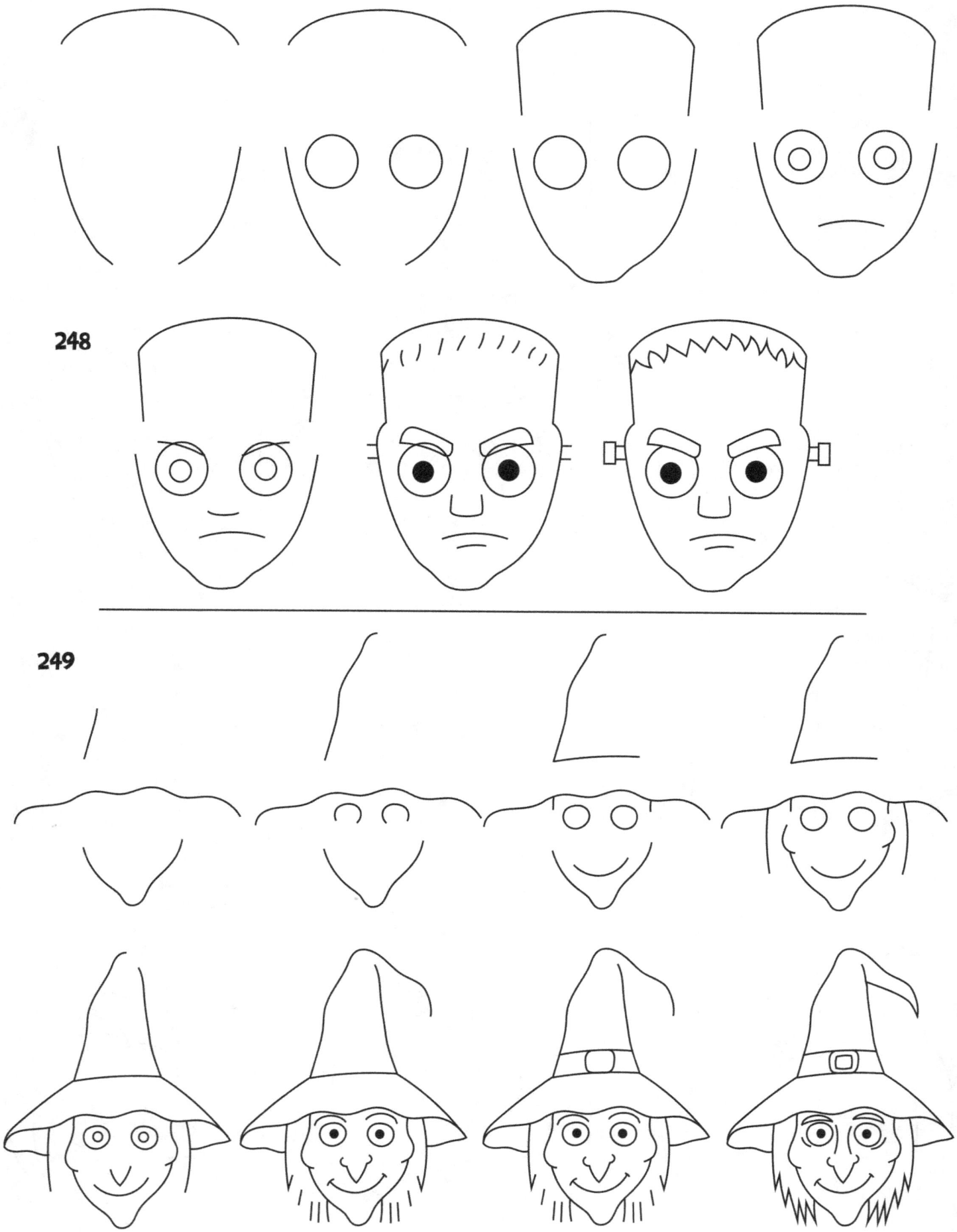
248
249

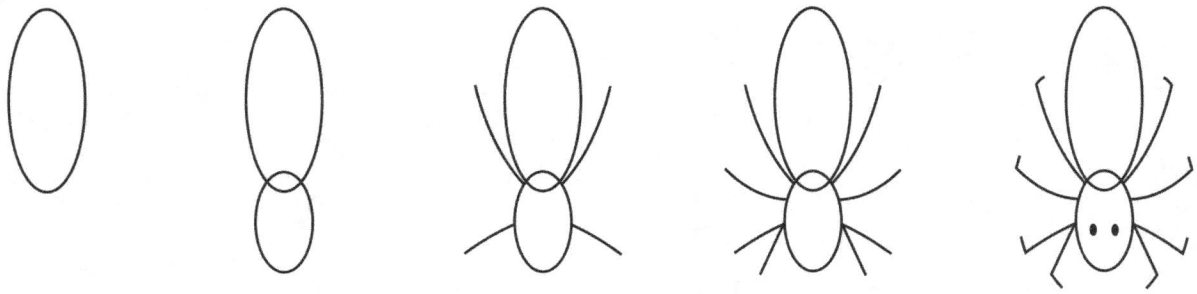

250

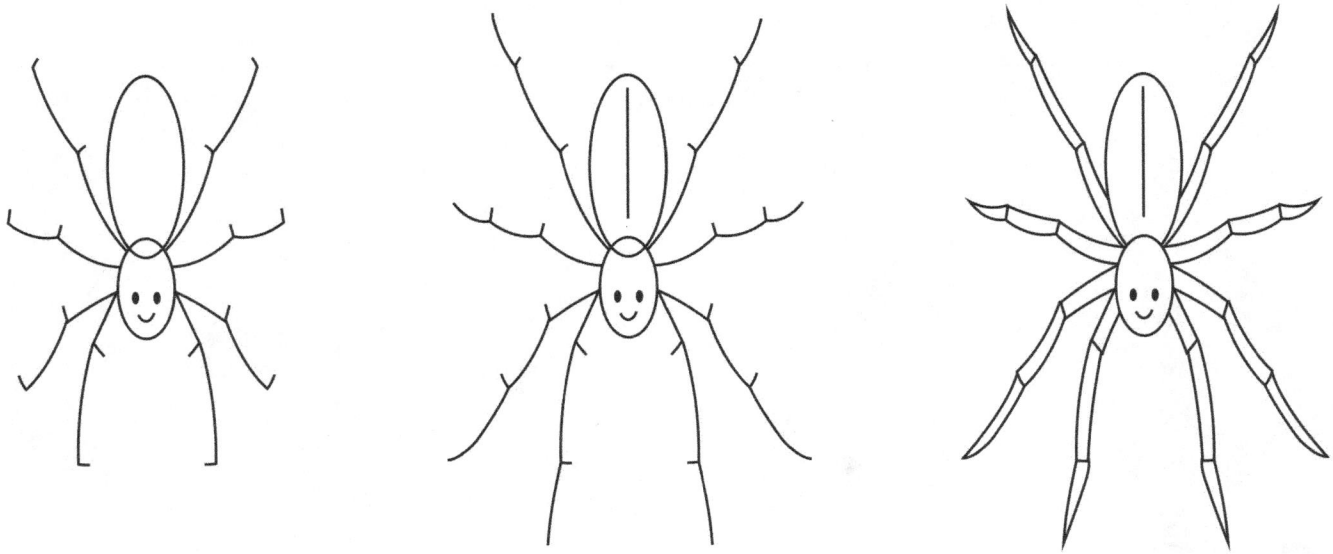

251

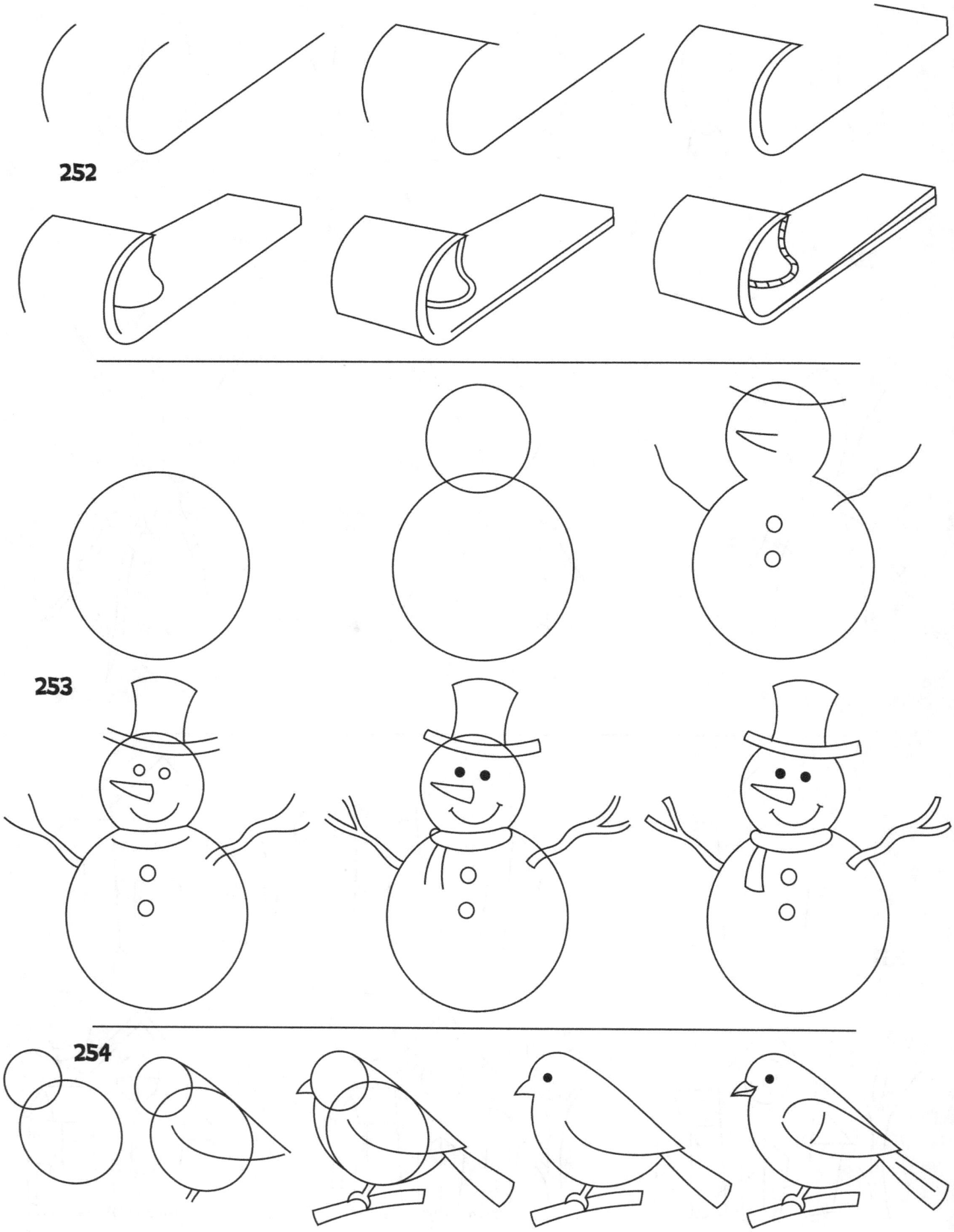
252
253
254

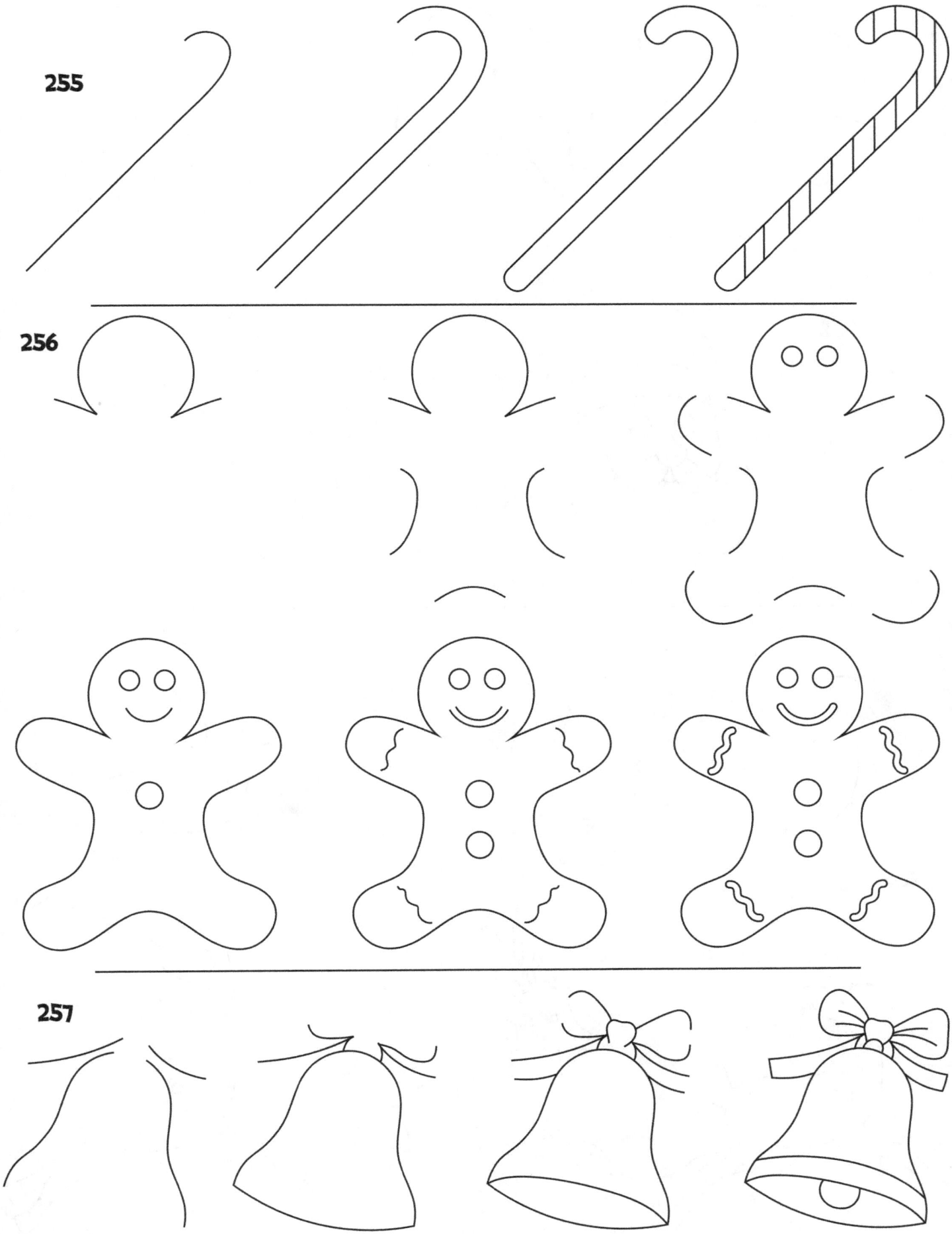
255
256
257

258
259

262

263

264

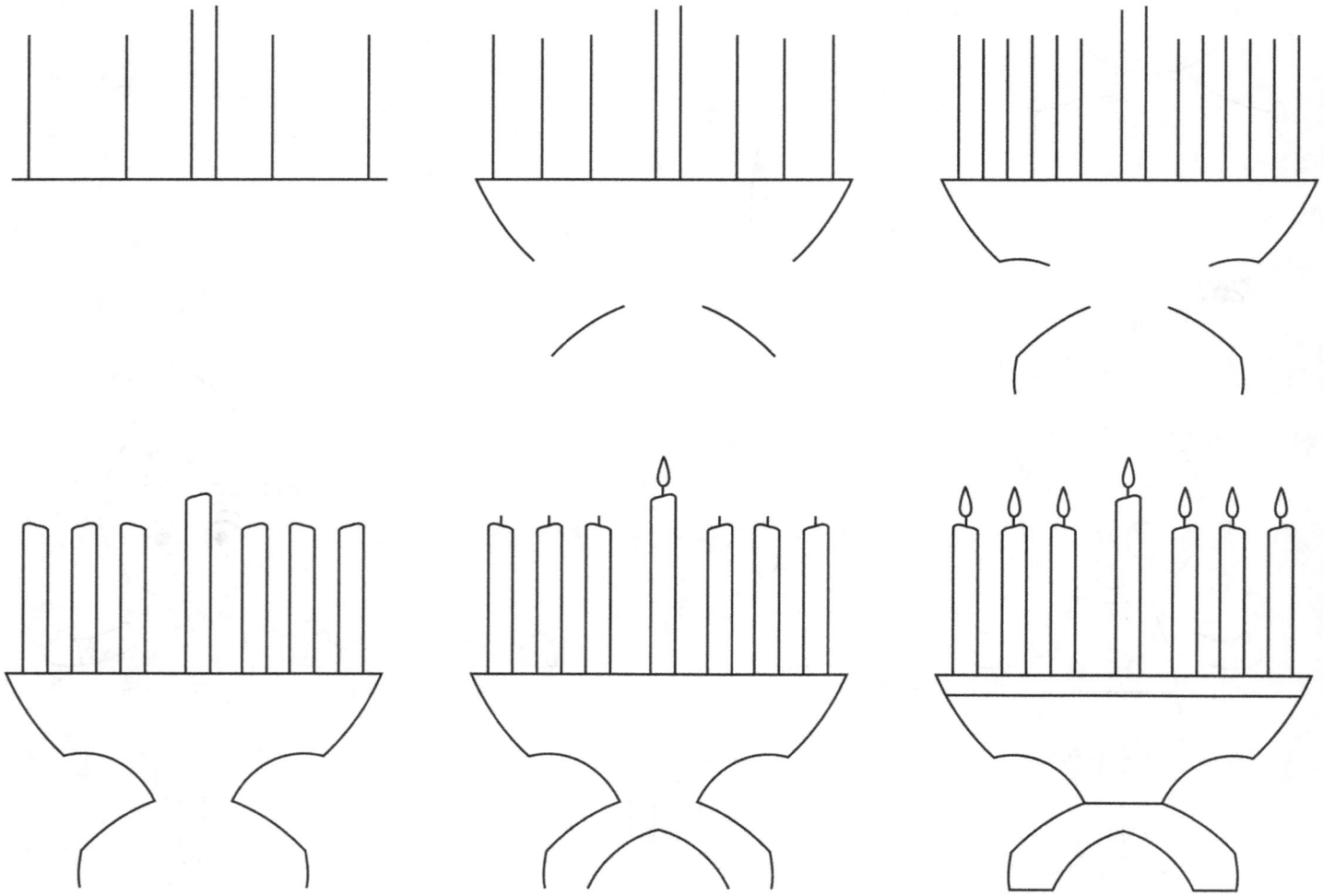

265
266

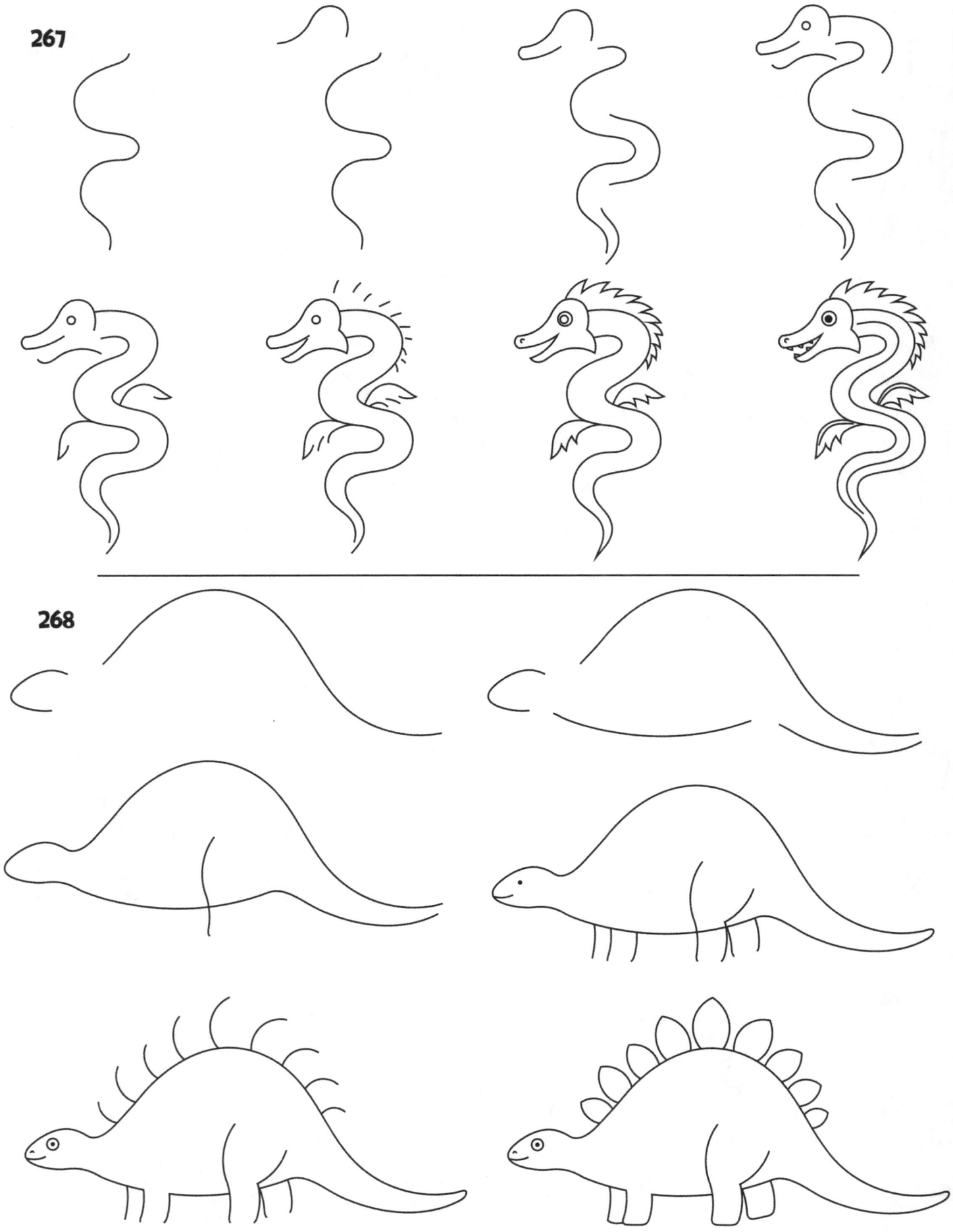
267
268

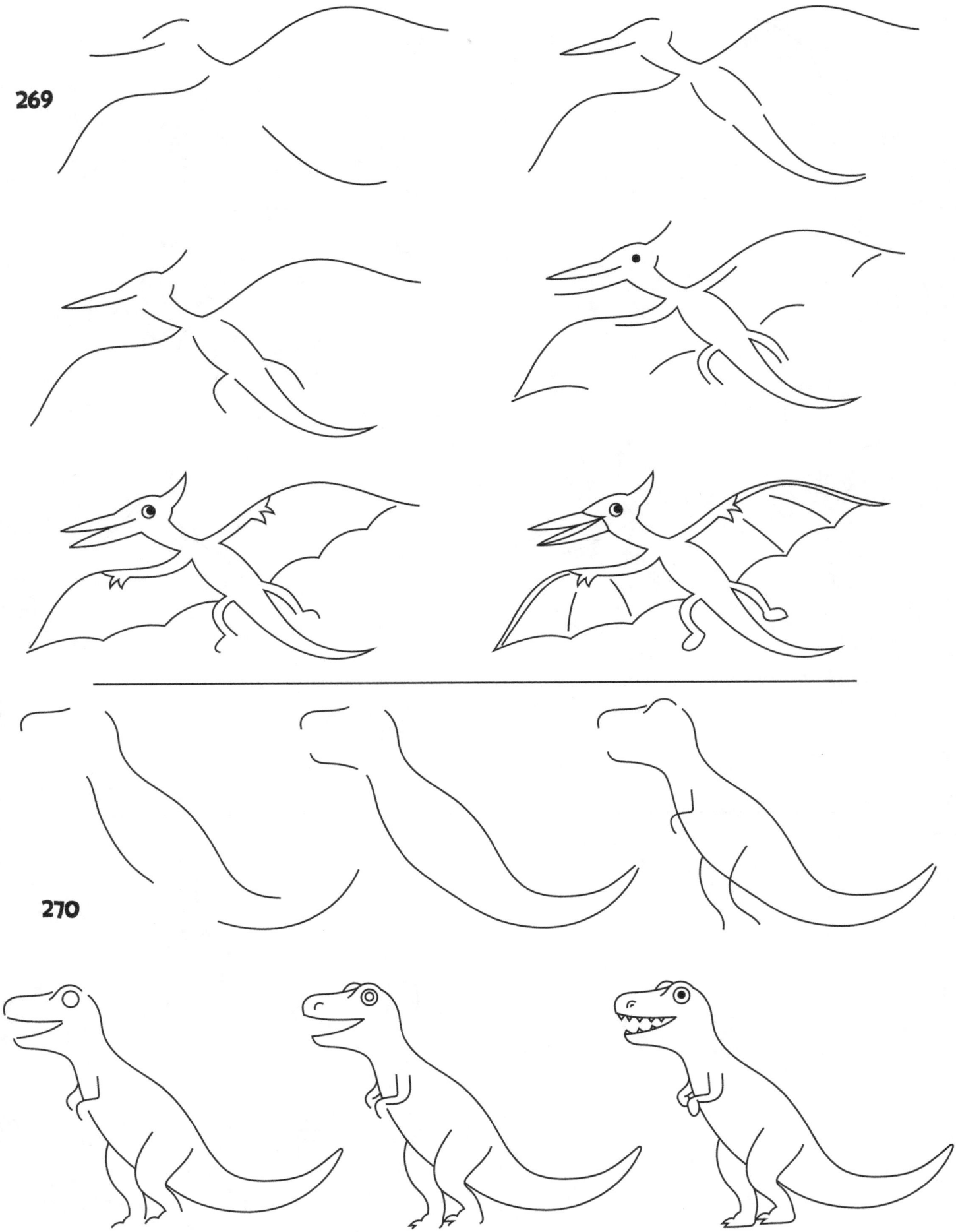
269
270

271
272

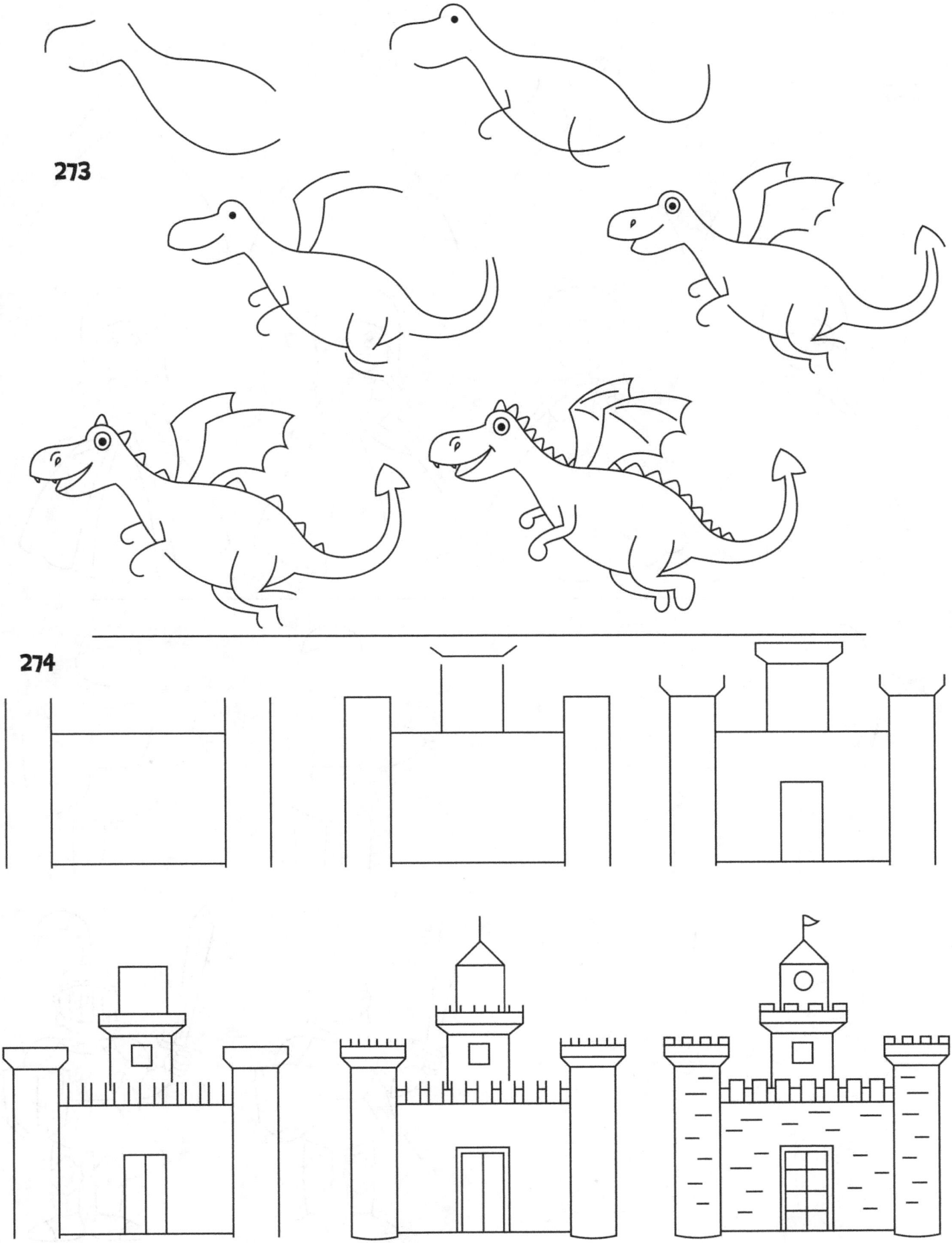
273
274

275
276

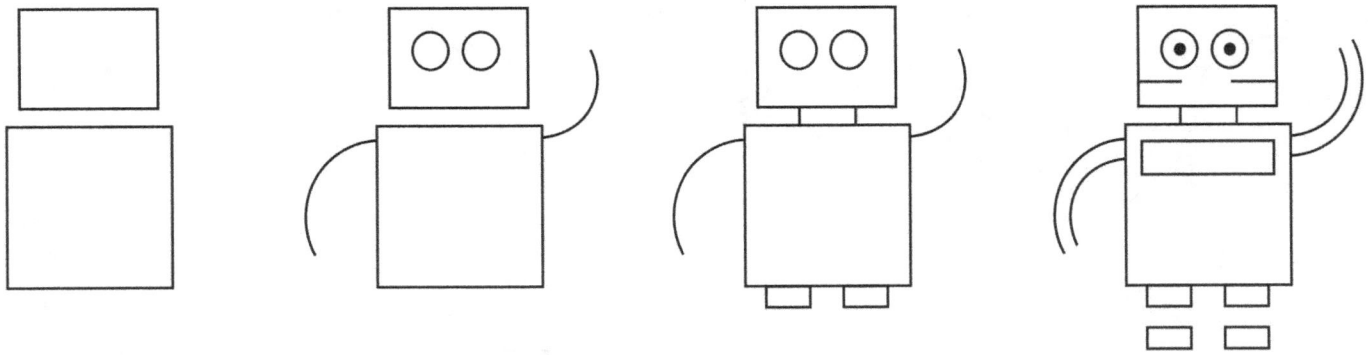

277

278

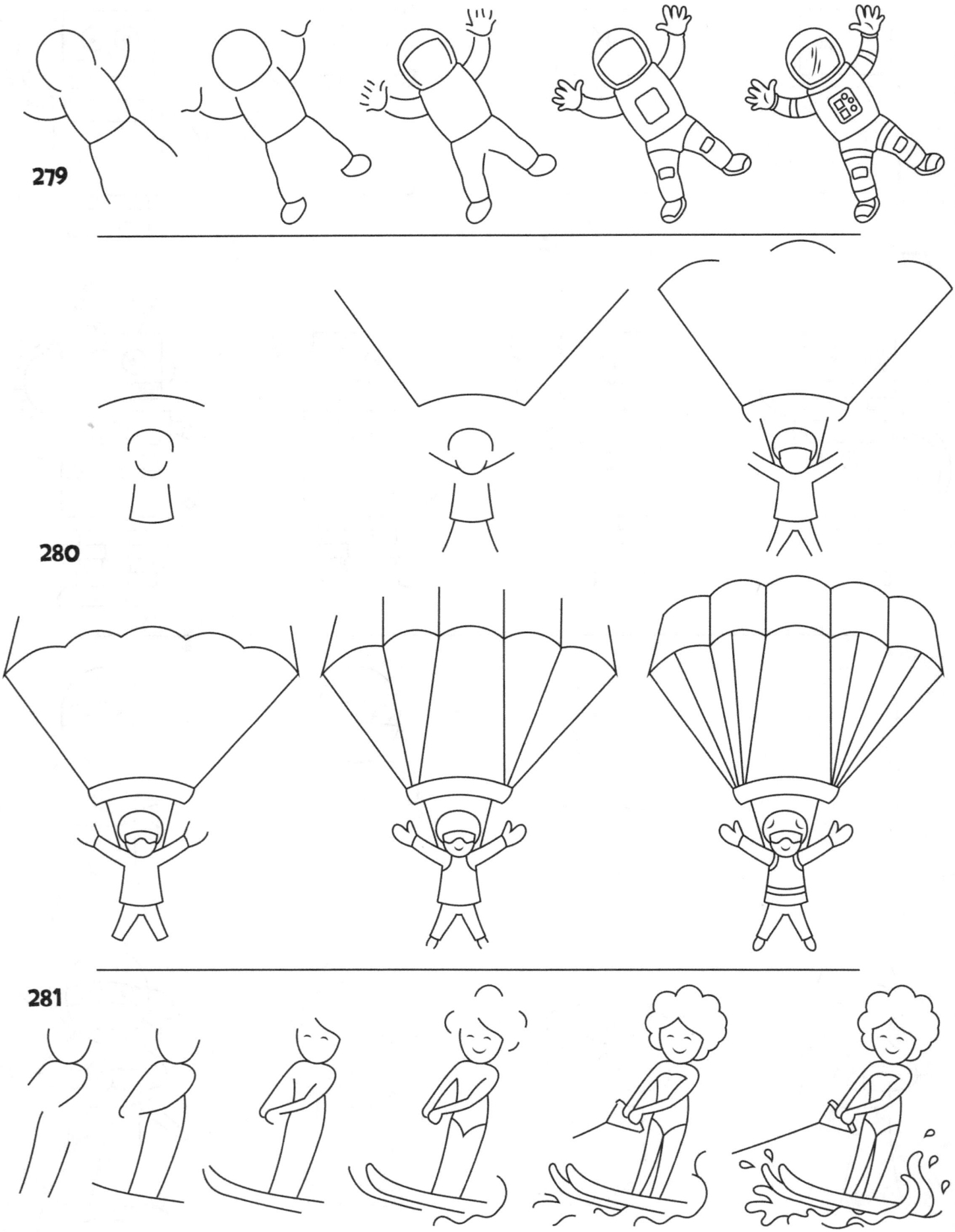
279
280
281

282

283

284

285

286

287

288

289
290

291
292

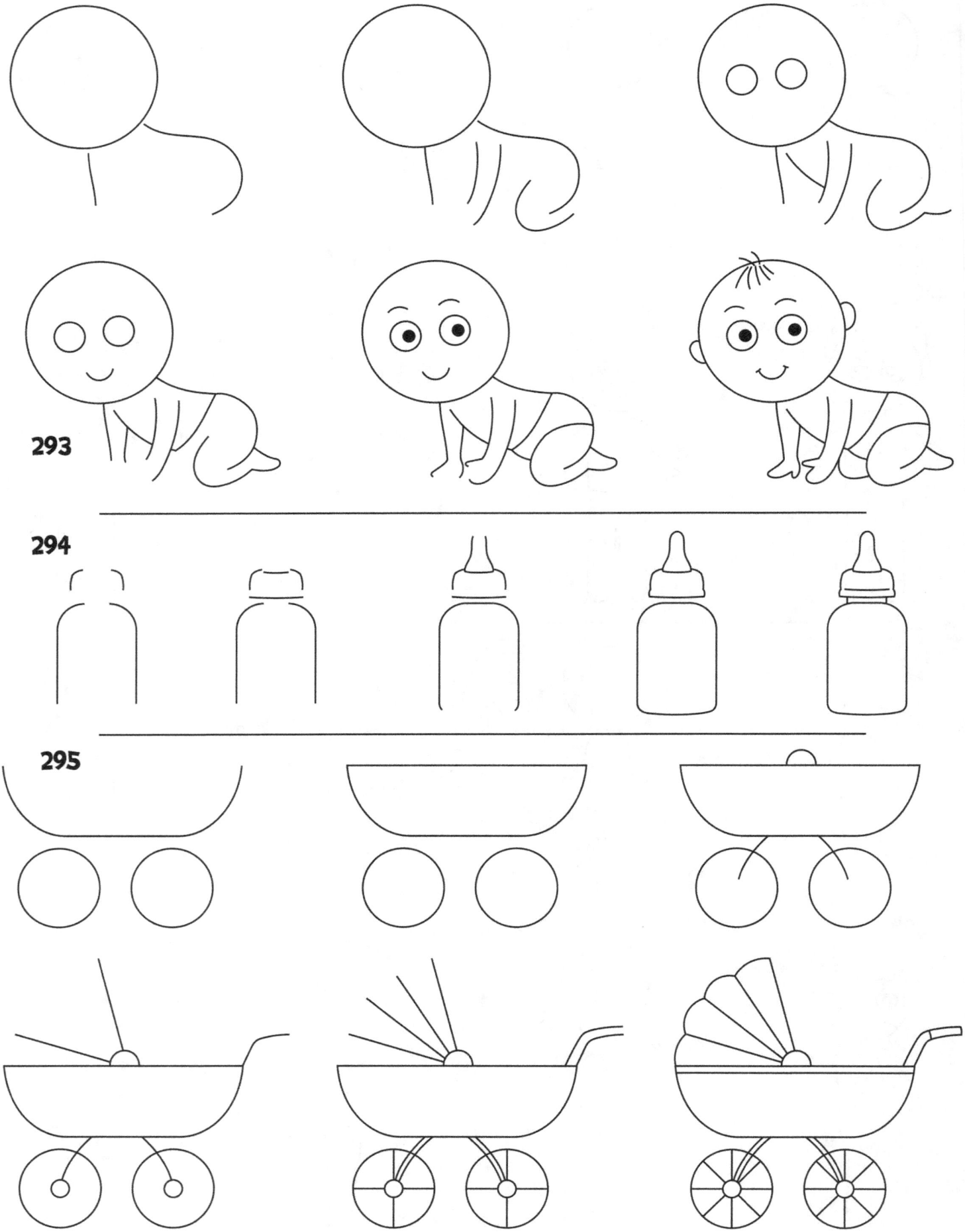
293
294
295

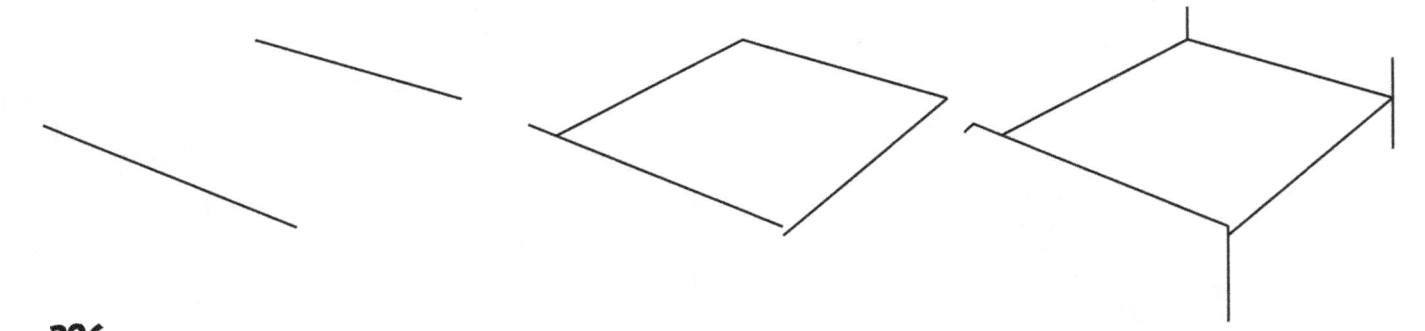

296

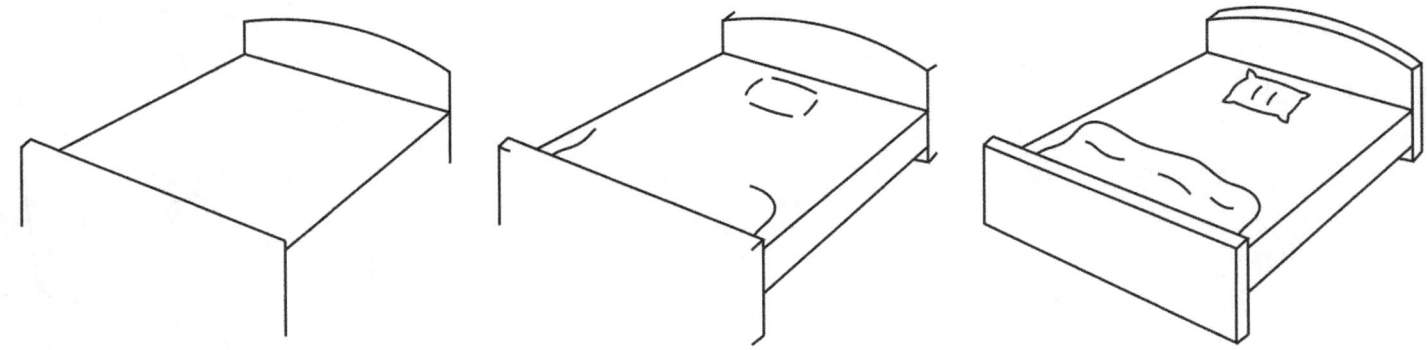

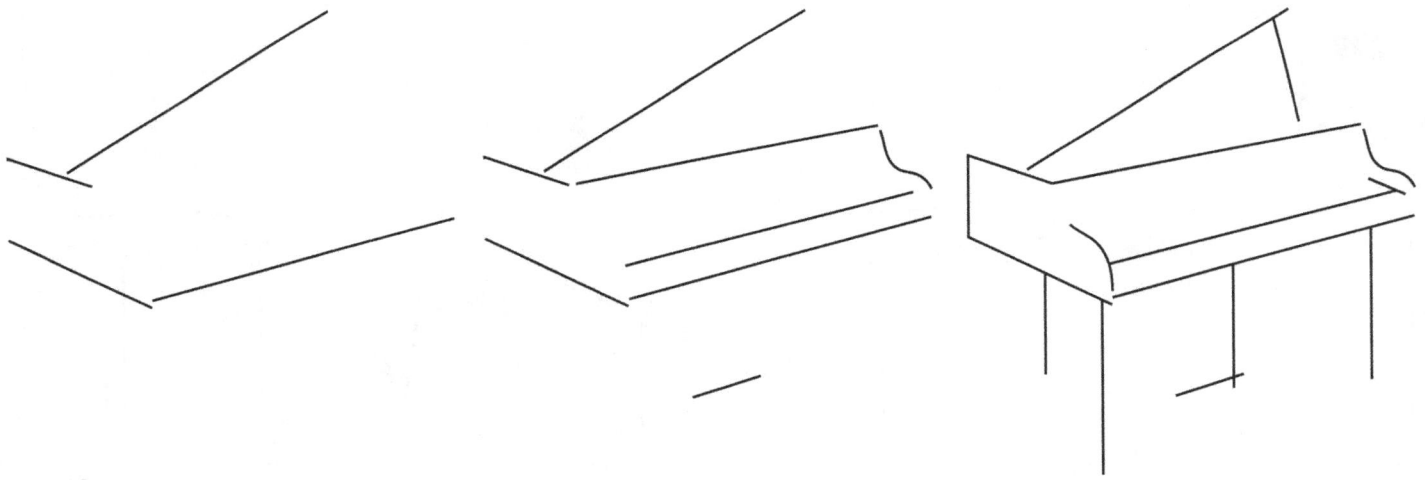

297

298

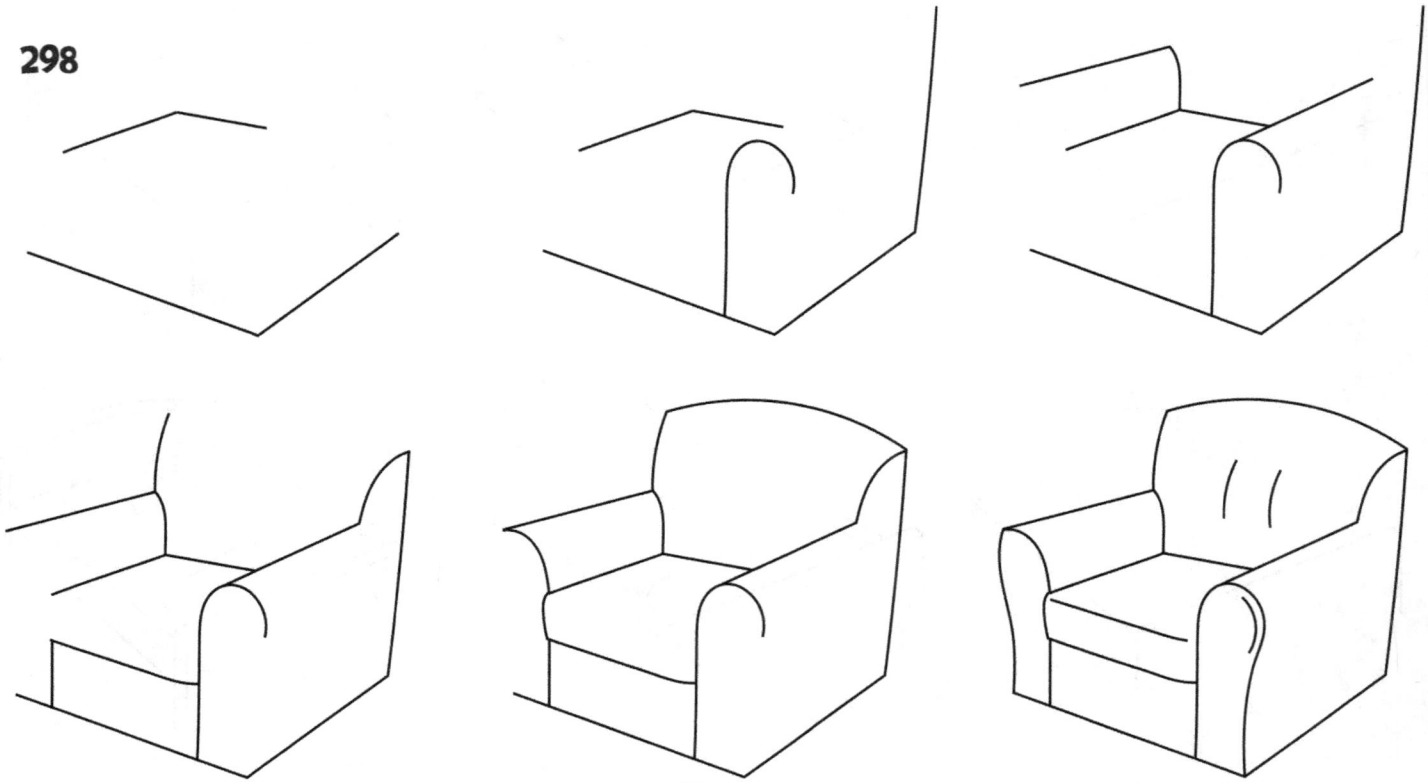

299

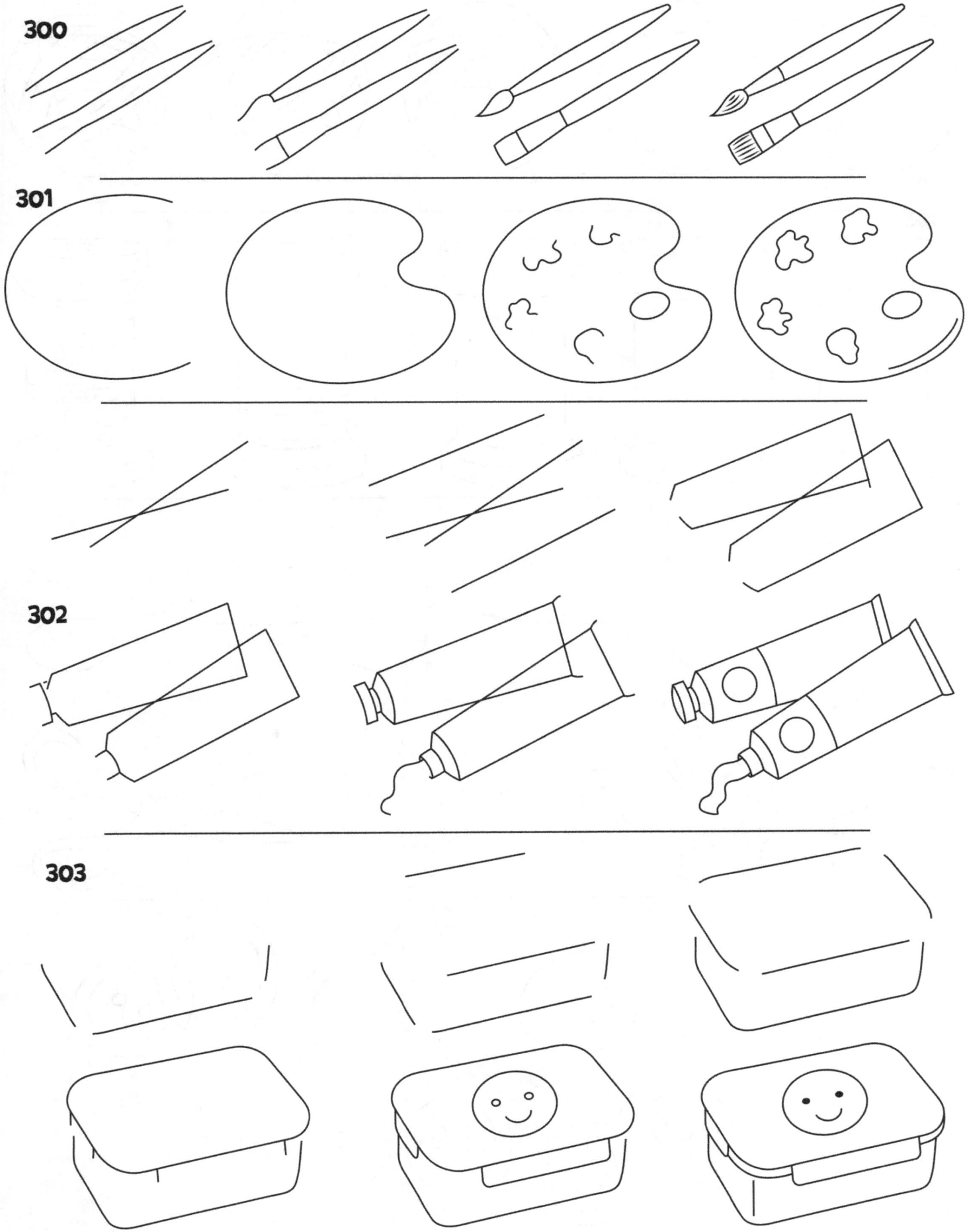
300
301
302
303

304

305

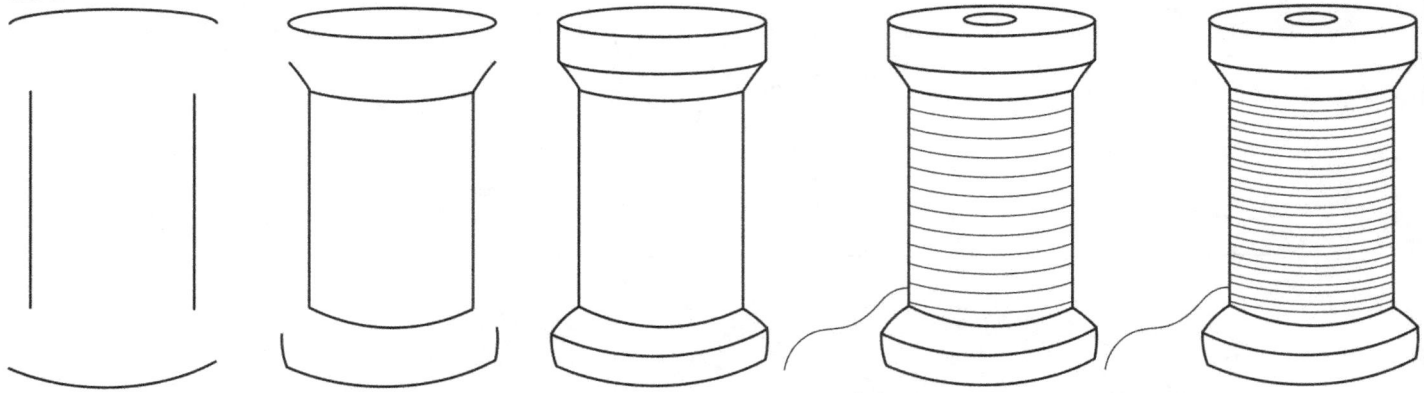

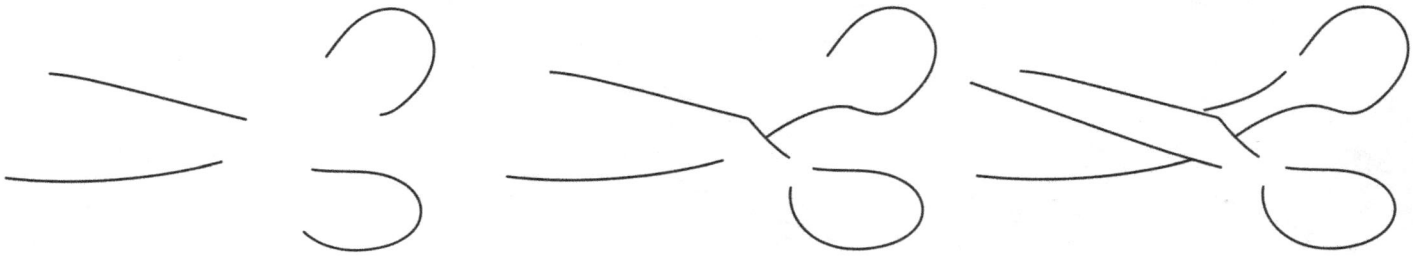

306

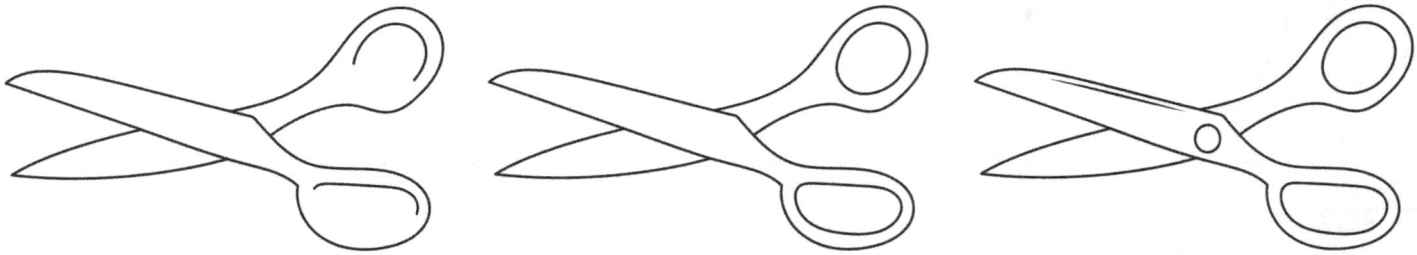

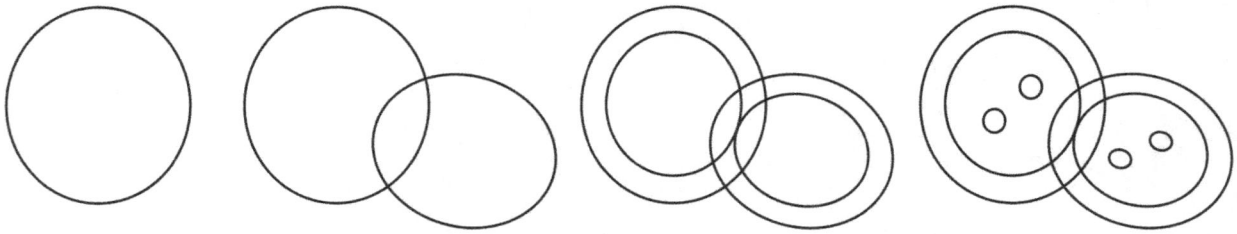

307

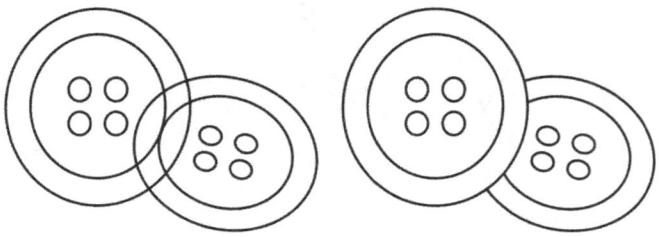

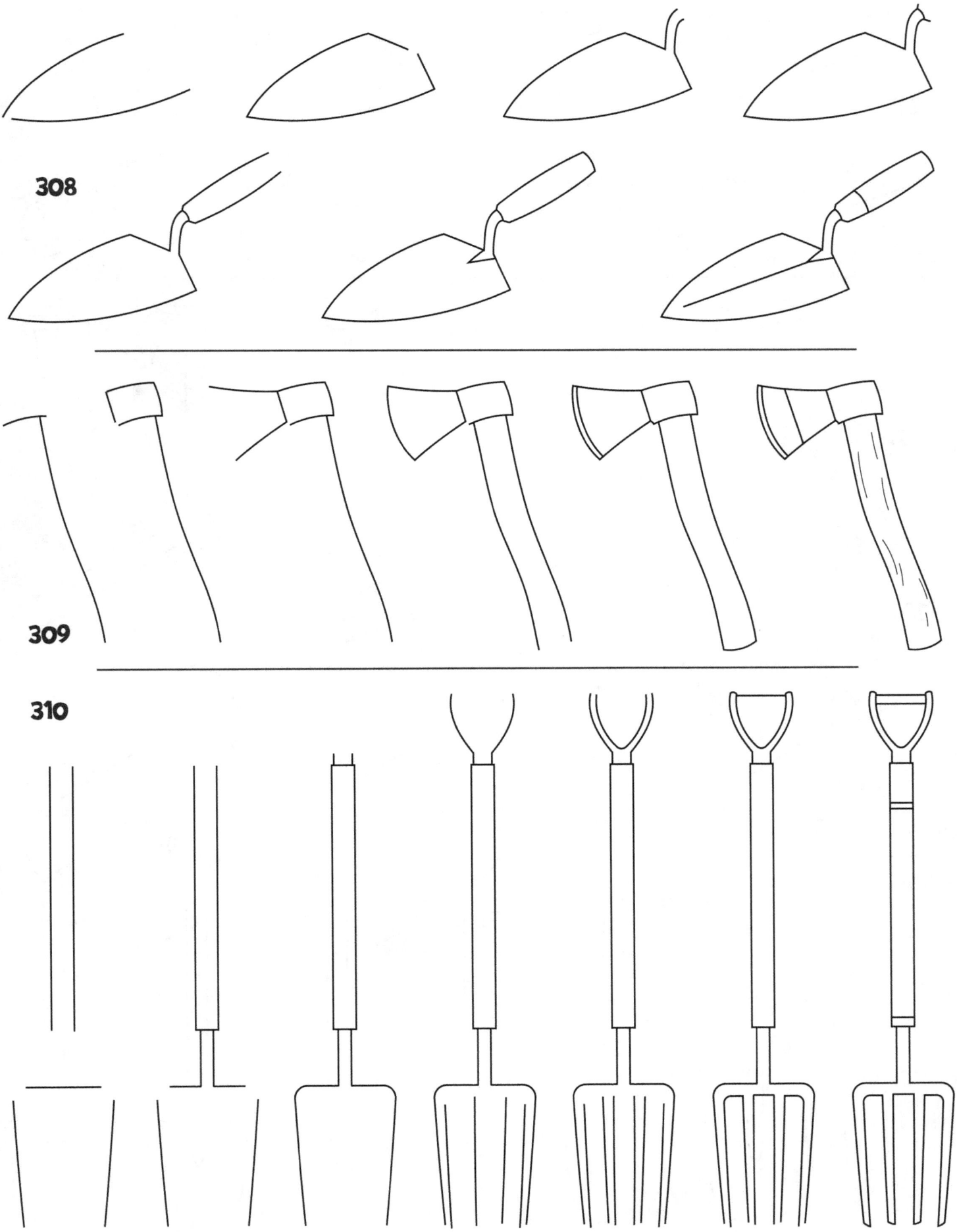
308
309
310

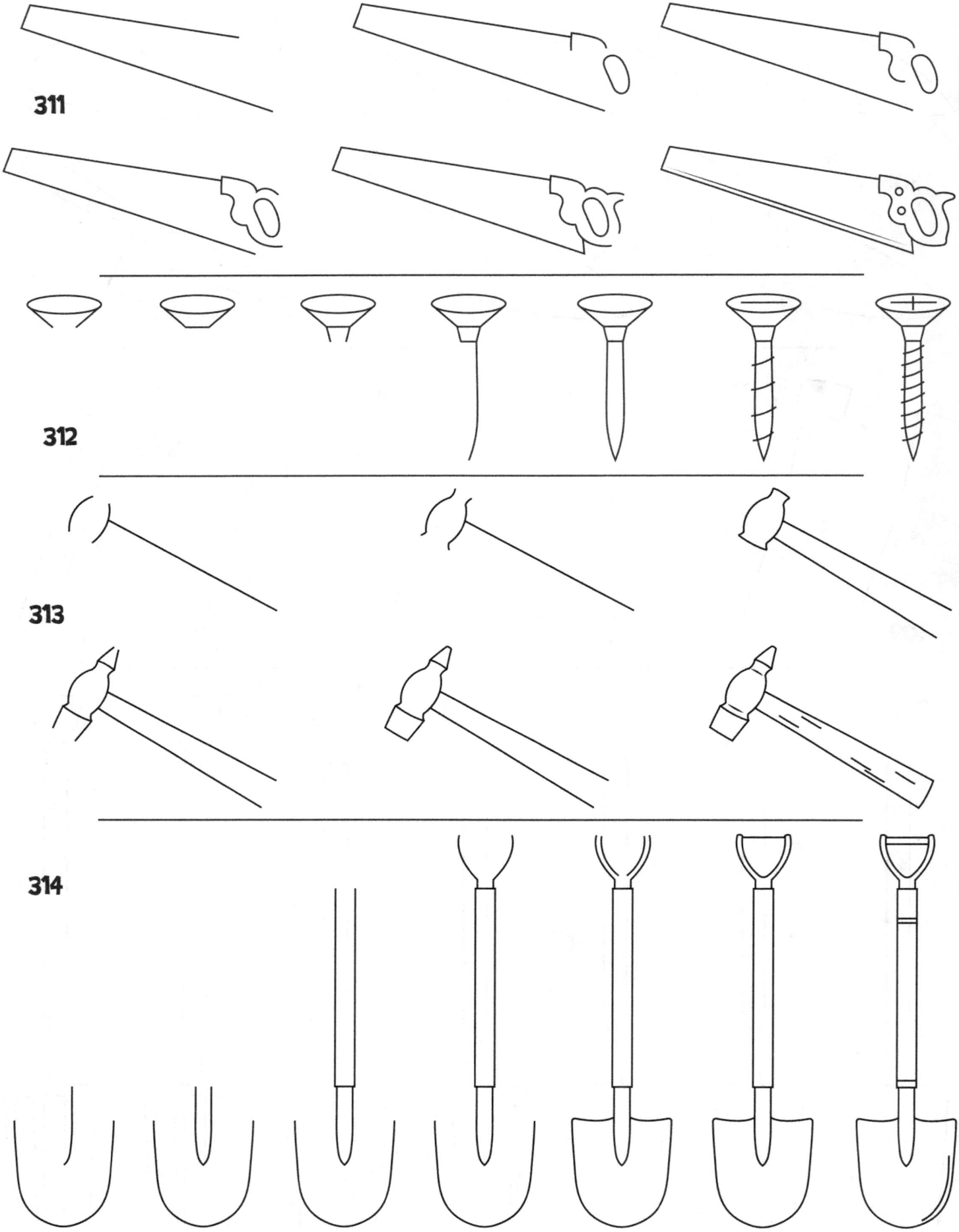
311
312
313
314

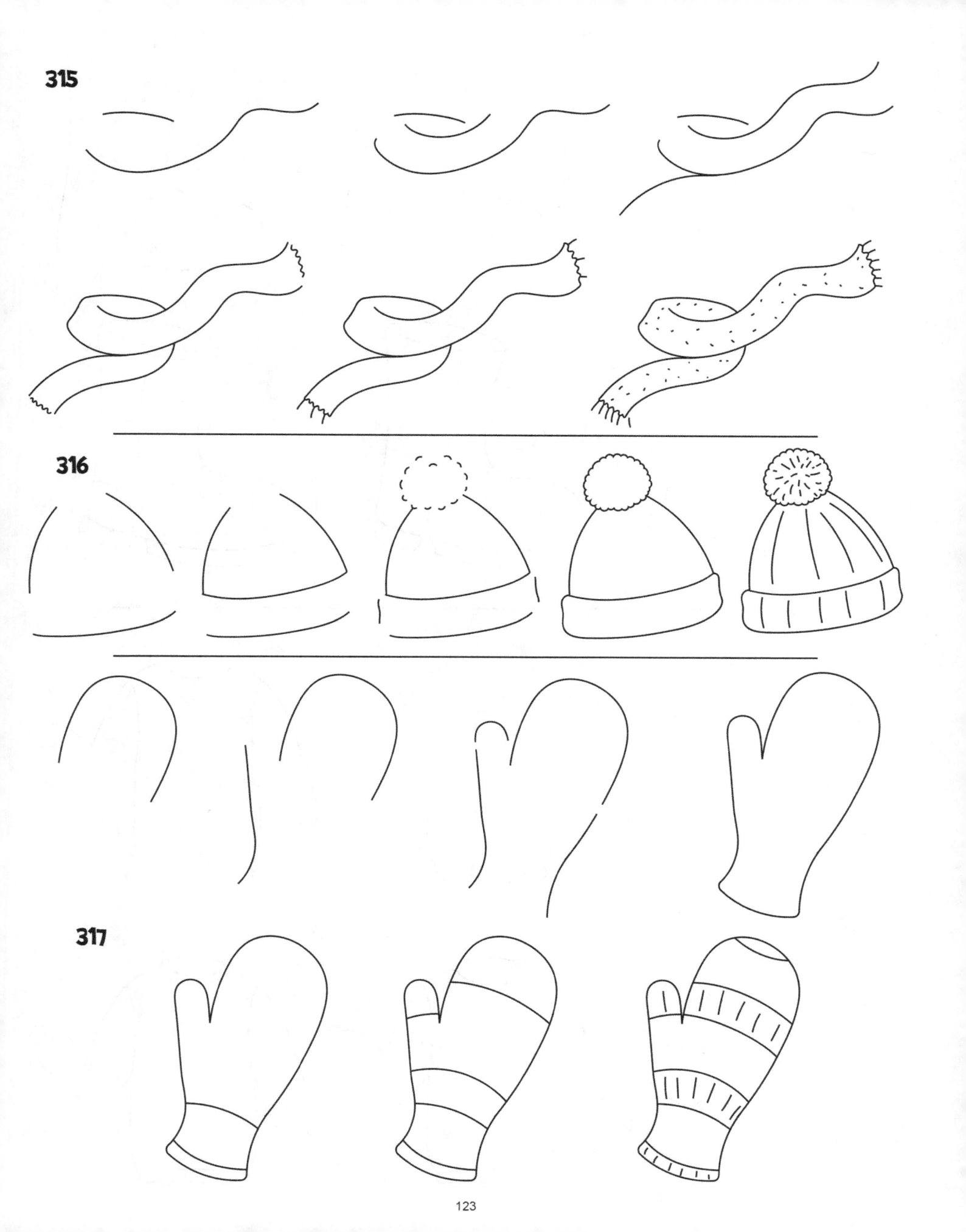
315
316
317

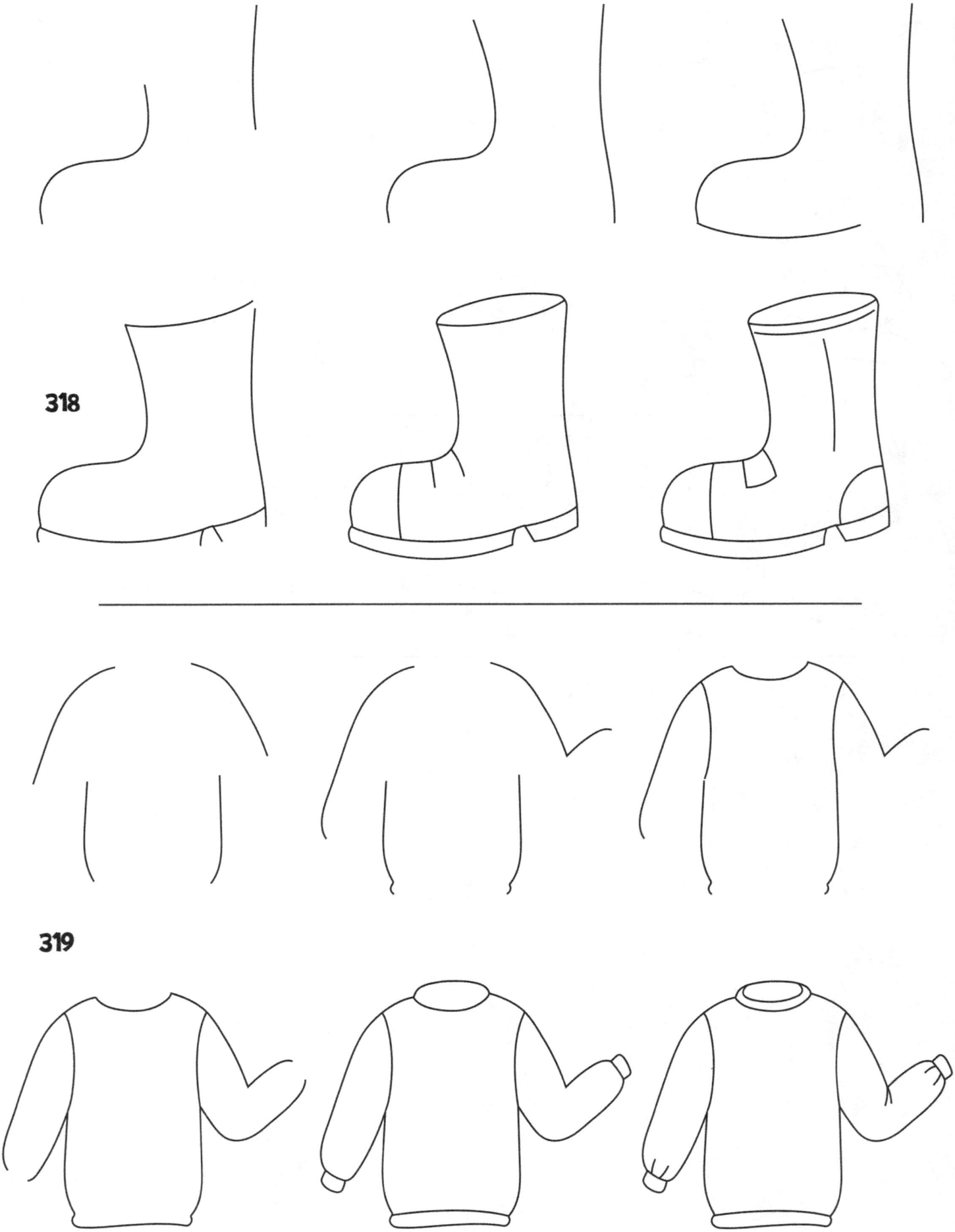
318
319

320
321

322
323
324

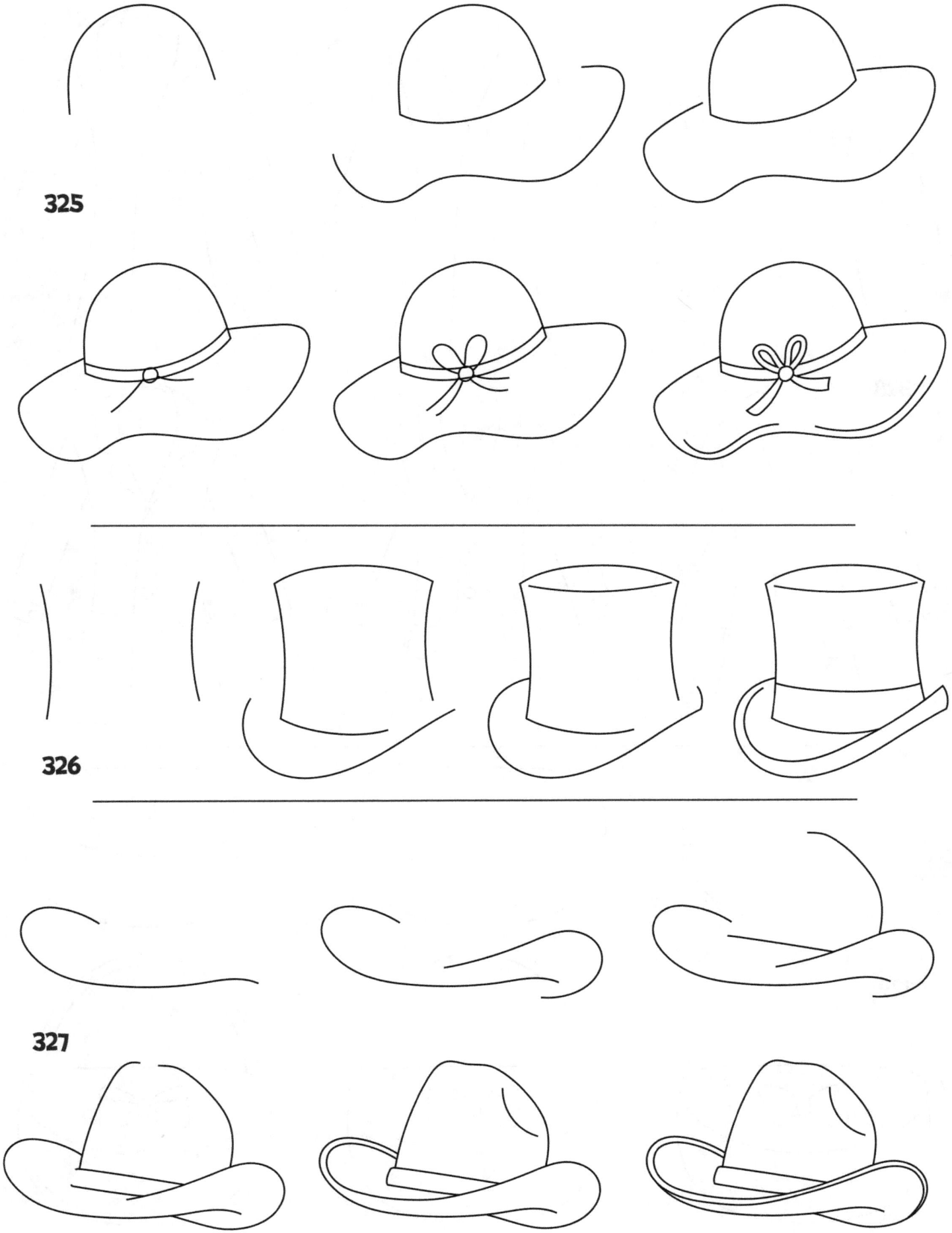
325
326
327

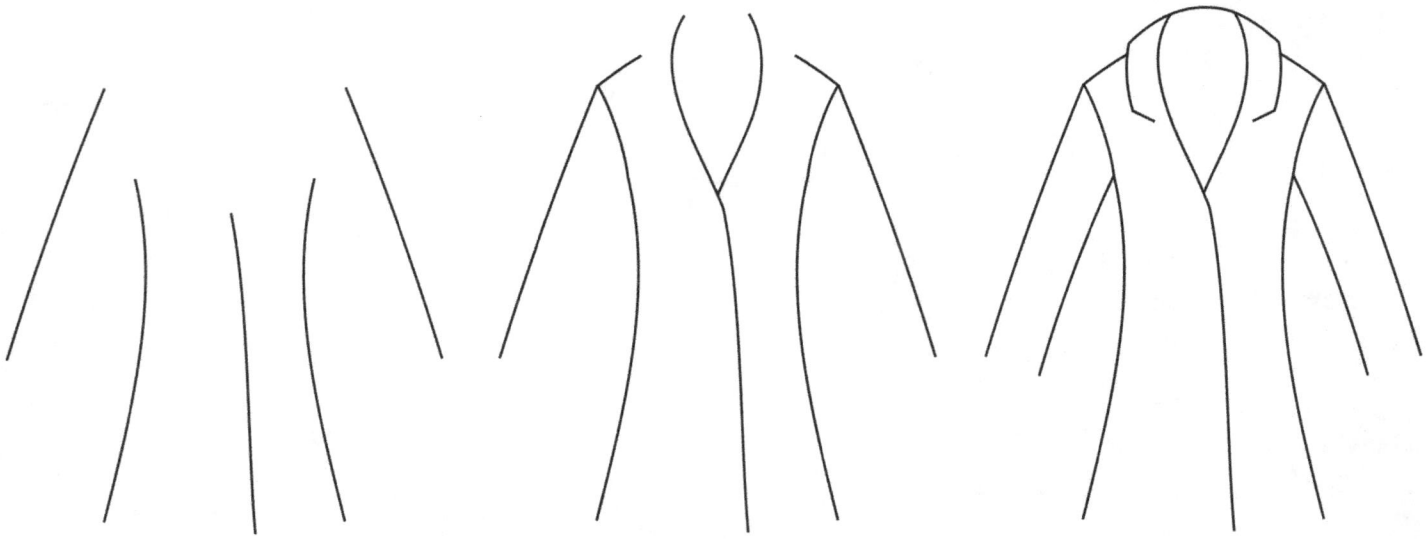

328

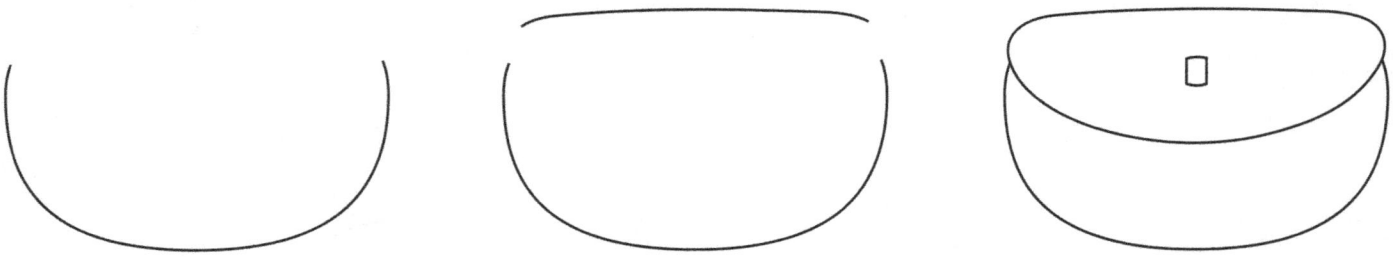

329

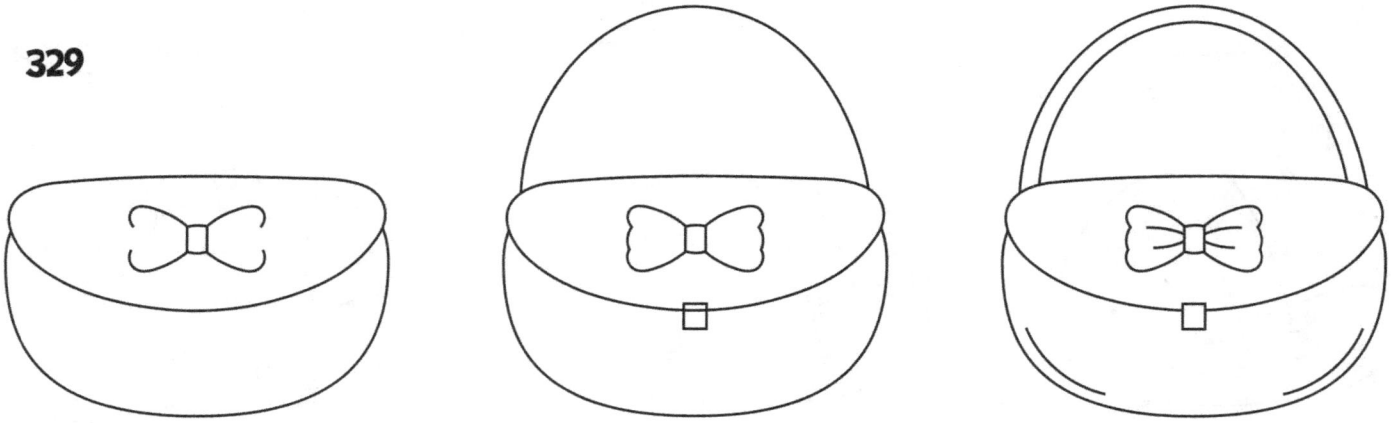

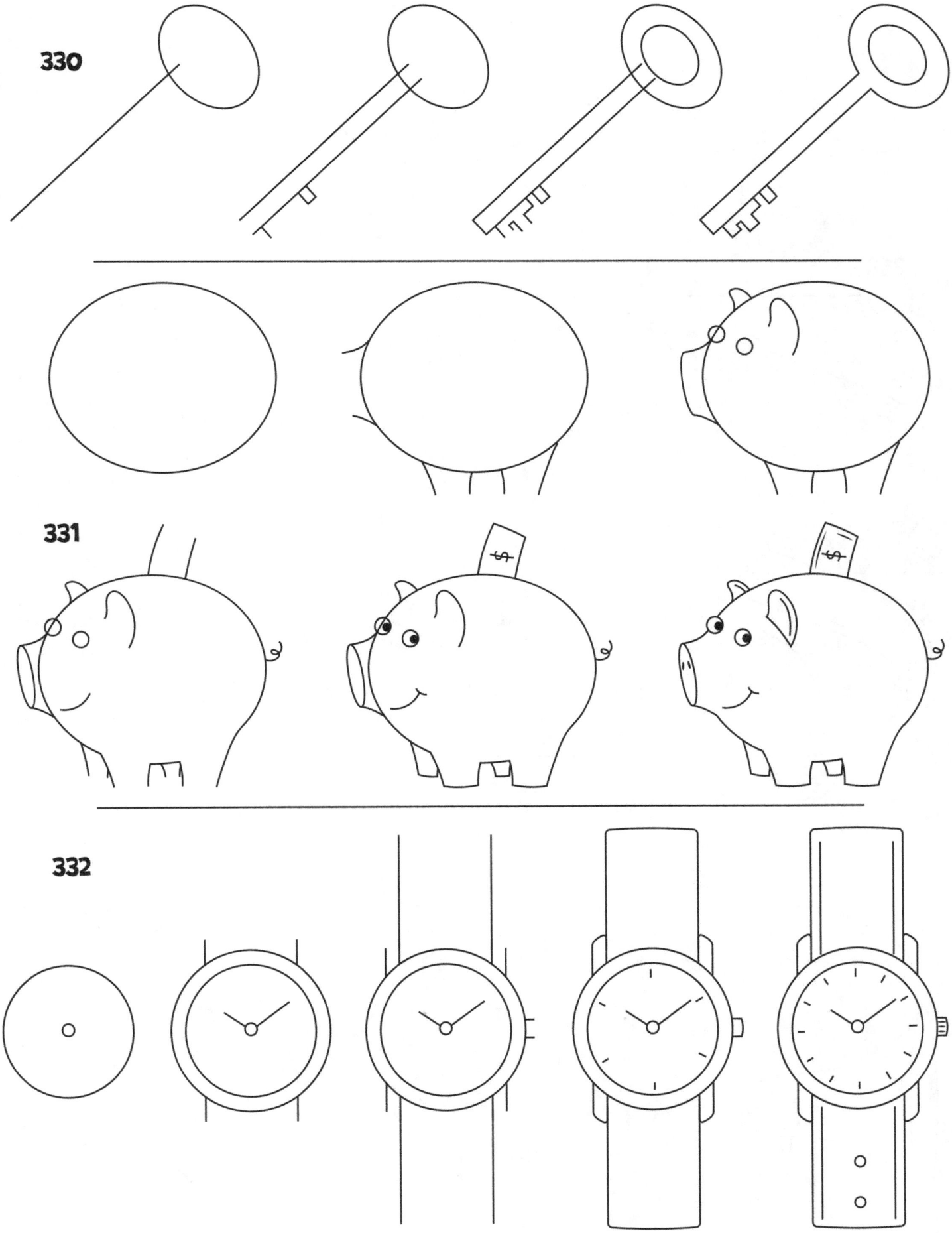
330
331
332

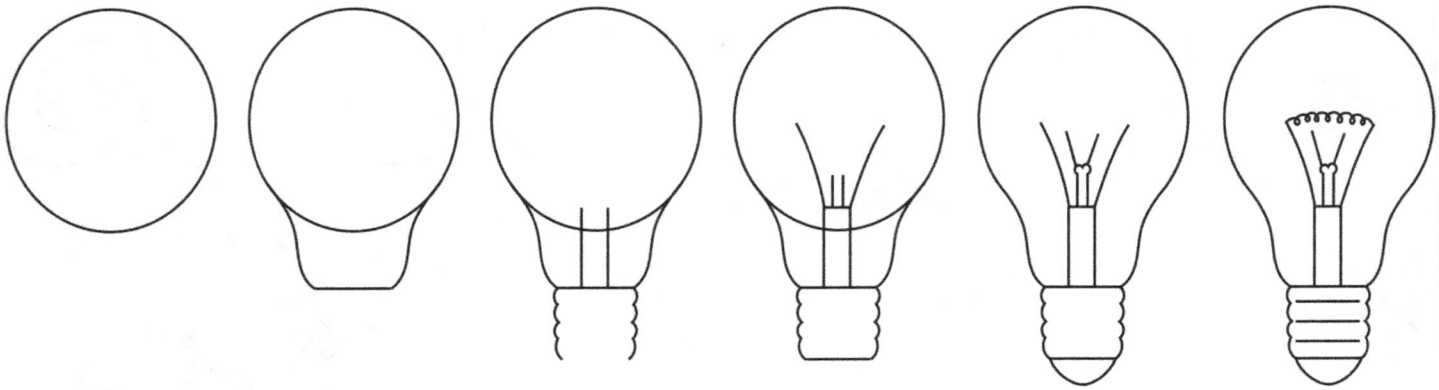

333

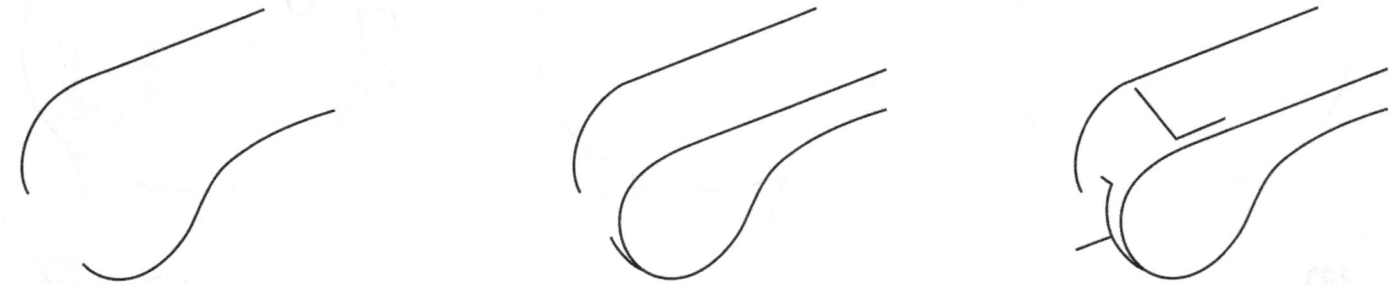

334

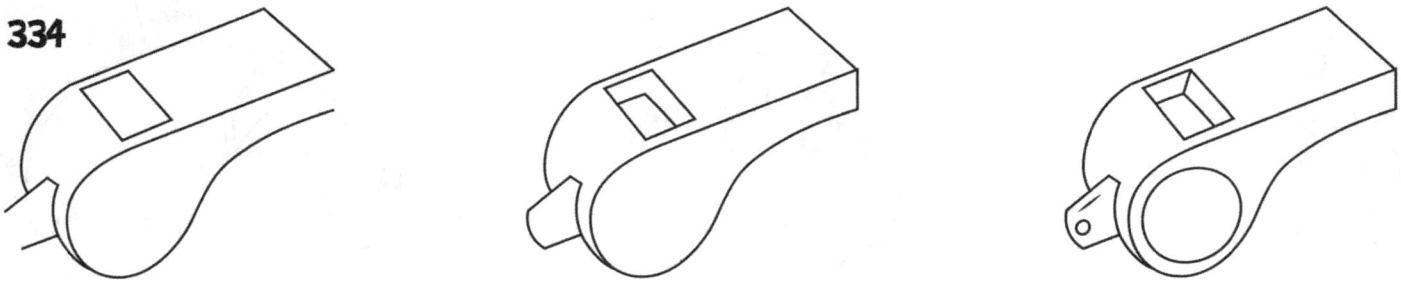

335

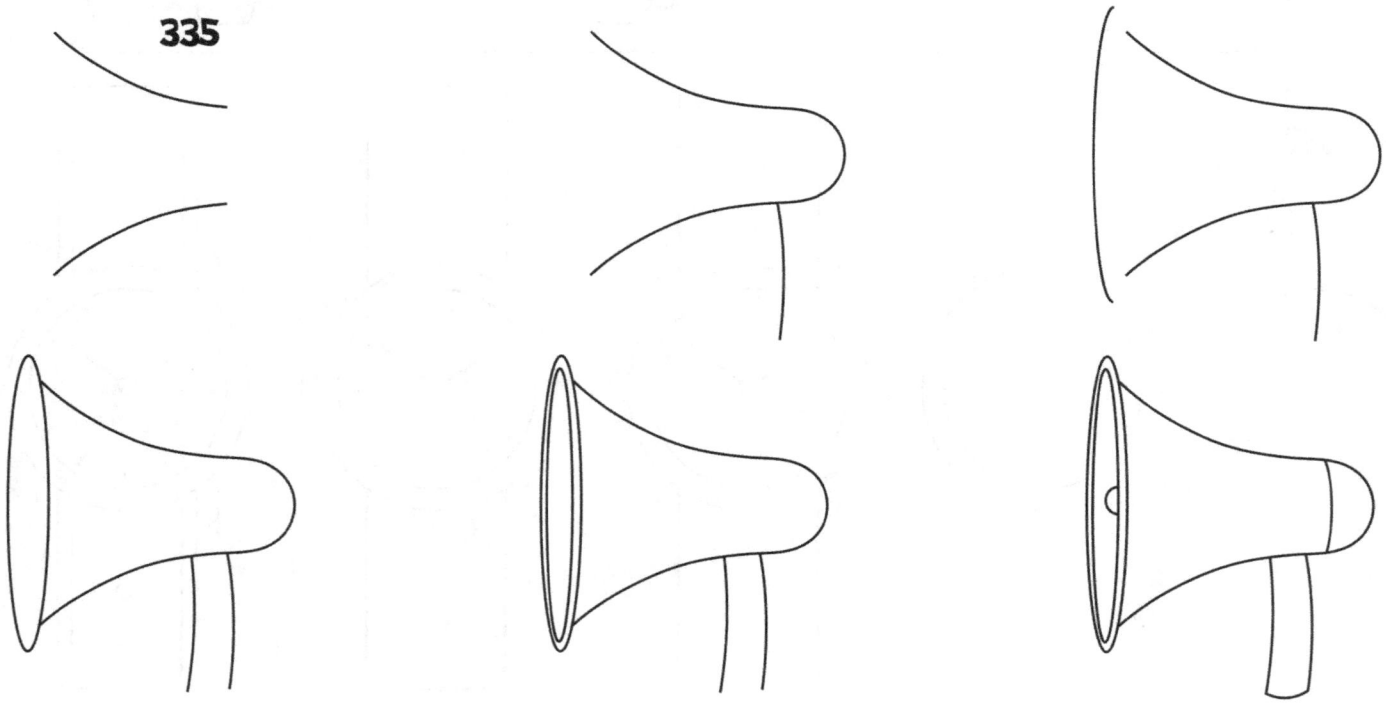

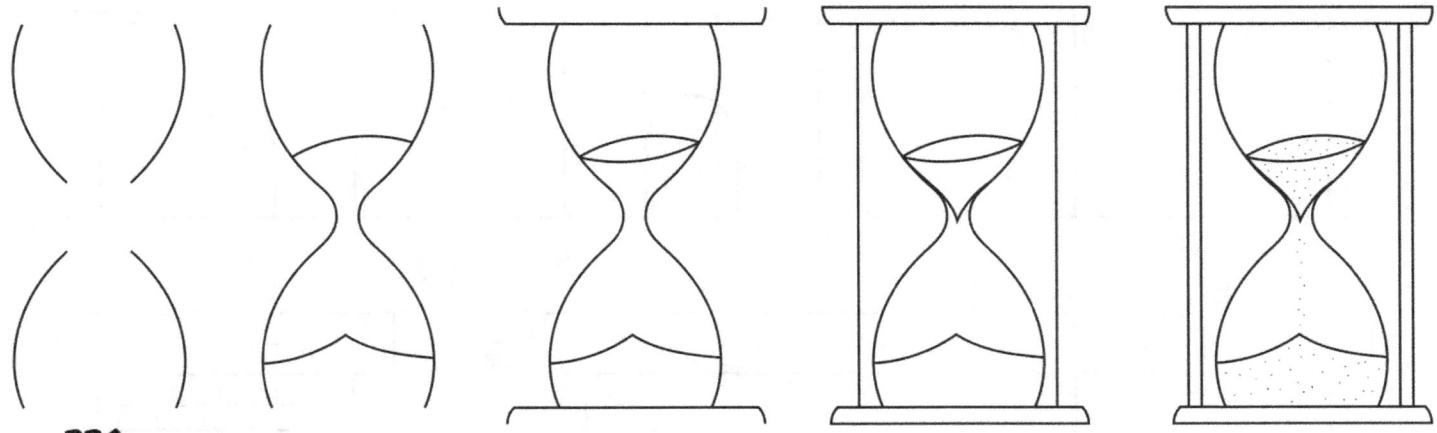

336

337

338

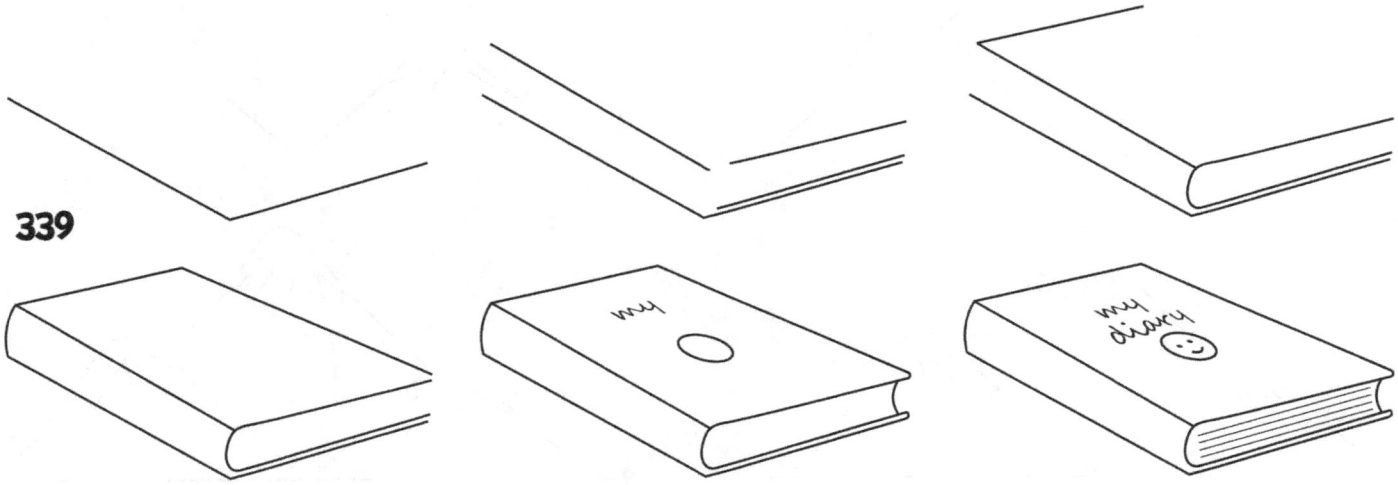

339

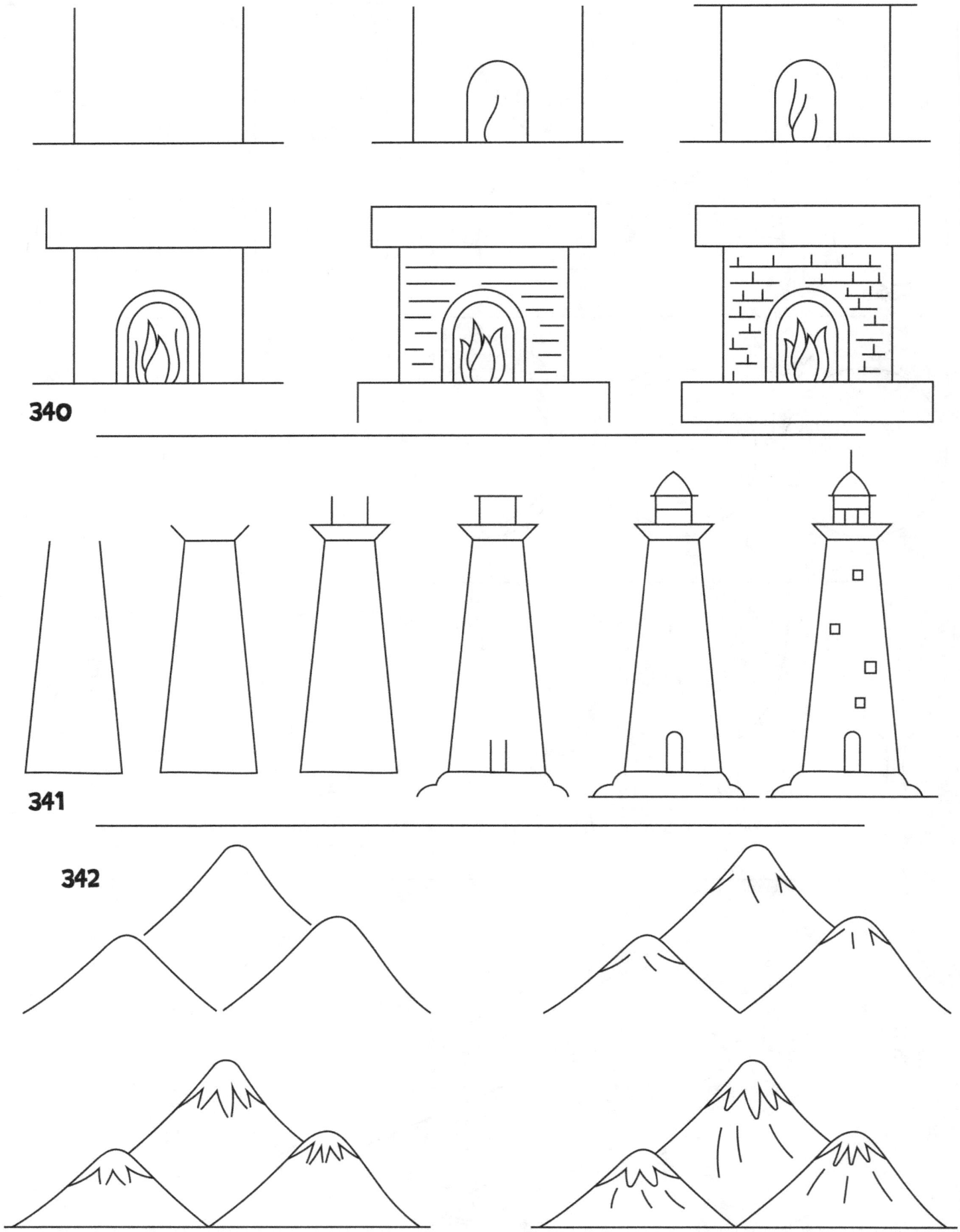
340
341
342

343

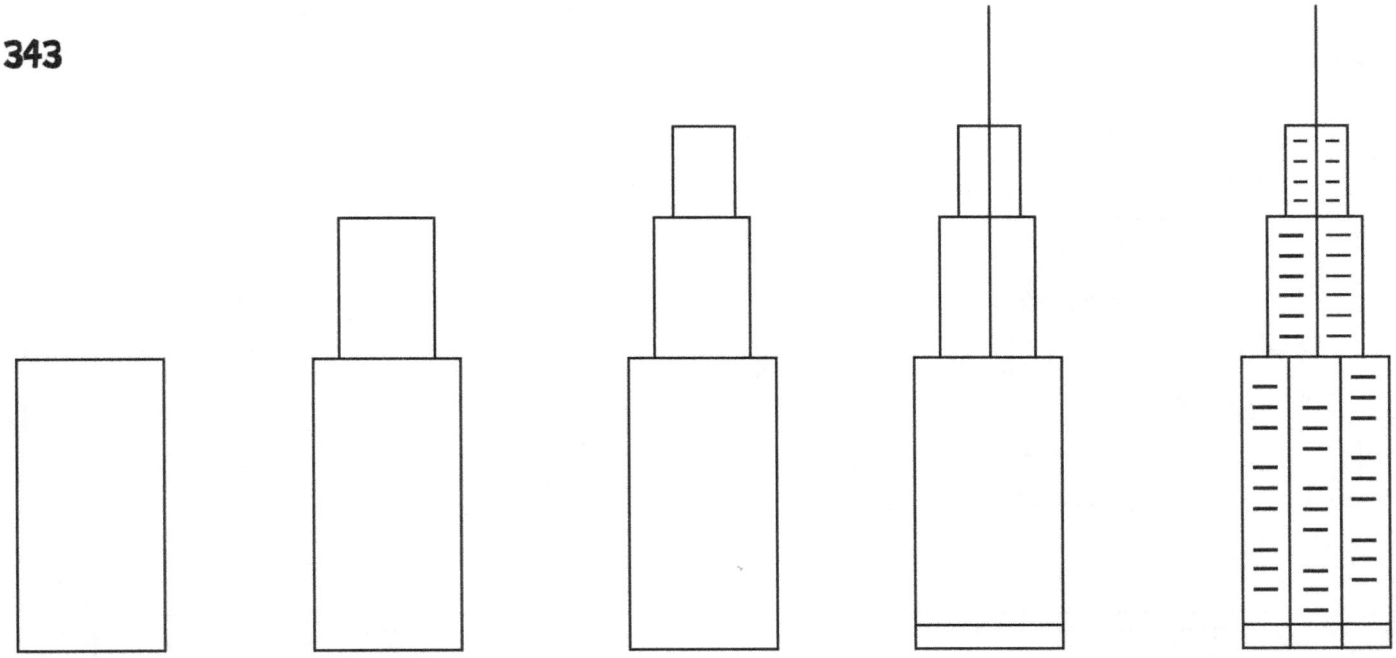

344

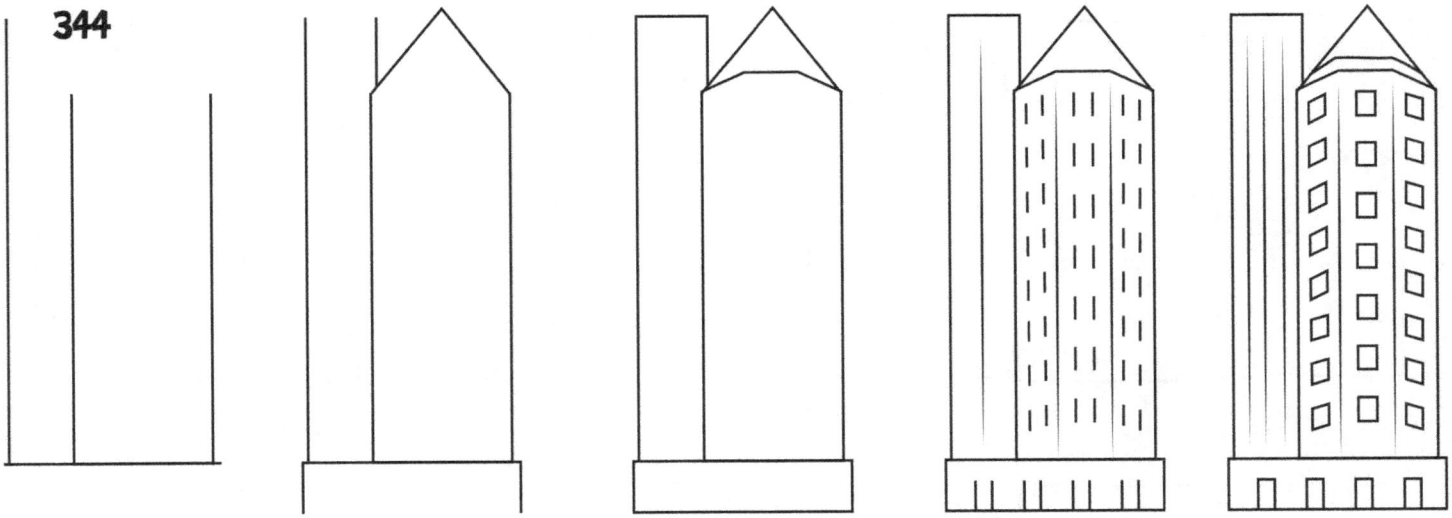

345

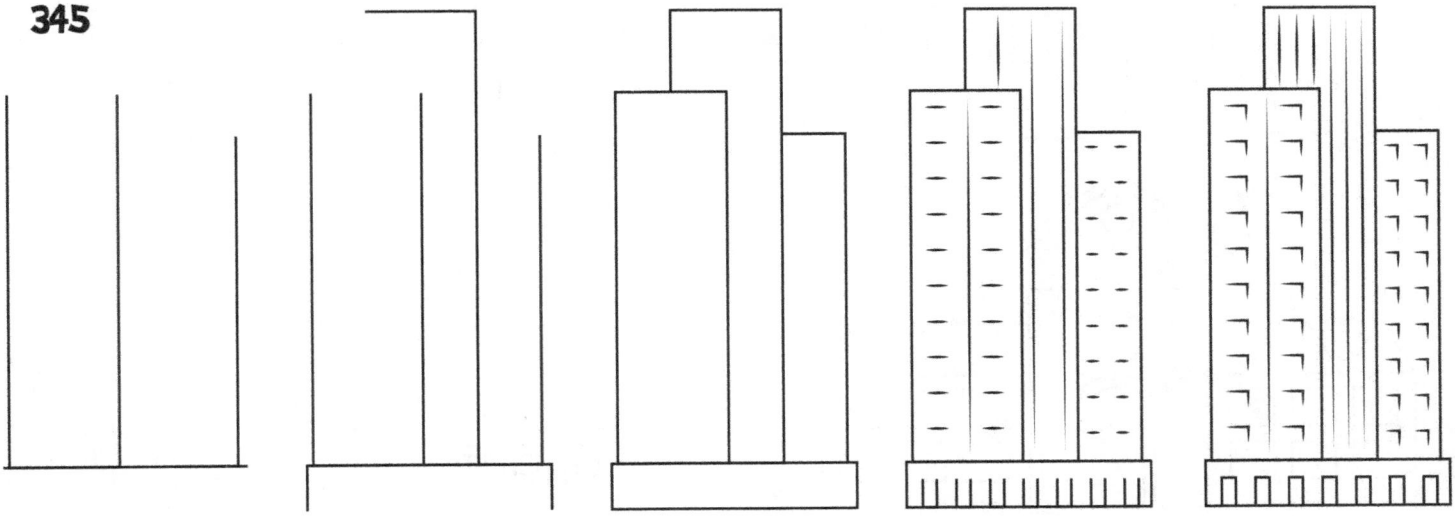

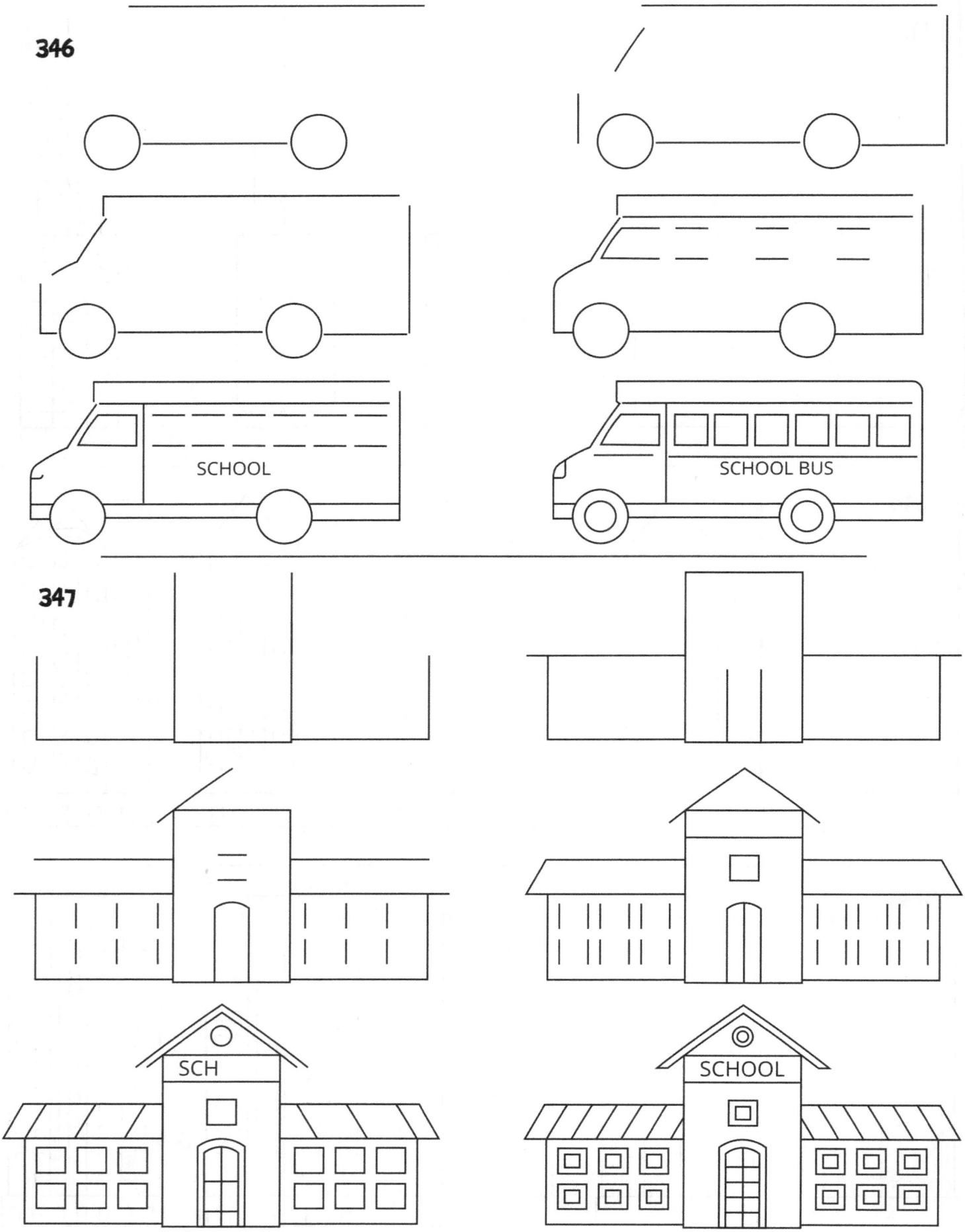
346
SCHOOL
SCHOOL BUS
347
SCH
SCHOOL

348
349

350

351

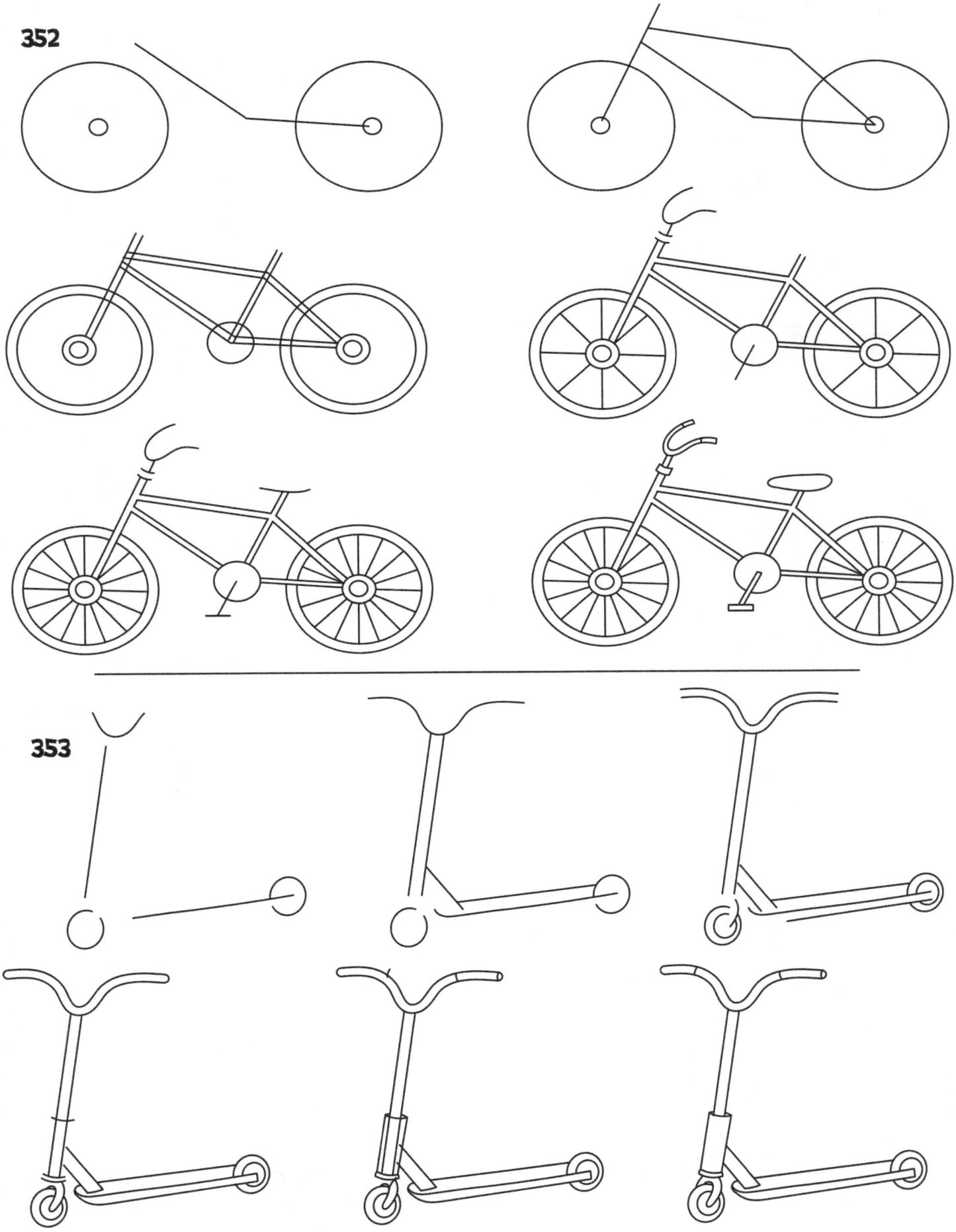
352
353

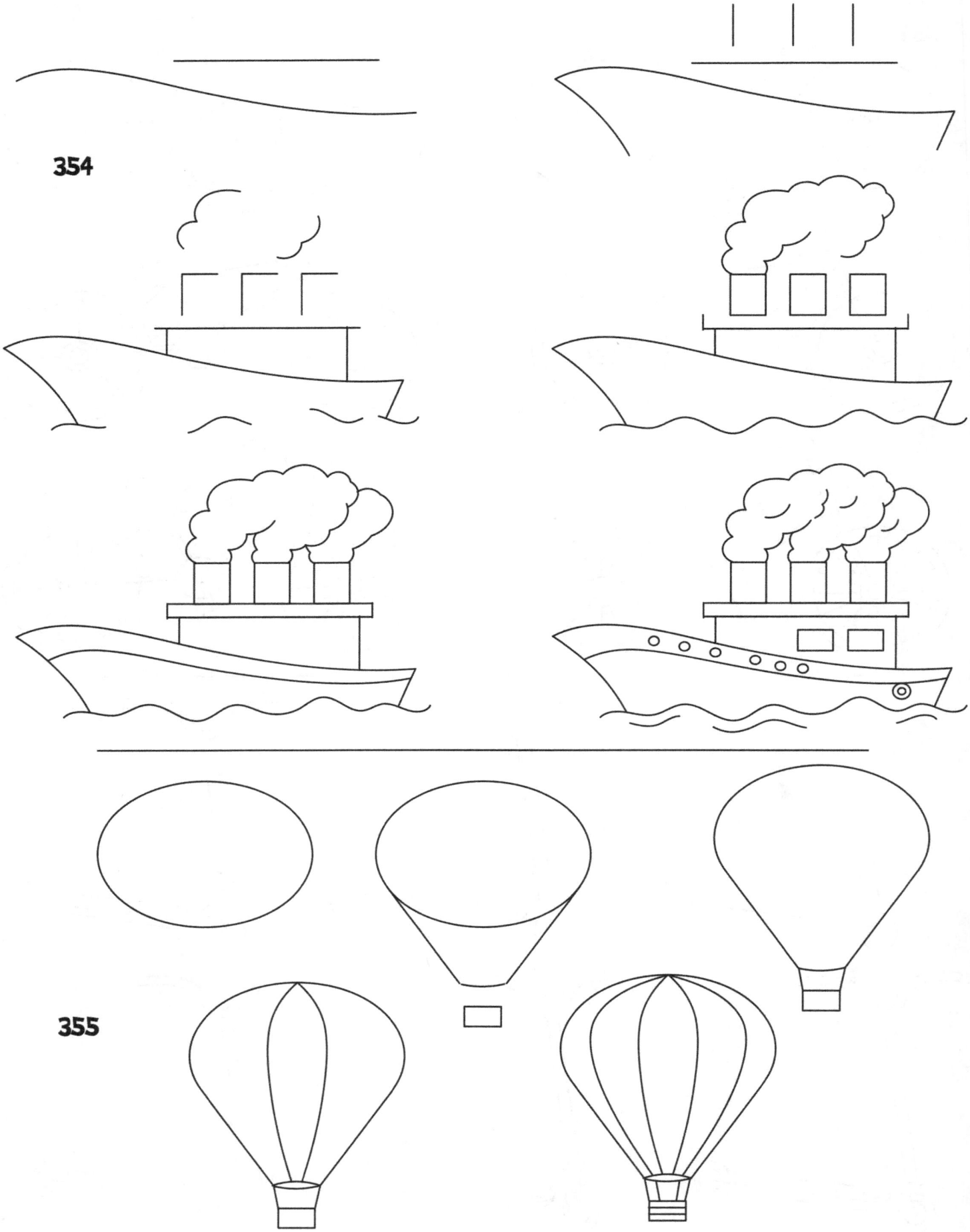
354
355

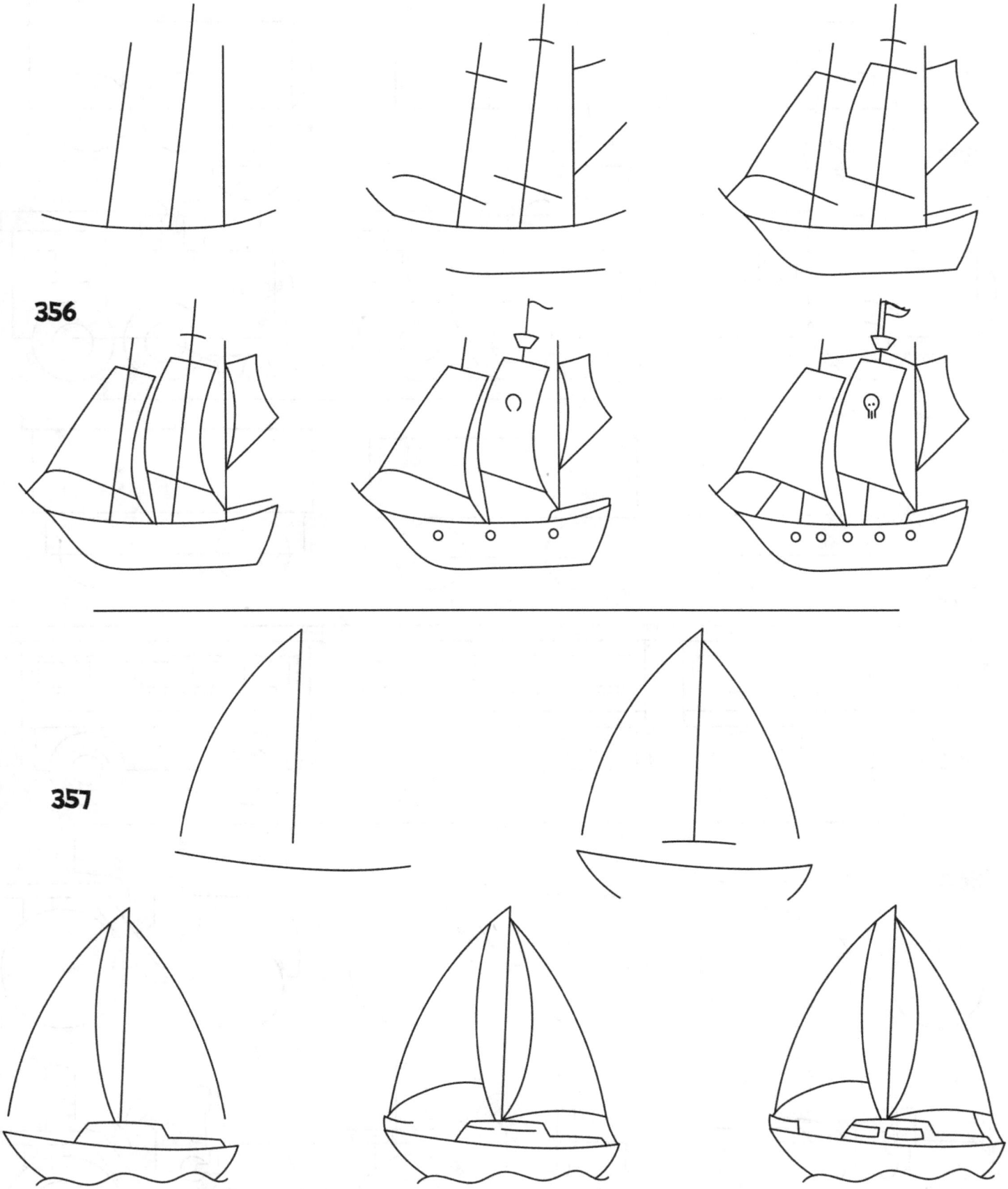
356
357

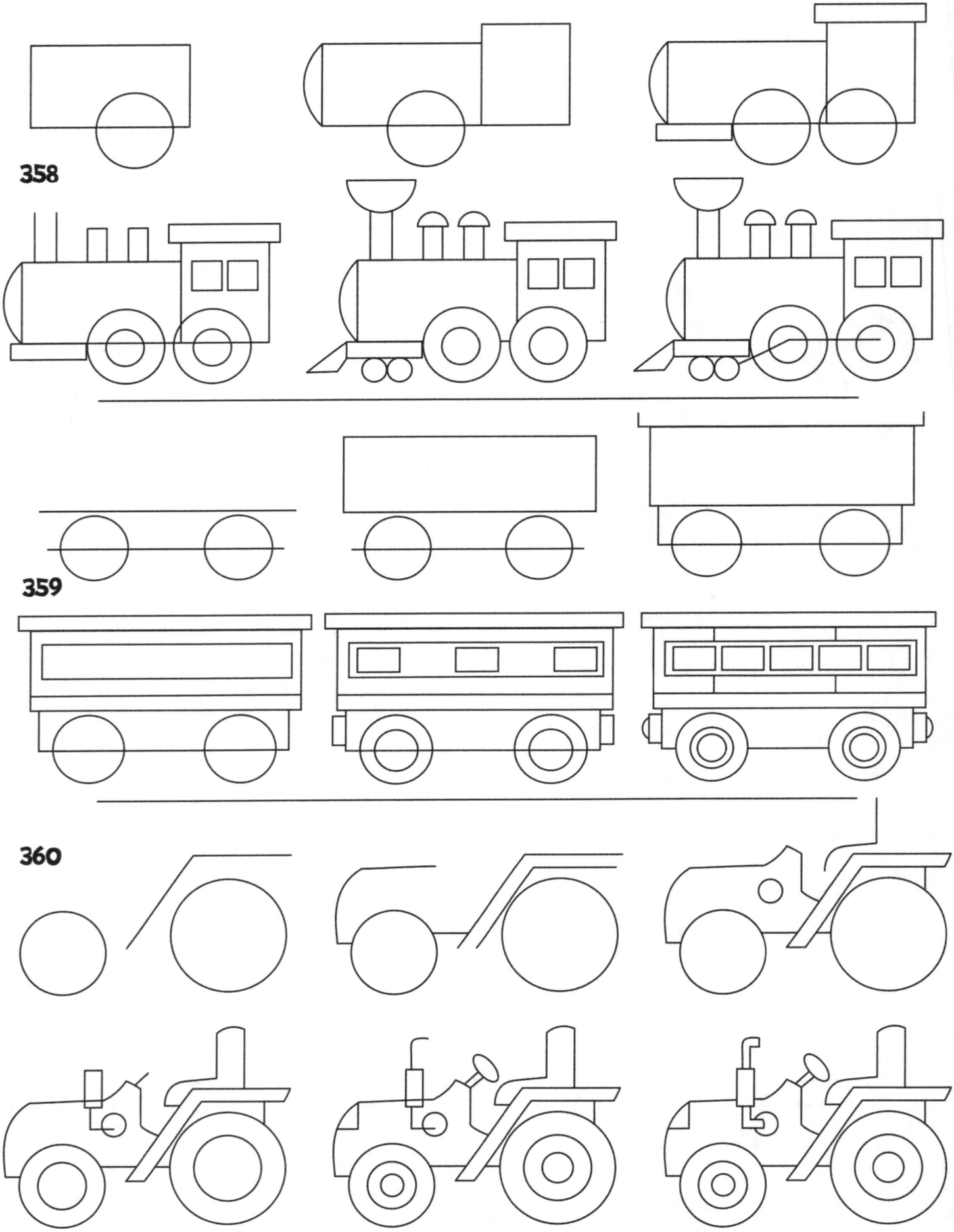
358
359
360

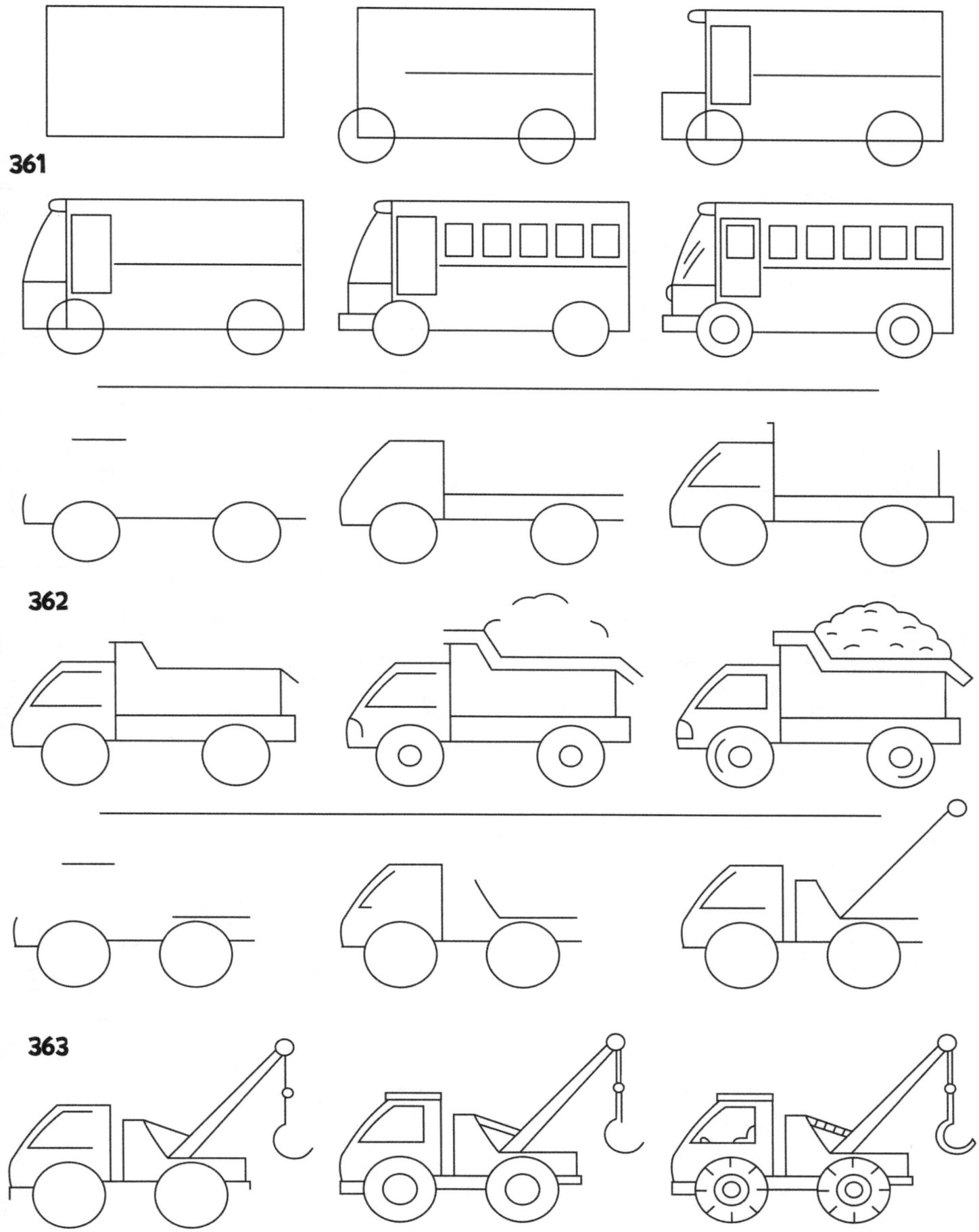
361
362
363

364

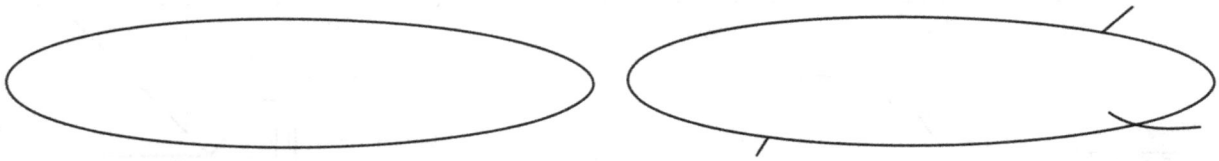

365

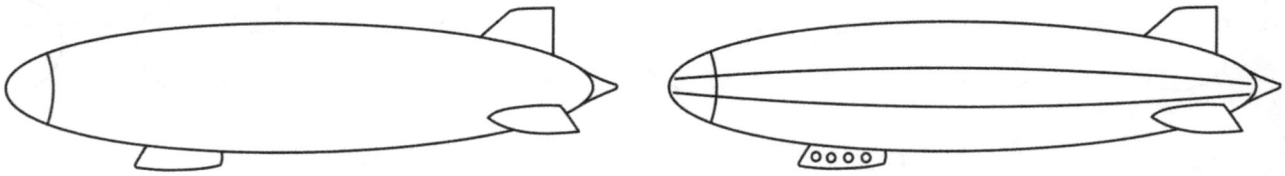

Free Download!

Like this book?

Join our VIP mailing list and get a *FREE* 70 page printable PDF *Holiday Activity Book for Kids*! It includes crosswords, word searches, picture matching, and coloring activities for ages 4-10!

Holidays include:

- Martin Luther King Jr. Day
- Valentine's Day
- St. Patrick's Day
- Easter
- Earth Day
- 4th of July
- Halloween
- Thanksgiving
- Hanukkah
- Christmas

Get started here:

www.woojr.com/VIP

CPSIA information can be obtained
at www.ICGtesting.com
Printed in the USA
BVHW011046220320
575658BV00016B/1096

9 780997 799378